Teaching and Learning about Computers

A Classroom Guide for Teachers, Librarians, Media Specialists, and Students

Joanne R. Barrett

The Scarecrow Press, Inc.
Lanham, Maryland, and Oxford
2002

CENTRAL MISSOURI
STATE UNIVERSITY
Warrensburg
Missouri

SCARECROW PRESS, INC.

Published in the United States of America
by Scarecrow Press, Inc.
A Member of the Rowman & Littlefield Publishing Group
4720 Boston Way, Lanham, Maryland 20706
www.scarecrowpress.com

PO Box 317
Oxford
OX2 9RU, UK

Copyright © 2002 by Joanne R. Barrett

All rights reserved. No part of this publication may be reproduced, stored in a retrieval system, or transmitted in any form or by any means, electronic, mechanical, photocopying, recording, or otherwise, without the prior permission of the publisher.

British Library Cataloguing in Publication Information Available

Library of Congress Cataloging-in-Publication Data

Barrett, Joanne R., 1960–
  Teaching and learning about computers : a classroom guide for teachers, librarians, media specialists, and students / Joanne R. Barrett.
    p. cm.
  ISBN 0-8108-4450-8
  1. Computers. 2. Electronic data processing. I. Title.
  QA76.5 .B29624 2002
  004—dc21   2002008350

∞™ The paper used in this publication meets the minimum requirements of American National Standard for Information Sciences—Permanence of Paper for Printed Library Materials, ANSI/NISO Z39.48-1992.
Manufactured in the United States of America.

Contents

Introduction		v
1	The History of Technology	1
2	All about Computer Graphics	23
3	Word Processing	39
4	Spreadsheets	53
5	Creating Charts and Graphics	67
6	Databases	78
7	Multimedia Presentations	100
8	The Internet	119
9	The World Wide Web	136
10	Creating Web Pages Using HTML	157
11	Developing Web Pages	181
12	Introduction to Programming	199
13	Viruses	218
14	Copyright and the Classroom	226

Appendix 1—File Formats	239
Appendix 2—Some Great Sites for Historical Information by Decades and Centuries	241
Glossary	243
Index	251
About the Author	255

Introduction

Ours is a society that craves new technology. Technologies have a most curious fate. While some technologies get woven into our daily lives, others may disappear as mysteriously as the dinosaurs. Some technologies, while breakthroughs at the time of their introduction, become common aspects to our lifestyles. Children of the baby boom generation listened incredulously to tales of life without television from their grandparents. Children of future generations will be just as incredulous thinking about life without cell phones or the Internet.

One technology that has been rapidly expanding into our lifestyle is the personal computer. The things that can be done with a computer and its applications have made obvious (and not so obvious) changes in the business office. The potential for ways to use the computer in the classroom is vast. Technology is providing many opportunities and challenges in how teachers can deliver their messages.

Technology texts tend to focus on one type of application or product. This book hopes to take a look at different applications, with the goal of providing information to help the user become proficient to the level suggested by technology standards. Understandably, the business community was the first to integrate the computer into the business environment. The legacies are textbooks and examples that mirror the business environment. This book seeks to create practical examples of interest to teachers and students. Technology projects that add value to another discipline or to part of the curriculum provide the most benefits. While a computer curriculum is important in its own right, an educational project that builds on the lessons of another discipline while mastering a new application provides the best of both worlds. Hopefully, the reader will be able to use the assignments provided with the chapters and incorporate them into many areas.

While there are dozens, if not hundreds, of websites to turn to for learning about many computer applications, it is sometimes difficult to find one at just the right level of proficiency for the user. Likewise, there are dozens of sites that provide really great ideas for lesson plans. While most media specialists are now experts at finding this type of information, the typical classroom teacher lacks one fundamental ingredient to be able to use many of those websites: time. The time to surf, narrow the focus, and find just the right websites is sometimes more than the average teacher has to spend. The information provided in this text is, therefore, intended as a time-saver.

One of the most important concepts of this book is that it is designed for teachers and learners. Technology brings with it ample opportunities for teachers to be learners, as well as for the learners to become the teachers. Sometimes the most effective technology-enabled classrooms are those where the instructor is the expert in the content area, but not necessarily the expert with the technology. Technology is advancing so quickly that oftentimes you find that it is the students who are the technology experts, and that they are more than willing to become the teachers. It is with a great sense of pride that a student will show you how he or she has figured out a shortcut or a neat way of doing something.

Remember back when you were younger. Was there a technology that you now take for granted that didn't exist then? How did that technology change your life? Many have left their mark and changed the way we live. I can remember my grandmother telling me on the way to the laundromat about life without washing machines, where a dryer was a rope, a couple of poles, and clothespins in the yard. I find it hard to fathom getting through the week without them. How did refrigeration change the way we live? We cannot imagine living without a refrigerator in our homes, not to mention what it has done to our capabilities for food distribution and delivery.

There are examples of technologies that have come into our lives and are here to stay. Indeed, it is hard to imagine life without them. There are still others that have been quickly surpassed or outdated by the advances that have come on their coattails.

Introduction

Popular culture is a funny thing. While fads and trends quickly fade or come and go, some people predicted the same fate for the computer. Some teachers may still feel resistant to bringing technology into the classroom. Still others are wondering who they can successfully add it to their repertoire. This book is for those how want to learn more about the various helpful applications. It provides chapters for all of the applications that can be applied to educational technology. There are still folks out there who think of the computer as a passing fad, especially in education. While I don't agree with them, they may be right, but only because another technology that fulfills its purpose and adds some newer value might replace it.

This book comes out of my desire to get organized. Twenty years of working with computers and wearing several different hats has led to shelves full of binders and notebooks stuffed with all kinds of computer-related information. If I had taught computer science twenty years ago, the body of information I would have needed would have been much smaller. While we have witnessed explosive growth, the areas about which one can learn and understand technology have expanded right along with it. Procrastinating consumers waiting to buy their first computers were often rewarded by more computer power at a lower price. A book about computing presents the same challenge, but at some point it is time to dive in. Here are the essentials for all the applications and issues that you could choose to bring into the classroom today.

As a classroom teacher, I have been able to find numerous books on various technology subjects. It frustrated me that I could not find one book that introduced all the topics that I encounter in the classroom. Indeed, most materials are designed for advanced and post-secondary students. This text is designed to be a guide for technologists, teachers, librarians, media specialists, and students together. Chapters introduce topics that are addressed in the National Educational Technology Standards for Teachers, as outlined by the International Society for Technology in Education. Samples have been provided that utilize many different packages available on the market today. In addition, there are assignment pages available that have not been designed for a particular brand or vendor.

There is one more feature to this book that makes it unique. While there has been a lot of ink, both bottled and digital, devoted to the topic of the digital divide (focusing on economics), within the classroom, there is another important divide—that of gender. Nowhere is the gender gap more egregious than with the use of technology. The models and assignments in this text are purposely designed to be gender-neutral. The examples and assignments have been created with both genders in mind, not one at the expense of the other. We need to empower our children in technology, so let's begin now.

1
The History of Technology

In this chapter we will explore the concept of technology and trace the history of the computer. The language of computer science will be introduced and discussed. We will examine the different elements that make up a computer, as well as different types of configurations. Finally, we will explore the human side, or what types of things programmers can do to help make computers easier for people to understand.

TECHNOLOGY: WHAT IS IT?

So, just what exactly is technology? Technology provides a new manner of accomplishing a task by using technical processes, methods, or information. Applied technologies are the instruments that change our lives in some way. Some technologies perform minor tasks or perhaps remove an inconvenience. Generally, new technologies arrive to make our lives easier. Each generation has had new inventions, but then successive generations cease to identify these inventions as technologies any longer.

Students are often intrigued by thinking about life without many of the things in their lives that they take for granted. A six-year-old will look into your eyes and express great amazement that an adult could have grown up normally without a computer. Her sixteen-year-old sister may be just as astounded at the thought of a weekend that did not include the use of a VCR. Each generation is just as confused at the thought of a lifestyle without these modern inventions. I remember my own shock at the discovery that my mother did not have a television in her home when she was a child because they had not yet been invented. I remember many tales of my mother's childhood, including how my grandmother's family would listen to evening programs on the radio in the living room. The exception was Friday evening, when my mom would get a dime, walk by herself, and meet her girlfriends at the local movie theater where there would be only one movie to see.

It is true that many new technologies are quickly incorporated into our lives. When they become part of everyday life, we no longer seem to think of them as technologies. While so many technologies have undergone this transformation, there are many examples of technologies that were revolutionary in their time yet became obsolete almost as quickly as they came into our lives. New and exciting in their day, some technologies have simply gone the way of the dinosaurs. Consider the slide rule, reel-to-reel tapes, 45s, eight-track tapes, party line phones, and Beta video format. Also, ask students about the technologies that are new today but will most likely be obsolete by the time they have children of their own.

We have all heard in many settings about how cyclical life can be. When we are very young, we hear it in kindergarten when we learn about the seasons. When we are older, we hear it in many historical contexts. Each generation feels confident that they are living at the most technologically advanced time in history. Each generation also has the belief that they are technologically superior to their predecessors. As far as technology is concerned, it is interesting to point out that not only do individuals take modern technologies for granted, but collectively a generation can do so as well. The notions in figure 1.1 can be a starting point for class discussion or short essay assignments.

New technologies are only new for the folks who are purchasing them for the first time. Funny that once you assimilate them into your lifestyle, they cease to be considered new technologies. For children growing up today, it is impossible to imagine life without computers. For instructional technologists, it is very easy to remember life without them! Sometimes technology can change the way we live. As it becomes cheaper and attainable by more of the population, it becomes part of the fabric of our lives. Often it is at the price of another preexisting system. Usually underlying the success or failure of the technology, of

> - What are some of the technologies you can think of that have changed the way we live?
> - What kind of an impact did this technology have on businesses and families?
> - After this technology became commonplace, were there others that began to fade away or go out of business?
> - Did this technology change the way people lived or where people lived?
> - What type of technology can you imagine that could eventually replace this one?
>
> (Examples may include electricity, automobiles, the telegraph, microwaves, radio, television, calculators, telephones, ballpoint pens, and so on.)

Figure 1.1 Something to Think About

course, are its economics and feasibility. Just remember that as you plod through the history of technology, if it happened before you were born, then chances are you don't perceive it as something new.

When a new technology is introduced, it is often met with skepticism. There are those who will quickly embrace new ideas and there will always be those whom we could classify as resistors, or Luddites. The term "Luddite" comes from the resistance of English textile workers early in the nineteenth century who were opposed to the displacement of workers by machines. One thing remains constant: when you have a new technology, you will find changes that affect society. It can be very intriguing to consider periods of history and compare the technologies available within different time periods. There are so many areas that have been affected by technology, including:

- Communications
- Transportation
- Manufacturing
- Energy sources
- Engineering
- Health and medicine
- Food production

- Commercial trade
- Banking and economics

Any of these areas can be the basis for research and analysis of how the introduction of technology can result in changes to individuals and the society in which we live.

HISTORY OF TECHNOLOGY

Consider the 1800s. In 1844, Samuel Morse, after years of experimentation and attempts to convince investors and politicians of the importance of his invention, had an opportunity to send a message in front of a congressional audience. He successfully sent the first telegraph message, "What hath god wrought?" from the Supreme Court in Washington, D.C., to Baltimore, Maryland, a distance of forty miles. Within two years, the telegraph could send messages five times its original distance. Six years after the congressional demonstration, it had grown to be able to send messages to areas over 300 times its original size. Two years later, the geographic growth was 600-fold. The newspapers and magazines declared how no communications instrument had ever grown so quickly and affected so many! These cries are very reminiscent of what we hear today about the growth of the Internet.

The telegraph had its own set of slang and acronyms that worked their way into everyday vocabulary. There were rivalries between those who were first to embrace the technology and the "newbies." Romance had its place, and the first long-distance wedding was performed with the bride and groom located in separate states. There were also those who hoped to use the new technology for their own gain at the expense of others, and they found ways to use it for less savory outcomes.

Initially, the telegraph did not affect commerce. This changed almost overnight. Businesses discovered that they needed to embrace the new technology, or step aside to make room for others who would. Therefore, businesses looking for the competitive edge often paid premiums for any advantage. The telegraph also had a few unexpected gifts for society. Soon, the ability of telegraphs to surpass country borders created a regulatory mess. The Pony Express closed down in 1861, as there was no way for them to compete with the telegraph. People saw in the late 1800s that there was now a way to keep up with world affairs, for the newspapers used the technology for more timely delivery of the news. Now that there could be faster feedback when problems arose, surely that would eliminate conflicts or wars. In the late 1800s, for the first time in history, people felt connected to a larger global community.

In 1876 the first successful transmission was made between two telephones. Two years later there were twenty-one telephones. Five years later, the first commercial long-distance line was in place between Boston, Massachusetts, and Providence, Rhode Island, for a distance of forty-five miles. In nine years, society went from a total of 230 telephones to 250,000.

In the 1890s there were only a few dozen automobiles and virtually no paved roads. Many felt that the notion of automobiles becoming the primary means of transportation was preposterous. In Vermont a law was passed that an automobile had to have a person several hundred feet ahead of it in order to warn horseback riders because automobiles were known to scare horses. Congress tried to enact laws to ensure that horses remained the chosen mode of transportation. These were the results of lobbying done on the behalf of coachmen, blacksmiths, and saddlers. The effect of automobiles on succeeding decades remains profound. For society, cars enabled the development of suburban living. Economically, it had a tremendous impact in opening additional markets for trade as well as interstate commerce. On the negative side, a need had developed for a way to combat interstate crime. Other negatives, like pollution and being the number one source of untimely death, remain with us today.

Also new on the horizon in the 1890s was electricity. Advocates claimed it would change business. Certainly it changed much about how we live and manufacture. It is hard to imagine what it may have been like to be the first on your block to get "electrified," or to be the first on the block to no longer depend on a block of ice to keep food from spoiling!

As the new century approached, the changes that loomed on the horizon had huge effects on society. As we enter the next century, presumably with our superior technology, what will be the next changes? Certainly the next wave of major change is identified as the expansion of the capabilities of the Internet, and with it e-commerce. Once again, business has pinpointed the potential in this new media, and building upon the initial success of some of the Web pioneers we saw an explosion in the number of dot.coms (short for a Web address ending in .com, traditionally allocated to commercial entities). The Internet's effects on our society have only begun to be measured.

While the history of modern computers dates back over half a century, it is also important to identify that changes to society come with technology. When discussing the history of computers, many textbooks will refer to the abacus as the first computer. Yes, the abacus was a tool that could be used to perform calculations, specifically mathematical calculations. However, many students are uncomfortable with the notion of a machine that does not require some type of energy source as a computer. Instead, you may also choose to define a computer as a device that requires electricity to perform its functions. Some want to define a computer as an electronic machine that helps you with your work. Regardless, to look at the progression of computers, consider the inventions in table 1.1.

Computer systems have come in many packages to date. Howard Aiken, working at Harvard University in 1944, completed the first electromechanical computer. This machine and the ones that followed were the first-generation machines and were made with vacuum tubes. As well as being fairly large, vacuum tubes generated a good deal of heat. It was not until the 1950s that transistors were invented and became a good replacement for vacuum tubes. The use of transistors ushered in the second generation, which became mainframe computers, the first commercially available machines. By 1953 there were only about 100 of them in use in the entire world.[1] Mainframe computers were very large, filling up large rooms of space requiring special power and ventilation resources, and were extremely expensive. In the early years of computing, only the federal government and huge corporations could afford computers. The computer user would have to sit at a "dumb" terminal and communicate via keyboard or input device separate from the large housing of hardware to perform calculations. Eventually, as the technology advanced, it is no surprise that the machines became smaller in size and lower in cost.

Table 1.1   Highlights in Computer History

- Blaise Pascal designs the first mechanical calculator, the Arithmetic Machine, to help in tax collecting in 1642.
- In 1694 Gottfried Leibniz extends the capability of Pascal's invention to include multiplication and division with a machine that used cylinders rather than gears called the Stepped Reckoner.
- Joseph Jacquard invents the Punched Card Loom, a loom that is controlled by punch cards, in 1804.
- Charles Babbage invents the "difference engine" in 1835, the first automatic calculating machine he planned to call the Analytical Engine.
- Ada Lovelace collaborates with Babbage in 1843 to design the first program for Babbage's machine, using the binary number system.
- Dr. Hollerith won a U.S. Census contest by creating the Tabulating Machine to analyze data with punch cards in 1886. The company he began, Computing-Tabulating-Recording Company, would later become International Business Machines (IBM).
- Dr. Howard Aiken creates an automatic calculator in 1937.
- Dr. Aiken at Harvard collaborates with IBM and the U.S. Navy in 1944 to produce the first automatic computer, the MARK I.
- Eckert and Mauchly create a calculating device with electronic switches and vacuum tubes, the Electronic Numerical Integrator and Computer, or ENIAC, completed in 1946.
- John von Neumann proposed a design that would allow computers to store data and programs internally in 1946. In 1947 he creates the Electronic Discrete Variable Computer, or EDVAC.
- In 1947 the transistor is invented by Bell Laboratories and is more reliable than vacuum tubes.
- The first commercial computer model with a stored program, the UNIVAC I, is available in 1951.
- In 1952 IBM releases the IBM 701, the first commercially available computer built with vacuum tubes.
- In 1955 IBM introduces FORTRAN, the first programming language in which machine code is not required.
- In 1962 American Airlines links computers together via phone lines for their SABRE reservations system.
- Integrated circuits, invented in the 1960s, were improved and introduced into computers in the early 1970s.
- Large-scale integrated circuits allowed microprocessors to be built.
- In 1974 Miro Instrumentation Telemetry Systems sold the Altair 8800 as the first affordable desktop computer designed for personal use.
- In 1977 Tandy Corporation becomes the first major electronics firm to produce a personal computer.
- In 1976 Apple Computer, founded by Steven Jobs and Stephen Wozniak, enters the marketplace.
- In 1981, IBM introduced its personal computer, the IBM PC.

The next generation of computers is referred to as the minicomputers. Minicomputers were smaller than their predecessors, but still enormous by today's standards. At the time they were presented, though, they were thought of as miniature mainframes—hence the name minicomputer. Minicomputers became more affordable, and most were the size of one of today's industrial-size copying machines. They brought computing power to medium as well as large companies, school departments, and similar institutions and agencies.

Our present generation is that of the microcomputers. Microcomputers contain the latest advances in circuit technology: the integrated circuit chips. Microcomputers are also referred to as personal or home computers. The personal computer, or PC, name came from the expansion of computers from the business arena to the home or personal arena. Interestingly enough, the first groups to truly embrace the personal computer were businesses. With the introduction of the personal computer, computing power became much more affordable. Where previously a company would have a minicomputer and a small staff to maintain and perform its functions, they could now place a microcomputer on every employee's desktop. We have now reached the point where it not unusual for employees to have more than one computer at their disposal, as well as their own machine at home. Just as earlier generations may have been lucky enough to have one phone for their entire household, now every member of the family might have more than one phone. So, too, it is now possible for family members to have their own computers.

Much of this affordability has been realized as a direct by-product of "Moore's Law." Gordon Moore, one of the founders of Intel Corporation, has become famous for his observation in 1965 that the capability of our microprocessors was doubling every year. Remarkable as it may seem, his observation that processing power doubles while the price gets cut in half on the average of about every eighteen to twenty-four months still rings true today.

DEFINING A COMPUTER

A computer is an electronic device that can receive, store, process, and transmit data or information. One of the most im-

The History of Technology

portant aspects of a computer is that it is a tool that helps perform a task or function to help you complete a task or job. Specifically, a computer is any electronic device that can perform numerical calculations. Computers, however, are capable of storing and retrieving millions of pieces of information rapidly and accurately without thinking or making decisions. Artificial intelligence is a branch of computer science that seeks to create machines that would be able to perform the components that make up the human brain and assimilate knowledge in a human-like way. Human intelligence is composed of three components: the conscious, the ability to classify information, and the ability to reason based on prior memories. Today our computers are capable of performing four essential functions; input, memory, processing, and output. Taking the process step-by-step, the unit must first accept information. Next, it is stored, and then the information is processed by the central processing unit (CPU). Next, the instruction results in information that is output in some form. Performing these steps depends on hardware and software, which come together in a seamless fashion to today's user.

Hardware and Software

Just what is hardware? Hardware is all of the parts of the computer that you can see and touch. They are the solid tangibles. Software is comprised of computer programs, which are instruction sets to tell the computer what function to perform. Software can be divided into four main categories: applications, games, programming languages, and operating systems.

You need both hardware and software to have a productive computer system. There are components of the hardware that you can't see unless you take the system, or "box," apart. It is easy to understand that if a part were to break on the inside, we could open it and substitute a new one for the broken part. Remember that all of the internal components are part of the hardware. Now, what if every time you were to open a particular application (software) and then attempt to save something in it, it froze the system so that you could not continue with your functions. Does this situation represent something gone awry with the hardware? Because the hardware is no longer performing, it would probably be safe to assume that you had encountered a problem with the software. Software is a little harder to see, for most programs are now accessible in a way that does not require program manipulation. As software has progressed, the designers have succeeded in creating programs that are increasingly easy to use, or user-friendly. Part of being user-friendly is the simplification of the process so that the user no longer has to have an understanding of programming, however rudimentary, to manipulate the machine.

Typically, an initial release of a software package will be labeled as 1.0. A fictitious example would be Libraryware 1.0. As modifications, or patches, are made to the release, the version numbers might change to the right of the decimal point, like 1.01 or 1.3. As full-scale upgrades are made, problems will be resolved and new features will be added to the program. Upgrades usually increase the version number to the left of the decimal point. So, you can safely assume that if you purchase the last release of Libraryware 7.0, you are purchasing the seventh, and most advanced version to date.

Operating Systems

One of the most important software programs in a computer is the one known as the computer's *operating system (OS)*. The operating system remains present to control the environment throughout usage. It acts as a vital link between the hardware and all the other software. Operating systems are the first piece of software the computer uses. When a machine is powered on, the machine will perform a power-on self-test, which is like an accounting for what hardware elements are in place. Next, the ROM BIOS (read-only memory Basic Input/Output System) will direct the system by loading the remaining portions of its operating system. The ROM will first look for the operating system on any floppy drives, and if it does not encounter one, it proceeds to look to the hard drives. In the early days of computers, the operating system was contained on a single floppy disk, before the computer had any long-term, or hard drive, storage.

The two aspects to be concerned with in an operating system are its function and its appearance. The function of the operating system is to monitor all of the systems operations and coordinate the systems functions. The OS appears to the user for manipulation in the form of the desktop. The user interface, if it uses icons, is referred to as a GUI, or graphical user interface. This interface is the way the user communicates with the computer. Appearance factors can include the accessibility, the instruction sets that are present, areas of user assistance or help, as well as the physical layout of the icons and items.

The majority of home personal computers today run one of two operating systems, Macintosh or Windows, but there are others available, including Linux and Unix. Macintosh, or Mac OS, has been long known for being user-friendly. The Mac OS has allowed users to drag, point, and click to manipulate the system functions. Windows, the popular operating system from Microsoft, has come in many flavors. Initially, Microsoft created Disk Operating System (DOS) 1.0, which was the operating system for the earliest IBM PCs. The DOS versions advanced over the years, and with them the capabilities of the operating system expanded. At one point, Microsoft released Windows. The initial Windows program was not an operating system, but an application overlay that created a more user-friendly environment than was provided in DOS. In the DOS versions, commands would have to be remembered and typed in from the keyboard by the user. While programmers did not find this daunting, the average user did. Windows 1.0, through the later 3.0 versions, sought to correct this situation by placing the majority of commands on menus. It was not until the Windows 95 version that Windows became an operating system in its own right.

While Windows has been advancing, we are left with one "legacy" item: the file format. Files are the way the system stores the software. In the early days of DOS, all file names could contain a maximum combination of eight characters (letters, numbers, or certain allowed symbols, such as an underscore), followed by a period and a three-character extension. The extension essentially notifies the operating system of the file's type, or format, and in certain cases launches an associated application when opened. Today's versions of the operating systems still interpret the extensions to determine which applications to launch or associate with a file. This is an interesting point because while many file names may appear below an icon, or picture of an item, the extensions may not be listed in the file name, but the icon shown reflects the file type. Careful inspection of the properties of these files, in particular where the MS-DOS name is examined, will reveal the existence of the extension. Programs or applications can be identified by the ".exe" extension, which stands for "executable extension." Please refer to appendix 1 for a more detailed listing of file type extensions. Incidentally, the Mac OS did not have the eight-character limitation, but uses the extension convention for file type identification.

Peripherals

Peripherals are the separate devices that are attached to the main "box" that houses the microprocessor and other internal components of a computer. Interestingly enough, some items that are peripherals on one model can be part of the main system in another. Consider a desktop unit that sits on the floor. Here peripherals include the monitor, keyboard, and perhaps a printer. Now think of a laptop. With a laptop, you could attach an extra external monitor or keyboard, which would both be considered peripherals. The keyboard that is "inside" the unit when you close the monitor would not be considered a peripheral. In general, peripherals are used as input or output devices.

Input Devices

The primary input device for a computer is a keyboard. There are different versions of keyboards for computers, and the standard keyboard contains 101 keys. Keyboards can have different layouts or combinations of the keys. QWERTY, which identifies the top left row of the keyboard, is the most common. Function keys are specialized keys and begin with the letter F combined with a number between one and twelve. There are keys that have specialized functions, such as the tab, insert, delete, page up or down, arrow or cursor control, shift, and caps lock (which causes all keys to appear in upper-case letters) keys. The ESC, or escape, key is usually used to abandon a process or function. The enter key usually has the effect of confirming an entry and moving the user to the next point for input.

The mouse is an input device used for moving a cursor on a screen. The mouse tracks the movement made against a ball inside the device against an analogous point on the display. Typically, mice have a button or buttons and functions associated with the different buttons. Mouse movement and control is referred to as pointing, dragging, and clicking. Dragging is achieved by depressing a button and keeping it held down while moving the mouse on a surface. Clicking is the resulting action of pressing and releasing a button on a mouse responding to a cue on the screen. Different functions can be assigned to mouse actions for different computer requirements.

Scanners are input devices that allow the transfer of images or text from a flatbed or screen directly into your computer. The image bed can accept pictures, text, diagrams, and drawings. Anything that you can place on the bed will be transformed into a digital image or document.

Output Devices

Monitors and printers are examples of output devices. Monitors provide a user with a place to view the results of computations. Information is first processed, then displayed to the user through a monitor. Printers produce a hard-copy version of the processing that the computer has performed. Not surprisingly, printers have a wide range of capabilities, sizes, and prices. Some of the characteristics that change between printers affect the quality of the output. Some printers are capable of creating very professional looking documents and even photo-quality pictures.

Protocol is a word that is very important in technology. Think of protocol as a set of rules that can govern what you do. In science, a protocol is a detailed plan, treatment, or procedure to follow. Hardware protocols are all of these things, as well as a set of rules to describe how data can be transferred. When there is consensus to protocols, you have a way for different technologies to work together so that manufacturers of hardware and software know what definitions to use and follow.

Printers

Dot matrix printers use much of the same design as typewriters. An impression is made on the paper by striking a character against a ribbon containing ink. These printers are impact printers. Ink jet printers work by using a fine jet of electricity to charge a piece of paper. The ink is then sprayed on the paper and it adheres to the charged particles. Finally, laser printers use a laser beam of heat against a drum to make the toner, or ink, stick to the paper.

There are pieces of hardware that can perform as both input and output devices. A modem (which stands for Modulate-Demodulate) is a good example. Computers internally pass on signals that are binary or digital signals. Digital signals, on the other hand, are parallel, and phone lines utilize analog signal technology. In order for a computer to communicate using phone lines, the two types of signals need to be reconciled. Not surprisingly, when we sought to connect our computers to the rest of the outside world, we chose to take advantage of a preexisting infrastructure. Since telephones went just about anywhere we wanted to go with our computers, it made sense to find a way to convert the signals between the two media. Enter the modem. What the modem does is convert the outgoing signals to analog, and the incoming signals to digital. This process enables the computer to communicate using the existing infrastructure of phone lines that can reach many places on our planet. The speed of a modem will indicate the rate at which it can transfer bits of information. Speed is measured in bps (bits per second) for older speeds and kbps (thousands of bits per second) for the newer and faster protocols.

Long-term storage devices, or floppy disks, can be both input and output devices. Floppy disks are designed to store information outside of the microcomputer. Floppy disks, also called diskettes, are reusable storage devices and vary in capacity. The first floppy disks used in personal computers were 5.25" in diameter. The 5.25" floppy disks could hold about 100 typed pages' worth of information. The newer 3.5" disks hold about 400 typed pages' worth. Now there are even newer disk types available, Zip disks, which come with much higher capacity levels. Diskettes got the name "floppy" because the thin sheet on the inside that stored the information was a very flexible piece of Mylar. Today people are most familiar with Mylar as a fabric used in balloons. A floppy disk is arranged into magnetic bands that are first divided into circular tracks and then further subdivided into sectors. Information is stored on them as tiny charged magnetic spots. CDs, or compact disks, also work in the same fashion, but are more resistant to damage.

The other option for long-term storage is a hard drive. Hard drives, so named because they were made with a hard piece of aluminum that information was magnetically stored onto, are the drives that are not removable from a computer. Hard drives provide storage, but are not portable in the way that floppy disks can be. To remove a hard disk from a computer you would need to disassemble it.

Memory

The memory that is used while a computer is functioning is divided into two types. In some ways, it is similar to the human long- and short-term memory. The RAM, or random access memory, is the memory that the computer uses during a session. If an item is in the RAM and does not go to a place for long-term storage, when the computer is shut down that information will be lost. The RAM memory chips are placed onto memory cards called SIMMs (single inline memory modules) that plug into special sockets inside the computer on the main system or motherboard. The number of sockets available will determine how high the memory level can be increased or upgraded.

ROM, or read-only memory, is permanent memory that is installed in a computer at the time it is manufactured. The information in the ROM is not accessible to the user. Modifications can occur in the form of system updates and require special instructions and procedures, usually from the vendor.

The Microprocessor

The "brain" of the computer, where the actual processing occurs, is in the microprocessor chip. The microprocessor is also referred to as the CPU, or central processing unit. As the main processing unit, this is where all of the computations are carried out. All the processing power of today's microprocessors is the result of high-speed processes carrying out only previously defined functions. Our present-day systems are not yet capable of thinking or reasoning problems; however, research is actively being pursued in this area.

The microprocessor contains three main types of circuits. The first type of circuits, arithmetic logic units (ALU), are where numerical and logical operations are performed. The second type are registers, which act as memory to hold information during high-speed processing. The third type of circuits are control circuits. Control circuits control the sequencing of the processing being done and help determine what moves between the other circuits and when.

Information flows between the arithmetic unit and the control unit. Information may be stored in the memory between, before, or after the flow of these two units. The microprocessor chip is composed of a very thin wafer of silicon. Silicon is a common element found in sand, quartz, and granite. The silicon is etched with circuits, which are then encased in a plastic or ceramic case. Cache are special memory chips that store information frequently needed by the microprocessor. External cache resides on the motherboard, while internal cache is built into the CPU. Internal cache has been designed to speed up the computations necessary when the CPU would have to send data to the RAM. The internal cache is the first place the CPU looks when it needs to retrieve information.

Information flows from input devices into the processor, and eventually out through an output device. Information flows to and from the microprocessor by way of data busses. Bus technology has evolved with microcomputers, and there are many types of busses for a manufacturer to use in building a computer.

The speed of the processor is an important feature of a computer. Time or speed in processing is measured in nanoseconds, which are a billionth of a second. As microprocessor chips have advanced, the quantity as well as the speed of the processors has increased. There are several microprocessor chip manufacturers. Motorola designed some of the chips used in the first Apple Computers, while the earliest IBM PCs have used chips designed by Intel. Intel introduced the first chips to be used for commercial purposes in 1971. The website for Intel Corporation provides a great deal of historical and background information about its microprocessors at www.intel.com.

Bits and Bytes

Amazing as it may seem, the computer only uses two numbers to perform all of its functions. The binary number system is the language of the CPU. Its two numbers, zero and one, can be thought of as a simple light switch. The switch can either be off or on, zero for off and one for on. Of course it gets a bit more complex than this, but the binary number system is the basis for the language of computing. *Bits (binary digits)* are then put together in groupings of eight. Eight bits make up one byte. A word is made up of thirty-two bits. Binary coded numbers can be written by their "0 and 1" equivalents, or with hexadecimal notation. Hexadecimal equivalents provide us with a more compact way of expressing binary coded numbers. Every character contained on the keyboard can be represented as a distinct series of the eight-bit bytes.

Network Resources

So far, we have only talked about the computer as a single machine containing all of its resources within its own parts. When a machine is operating by itself, we refer to it as being stand-alone. However, it often makes sense to be able to share computing resources. The easiest way for sharing resources is to become part of a computer network. There are many different types of networks. However, all networks exist for the purpose of sharing information and resources.

It is a fairly simple process to make a stand-alone machine become a part of a network. A physical connection must be made through a network interface card (NIC). The network card contains a connection to the network. In wired networks, the NIC would have a physical connection to the cables. In a wireless network, there would be some type of receiver contained on the interface.

A network consisting of hardware in relatively close proximity is referred to as a LAN, or local area network. Another term that has become popular to describe local networks is an intranet. An intranet is a private computer network—generally one that is contained within a building or organization. Intranet is a term that distinguishes a local network from a larger network, like the Internet, that is not limited by corporate, state, or even continental borders. Networks that are geographically dispersed are also referred to as WANs, or wide area networks. The world's largest WAN is the www.

A bridge or gateway is the hardware interface for connecting different networks together. While a network protocol is the way the hardware communicates to perform its tasks, the protocol is the way the hardware and software can work together. A topology is the physical way that you lay out your cables for your network. There are different network topologies including the bus, ring, tree, star and mesh. Interestingly, a network does not have to be limited to a particular topology; rather, it can consist of combinations of the different options. In a bus topology, machines are connected in a row to the network. If one member of the network fails, all the other members beyond that position will no longer have access to the network. In a star topology, all the members are connected as branches coming from a central point. If one of the branches fails in the star, it does not affect the other branches. In a ring topology all of the devices are connected in the shape of a closed loop. The central point in the ring is the hub, and the hub directs the flow of information. The tree topology puts together multiple stars along a linear backbone. The mesh topology requires all nodes to be connected with every other node and is the most advanced.

Our generation technology has been advancing at breakneck speed. Now we are faced with a generation that has new challenges and issues never before encountered. While communication technologies have been advancing and breaking down barriers, with the Internet we see new obstacles never before encountered. For this reason the Electronic Frontier Foundation (EFF) was founded in 1990 by three of the biggest names in the computer industry. Founders Steve Wozniak from Apple Computer, John Gilmore from Sun Microsystems, and Mitch Kapor of Lotus Development wanted to create a foundation that would seek to protect the right of free speech in the digital era.

The global nature of the Internet presents another interesting issue. There are no international laws relative to commerce or copyright. How are these issues to be handled in the future? When creating hardware and software applications, the marketplace is now truly global. Creating things for a global audience is far different than creating them for an environment that you know. Consider choosing a new logo for your software application. You are lucky enough to be a fairly good artist and create a cute owl for the icon to represent the program. An owl makes sense because you feel it represents a wise and smart product. While this works well for your application at home, you have to consider what the icon could stand for in other cultures, for the owl that stands for wisdom in your culture may indicate black magic and witchcraft for other cultures. While diversity is an important issue for our time, it is ever so important in the world of technology. While seeking to cross divisions, we need to do so in fair and just ways. For these and other reasons,

Apple Computer devised an entire sourcebook on the topic of interface elements.

Interface Elements

In its sourcebook, Apple Computer set forth guidelines for developers to follow. Interface elements are the access points to the user and they should be designed to be very user-friendly. There are several ways to accomplish this goal. There are six different menu types: pull down; scrolling; hierarchical, which descends from a prior menu; pop-up, such as in a dialog box; palettes, which are used for items like tools and colors; and tear-off, which can be moved and dragged about the screen by the user. The developers felt the menu should remain at the top of the screen, and would provide shading to indicate menu choice availability. Menus should contain single-word options that are verbs. They only use adjectives in menus when referring to changing the attributes of a selected object.

In general, icons are better than words because they take up less space. Apple also felt that there should be reserved keywords, so that no matter the application, the keystroke combination used to initiate some actions should remain the same. Commands to cut, copy, paste, and quit are examples of the kinds of functions that should remain constant for the user.

Apple has also set forth human interface principles. These principles are the thought process that guides their decision-making in the creation of their applications. One such principle is allowing the user to have direct manipulation over the environment. An example of direct manipulation is dragging a document from one folder to another to move the location where it is to be stored. Applications should also have consistency. Users get familiar with the ordering of a menu. The menus in multiple applications should respect this idea and all provide the same order wherever possible. Third, Apple believes in providing the user with feedback and dialog. Examples of feedback would be error messages. Another principle is the notion of WYSIWYG, which stands for "What you see is what you get." Apple has several additional principles, but the point behind them is consistent. The developers don't require users to remember what aspects are available. In summary, they provide an environment that is comfortable for their audience.

There are also design considerations. Essentially, in designing applications and technology it is important to remember that technology serves a global audience. You need to remember that not all languages read the same way. In other words, there are languages that the reader reads from left to right, such as you are doing right now, and other languages read from right to left on a page. If you are designing a menu that will be used across cultures, you need to keep in mind that if you prioritize to match, you need to provide a provision to adjust your menus. Likewise, you need to consider colloquial and regional differences. Stick with standard language that can be translated easily. One of the best design considerations that Apple has had is to make connection to a network a transparent process to the user. They subscribe to the idea that users don't want to have to make decisions about what network resources are available. In their environment, they want resources to be available and to have the ability to be seamless to the user.

This concludes our look at the history and the hardware. The remainder of our chapters will focus on just what you can do with your computer. Successive chapters look at the results of using the different types of applications and even a look behind the scenes of an application with an introduction to the art of programming languages.

The activities that follow for chapter 1 can be used according to your situation. You can use them as guides to be completed on a computer or with older, conventional sources.

NOTE

1. *Compton's Interactive Encyclopedia*, 1994.

Activity Sheet 1.1

Inventions and Technology

Name: _____ Date: _____

For this activity you will need to refer to the information in table 1.1. All of the events in table 1.1 represent dates in the history of computers.

1. Choose five events in the history of computers.
2. Choose an additional five events in history. You can select things like the beginning or ending of wars, assassinations, presidents, natural disasters, and accomplishments in sports or in medicine.
3. Now create a timeline to show the events you have selected. Arrange your timeline so that the events are all above the timeline, and label the years below the timeline. Be sure to arrange your events along the timeline at intervals that are fairly accurate. For example, if your timeline ranges from 1880 through 1980, the point halfway along the line would be 1930, and three-quarters of the way would be 1955. Place your events on the timeline in a way that can identify them as a "historical event" or a "development of the computer." You may choose to place them in different colors or use different patterns, shapes, or shading. Be sure to include a key that identifies your selections.

Key

☐ Historical Event
■ Computer History

Activity Sheet 1.2

Inventions and Technology

Name: _____ Date: _____

Name an invention or technology that you think has made an impact. (Choose an invention that would be interesting for you to learn all about.) Look up information and facts about the invention that you have chosen.

1. In what year was your invention made or patented?
2. Who was the inventor?
3. How did this invention affect businesses?
4. How did this invention affect individuals?
5. How did this invention affect families?
6. How did this invention impact society?
7. Has this invention been replaced by another invention?
8. Do you think this invention will be replaced by another future invention? Why or why not?
9. Who was president at the time your invention was invented?
10. Name a historical event that happened around the time of your invention.
11. What has been the most significant impact of your invention?

2

All about Computer Graphics

> This chapter will introduce the topic of computer graphics and explain the terminology associated with graphics. First, computer monitors and how they have improved over time are discussed. We will talk about the capabilities of different graphic image files and focus on the types used on Web pages. We will identify the peripherals most often used to create graphics. Finally, we will briefly introduce some popular graphics applications.

To begin to understand computer graphics, we first have to take a look at the technology on which they are dependent. Computer monitors have borrowed some of their technology from television. The monitor contains a surface of phosphor. The pixels are then turned off or on by an electron beam that, when on, causes them to glow. The image must then be continually refreshed to the screen. A typical refresh rate is about thirty times a second. Higher refresh rates are imperceptible to the human eye. Sometimes, monitors appear to flicker. This flicker effect is when the refresh rates are slowed down, and the eye can begin to detect the effect of the image being refreshed.

Before there were color monitors for computers, there were monochrome, or one-color, monitors (just as before we had color television, we had black and white television). Monochrome monitors are capable of displaying only one color: usually green, white, or amber. Interestingly enough, the monochrome monitors created the shade by mixing three bits of information together. The result of mixing these bits creates eight gradations from white to black. Keep adding small drops of black to a large drop of white, and you can imagine the resulting steps on the scale. This scale is referred to as a gray scale.

Color monitors produce colors in a very similar fashion. The first color monitors, using the color graphics adaptor (CGA), were limited to displaying red, blue, and green. By controlling the amounts of the three colors, the monitor can display many more colors. Initially the EGA, or enhanced graphics adapter, was capable of displaying sixteen colors at the same time. Just like with the gray scale, little amounts of the additive primary colors of red, green, and blue will result in the color palettes that we experience when we view colored images on a color monitor. Because the colors are created by mixing red, green, and blue, monitor colors are often referred to as RGB color. Earlier CGA color monitors were only capable of displaying eight colors—similar to the capabilities of the gray scale. The next color monitors, the video graphics array (VGA) monitors, used similar techniques and were able to display 256 colors. With the introduction of high-resolution monitors, you now have the capability of combining the three colors each in 256 gradients, for a total of 16,777,216 (or 256 x 256 x 256) colors.

Gamma is the overall brightness that a monitor is capable of displaying. Gamma settings vary on different hardware platforms. A higher gamma value results in a darker display. This difference is responsible for some images varying between terminals. The technical term "gamma" is really a description of the relationship between light intensity and electrical voltage requirements.

Color settings can be represented by RGB values. Graphic files can be created in eight-, sixteen- and twenty-four-bit scales. In the decimal scale, they can range from the darkest (0) to the lightest (255) for a range of 256, or 2^8, values. We then refer to the hexadecimal equivalents to determine the actual values for each of the three main components. This allows the equivalents of the R, G, and B components to be expressed as a six-character string. Therefore, black is written as 000000 and white as FFFFFF. Red is FF0000, blue is 0000FF, and green is 00FF00. This way of putting the R, G, and B together is a hexadecimal triplet (nicknamed "triplet"). All the other colors occur somewhere within the parameters of white and black. Because not all monitors are capable of rendering the intermediate values if they are using the older standards, or even if they are new monitors set to an older setting, there are colors that are referred to as being Web-safe. The Web-safe colors are the basic colors that all color monitors are capable of displaying.

Monitor sizes are measured diagonally across the screen. The most common sizes for monitors are fourteen, fifteen, and seventeen inches. Special monitors are also available in other sizes. While the size differential between a fourteen- and fifteen-inch monitor seems really small, the reality is that the fifteen-inch monitor will provide 20 percent more viewing area. Realize, too, that the size of your monitor will determine limits on the resolution. Also important in choosing monitors is the refresh rate. Refresh rates below seventy-five Hz can cause eyestrain and will appear to flicker to the viewer.

Printers that do color printing use a similar process. Printers need to mix the primary colors on paper. When you add in the reflective effect that paper has, it is easier to create colors on paper utilizing the subtractive primary colors of cyan (blue), magenta, and yellow. The first cartridges created for printing were black. Today, color printers will label cartridges as CMYK, for cyan, magenta, yellow, and black. The combination of CMYK in printing is often referred to as the four-color process.

Realizing that the colors are mixed in similar fashion, but with different primary shades when printed in color, helps us to understand why sometimes a graphic or page on a monitor can look very different on a printed copy.

A pixel is the smallest rectangular unit of a picture. Unless magnified, they appear to the human eye as a dot. If you imagine the screen to be a grid consisting of rows and columns, the pixels would be the points of intersection. A raster is a horizontal row of pixels. The intersections, appearing as dots, are then either off or on. A term that is often heard in conjunction with computer graphics is resolution. Resolution is measured in pixels per inch, abbreviated as ppi, or dots per inch, abbreviated as dpi. Monitor resolution refers to the total number of pixels available on a screen. The higher the resolution, the greater the number of pixels that are packed onto the screen and the better the quality of the image. While the resolution number is related to the size of a monitor, monitors are capable of displaying different resolutions. The term "dpi" is a measure of how closely the dots can be placed when printing a graphic. Printers will declare their resolution in dpi values. Funny, though, that many people do not make the distinction and will use the two terms interchangeably.

It is important to remember that monitors differ in the number of colors that they are able to display. In general, the following pixel rates imply the images can have the following number of colors:

1-bit → 2 colors
4-bit → 16 colors
8-bit → 256 colors
16-bit → 32,768 colors
24-bit → 16,777,216 colors

Dithering is a mixing process similar to that of combining colors for monitors and printing. Dithering is a graphics and printing process where a dot is created by mixing different colors within a matrix of eight pixels. Combining the colors within a pixel produces many shades of a color.

THE MANY PURPOSES OF COMPUTER GRAPHICS

Computer graphics can be created for many purposes. Video games rely on computer graphics and are created for several different media. Computer animation is the result of displaying graphics in a sequence that has the effect of simulating movement. Graphics can also be created with many different types of applications. Some graphics applications are designed for a specific purpose.

Among the first graphics application programs created were those that allow the user to paint creations. With paint programs, the user can select tools and shapes and color them at the pixel level. The paint programs were simple, and it was very easy to master all of the capabilities offered within them. The next generation of the paint tools was the drawing program. Drawing programs included much of the same capabilities as the painting programs and added a new dimension in treating the created graphics as objects. Draw programs evolved the capabilities of earlier paint programs by allowing the objects to be rotated, shrunk, and enlarged, as well as allowing the user to change the dimensions and providing more detailed effects.

Computer-aided design, referred to as CAD, is a specialized form of graphic computing. CAD takes the needs and graphics requirements of engineers and architects and applies them to mechanical and computer science. CAD systems are typically specialized, and with that specialization comes greater expense. CAD has allowed the field of engineering to make remarkable advances. To the average consumer today, typical CAD applications can be seen in many home improvement and hardware stores. Arrive at the store with the dimensions of your kitchen and the locations of your appliances. The store, using its CAD system containing scads of geometric information, can then provide you with a screen, and perhaps printed, version of what your new kitchen would look like. Further, they can provide you with images from different angles and perspectives that give you the feeling of being in your new kitchen while sitting at the "drawing" board. This technology helps the homeowner avoid potentially costly mistakes. Imagine what CAD must be doing in the manufacturing markets. Similar to the CAD software is ray tracing, which creates realistic images of the effects of lighting. Ray tracing would allow you to take a picture of your kitchen and show you the effects of adding a skylight above the kitchen sink. The process of ray tracing calculates how light rays will be reflected and refracted from sources, taking into account the capabilities of the human eye. As the two-dimensional screen images become more realistic, we refer to this approach as photo-realism. Photo-realism is a term used to describe graphic images generated by computers that seem to be realistic.

Presentation graphics are applications that create images that are used for formal presentations. Some may accompany a speaker, while others are created as a presentation in their own right, such as animated movies. These animations, while they can look three-dimensional, remain two-dimensional drawings on the media they are created. The use of shadows and colors simulates a third dimension in the pictures.

Digitized video is a technique that captures video and allows the playback of graphics and images. With digitized video, the image is captured at a fairly high rate into frames. The images can then be saved and even compressed to save disk storage space, then played back later. There are many applications that can be used to view digitized video, and a number of these viewing programs are available for free. One of the first applications that were created for digitized video was QuickTime. QuickTime is still a popular video application for several purposes. In fact, many other software applications include a copy of QuickTime to enhance the capabilities of their packages. Today, many of these programs provide free versions that can be downloaded or installed to a computer by clicking on the appropriate place at the host program's website. Many of these viewers also have more advanced models with more advanced features available for purchase. Currently, many websites that send or "stream" video as part of their broadcast will direct the user to the websites to install these applications. Among the market leaders are Real-Player from RealNetworks, Inc., and MediaPlayer from Microsoft. The streaming video that can be viewed on the Web is not yet as clear as the picture quality of television. The rates at which the images can be shipped on the Web are dependent upon the speed of one's Internet connection. Additionally, there can be traffic problems at popular sites, which slows down their streaming video delivery. Currently, streamed video of fairly still images is pretty good, but movement is often accompanied by blurring of the images around the edges. Look for the quality of streamed video to improve dramatically in the next decade. The generation that is growing up with computers as a part of daily life is not going to accept quality that is considerably lesser than that available on the television.

Thumbnails, or tiny pictures that represent larger images, are miniature versions of graphic files that have many uses. They can be used to save storage space and to save processing time that a larger image would need. The thumbnails also allow you to view a "menu" of little pictures on the screen at one time. There are many applications that use thumbnails as a link to a larger image. Selecting the thumbnail will bring an enlarged version onto the screen.

Digital watermarks are sometimes included as a proof of authenticity of a file. Watermarks are created for computer program detection, but are often not visible to the viewer. Usually watermarks contain information about the author, creation date, and any copyright information. Often watermarks are embedded into digital images. The main reason for using a watermark is to protect ownership and to protect against unauthorized usage. There are graphics applications that can create and embed watermarks for any images that you create.

DIFFERENT TYPES OF GRAPHICS FILES

Computer graphics can be divided into two basic types. A raster graphic is composed of square pixels arranged on a grid. The image exists as it is defined by the pixels. Raster graphics are also called bitmap images. A vector graphic is made up of objects as well as information about the location and makeup of the object. Location information consists of start and end points, while makeup information can include information about colors, patterns, and other characteristics. Vector graphics are often made up of layers. The layers are stacked together and contain the information at each level. Usually you will find that simple graphics packages deal with raster images, while advanced graphics packages work with vector images.

Not surprisingly, there are tons of different types of graphic file formats available today. Just about every application likes to create its own unique file type. Determining what format to use can be a bit daunting even for the most experienced users. While there are some formats that are proprietary, meaning they can only be used within a certain application, there are many others that are common to more than one application. Currently, there are three different graphic file formats that are used on the Web. Remember that if you are creating graphics for the Web, you only need to create pictures with a low resolution. For the most part, higher resolutions will require longer times when loading a Web page. Even the newest Web users have experienced the frustration of having to wait what seems like days for a Web page to load. Today, designers are encouraged to check the load time of a Web page. If it crosses a particular threshold, pare the page back or shift it onto multiple pages, because viewers that are expected to wait will often cancel the loading and quickly move on to another link or location! This is why many of the browser applications, which are the programs designed to view Web page content, give an option to turn off the graphic images and load exclusively text-based materials. Little place cards or holders mark the locations where the graphics would be if they were turned on, and in addition, there can be alternative text displayed in place of the graphic as defined by the Web page designer.

GIF

The first of the three formats in use on Web pages is the GIF (graphic interchange format). GIFs were the first image files to be displayed with Web browsers, are limited to 256 colors, and are best for images that are less elaborate. There are two forms of GIF: 87a and the newer 89a. The original form, 87, was released as a free utility for CompuServe in 1987. Both 87a and 89a use .gif as their file name extension and are fully supported on most browsers. The most important feature to GIF files is that they are considered "lossless" compression. This means that when they are compressed to save disk space, there is no loss to the image. GIFs use LZW (Lempel-Zev-Welch) compression, a technique that was developed by Unisys, which together with CompuServe is the current patent holder on the LZW technique. LZW is an extremely efficient way to compress an image. In 1994, there was a bit of controversy over whether Unisys would begin to charge for the use of their patented technique. It was during this controversy that the newer PNG format was announced and released—when users feared they would have to start paying licensing fees for use of the earlier GIF format. In the end, Unisys never charged users for using the GIF technique.

Normally a graphic image appears on a Web page one line of the image at a time. This procedure continues through the entire graphic, line-by-line, before it is loaded. GIFs, on the other hand, take advantage of a process known as interlacing. With interlacing, an image is displayed by passing over the image in four passes. The image appears at first as a ghost and gradually becomes clearer on each successive pass. Interlacing is a good option to increase the speed that it takes for an image to load. GIF images also have the capability to be presented with a transparent background. The transparent background allows other images and text to show through.

The newer GIF89a format allows multiple images to be compiled or grouped into one single GIF image. The resulting effect is a stream of images when viewed through Web browsers. This effect, when repeatedly played over and over, has the effect of making the

GIF move. This is a very basic animation technique that emulates an artist taking a flip pad and drawing the same image over and over on each page with only a minor change, so that when the pad is flipped the image is animated and appears to be moving. There are special applications that can be purchased fairly inexpensively to make animated GIFs.

JPEG

The JPEG (for Joint Photographic Experts Group), pronounced "jay-peg," is the most popular graphic file format for photos on the Web today. While the extension is most properly JPEG, you will also see this abbreviated as .jpg to accommodate older operating system naming conventions. JPEGs are composed of twenty-four-bit color, which you can combine to form millions of colors. The trade-off to the amount of colors, however, is that compression is considered to be "lossy." This means that each and every time a JPEG image is saved, it experiences a degradation of some of the original color and clarity. While the loss is fairly small, it is present nonetheless. JPEG images can compress an image to about one-twentieth of its original size.

PNG

The PNG (for portable network graphic), pronounced "ping," is the third format that is used on the Web. This format is fairly new and is still a bit rare on the Web. Developed in 1995 by Thomas Boutell, it was posted as an alternative to GIF files when it looked as though Unisys might begin charging for the use of GIFs. PNG capabilities are far greater in that they can support eight-bit through twenty-four-bit color, and they offer a lossless compression technique. Ultimately they are clearer images that are smaller in size than comparable JPEG or GIF files.

BMP

BMP, or bitmap, images have no built-in compression techniques. Bitmapped images are excellent for storing clipart and are excellent for certain art projects like screensavers and wallpaper in a DOS or Windows environment. They are called bitmaps because they contain information about what is in each bit, like a matrix on a screen.

Bitmaps were often the file types that were created in the early paint programs. Almost all of the painting programs today allow creation of .bmp files.

PERIPHERALS USED TO CREATE GRAPHICS

Scanners are peripherals that are used to import pictures and documents into a computer. Scanners can also be used to import photo negatives and transparencies (slides). They consist of a "bed," which is the flat surface that translates the image into the computer (much like the flatbed on a copy machine). Scanners vary tremendously in their price and capability. The features that set scanners apart are their dynamic range and the optical density.

Dynamic range is a brightness value that measures the sensitivity of the sensors to convert analog-to-digital. The minimum depth for photos is twenty-four bits. Optical density (OD) measures the breadth of the range of brightness values that a scanner can capture. The highest OD measures are the best. OD is based on a logarithmic scale, so even a small jump numerically represents a large jump in order of magnitude. The majority of consumer scanners on the market today have a range between 2.8 and 3.0 OD. These rates are more than adequate for scanning photos. Negatives and transparencies require at least 3.2 OD.

Some scanners have features for working with extra-large or extra-small originals. There are also extremely pricey scanners that are designed to quickly process pages, and these high-volume machines can process up to eighty-five pages per minute.

What is interesting is that dpi calculations in scanners represent the number of sensors in a single row. What is important to consider is that, typically, monitor screens are bigger than photos. Increasing the resolution will increase the size of the image on the screen. It is important to know the size of the image you are scanning and the dimensions of your screen. You adjust your resolution to allow for the photo to fill the size of the monitor as desired. As an alternative, you can set the resolution as high or as low as you might want and then adjust the image's viewing size (by percentage) to make it fit the screen. Most of the software interfaces for scanners provide a setting whereby the height and width can be determined by pixels or inches. What you need to determine when scanning is how large the item is to be scanned, and what size you want the final image to be. You may then adjust the resolution to resolve the two items. Adjusting the size to fit different monitor resolutions is often referred to in the software as scaling options.

With regard to size, it is important to remember that with graphic images it is always better to resize images to be smaller. Shrinking images will be far preferable to enlarging. You will always maintain better quality by shrinking an image rather than by enlarging an image, as enlarging makes the space between the pixels expand and become more detectable, and as a result, blurrier.

Scanning images from printed materials like magazines introduces a special problem called a moiré pattern. The pattern is revealed as a crosshatched or herringbone appearance on the scanned image. The pattern is caused because both the scanned image and the printed image are made up of small dots. Some scanning software applications allow a screen filter to adjust for this problem.

The software that accompanies scanners will often allow the user to determine the file format of the graphic. Remember that choosing JPEG, which is good for photos, results in some compression losses. For this reason, many scanners use TIFF (tag image file format) with a .tif extension. TIFF was originally developed by the software company Aldus, which was later acquired by Adobe. TIFF creates a large file, but it does not suffer from compression losses.

Digital Cameras

One of the neatest developments in computing in the last couple of years has to be digital cameras. Digital cameras can take a picture and immediately store it as a digital image. The images can then be transferred or downloaded to a computer to be used in many different ways. Once downloaded, images can be manipulated in graphics programs and printed. One of the nicest features of digital photography is that it has eliminated the need to develop film. Unlike Polaroid film, you do not have to wait for the picture to process and appear. In fact, many digital cameras include a miniature monitor that allows for a live preview of a picture. In addition, when you review your picture in the camera, if you do not like it you can simply delete it and snap another! The immediacy of working with these images is really fun.

TWAIN

TWAIN began as an initiative launched in 1992 by a group of industry vendors who saw the need to standardize the way software and imaging peripherals communicated. This nonprofit organization, which can be found on the Web at www.twain.org, has done a great job in standardizing the applications programming interface (API) that is used. The word TWAIN was based on Rudyard Kipling's phrase, "[A]nd never the twain shall meet." It is a tongue-in-cheek idea because the organization and their resulting interface are an attempt to be sure that all graphics can be shared and can meet in common ways. TWAIN drivers are distributed by the hardware vendors and are included when you purchase a scanner or camera. Likewise, software applications utilize TWAIN to pull images into the program for you to work on.

CREATING A GRAPHIC IMAGE

There are several graphic applications from which to choose when creating a graphic image. While many have advanced and specialized features, there are others that have only basic painting options. Some application programs can be downloaded and installed directly from the Web, while others will require the purchase of a CD. Not surprisingly, some programs provide better documentation and manuals than others. Choosing a graphics application really depends on the needs and budget of the shopper. Among the popular alternatives are Adobe's PhotoDeluxe and Photoshop products, Corel PhotoPaint, Microsoft Photo Editor, Jasc Paint Shop Pro, Micrographx Picture Publisher, ULead iPhoto Express and PhotoImpact, and Macromedia FreeHand. We will take a brief look at a couple of the programs available: Microsoft Paint accessory and Jasc Paint Shop Pro.

Microsoft Paint

One of the simplest ways to create a graphic in the Windows environment is to use the paint accessory that comes with the operating system. The most recent version allows for the creation and storing of more than just the .bmp default file format. The tool

Figure 2.1   Desktop of Microsoft Paint Program

palette in paint is very simple to manipulate. The hardest aspect of the program is getting used to drawing with a mouse or cursor key. Figure 2.1 shows the desktop of the paint program.

As shown in figure 2.1, the color palette is at the bottom of the screen, and the tool palette is on the left-hand side. The available tools are a fairly simple set including a pencil, spray paint can, paintbrush, eraser, eye dropper, paint bucket, text tool, and a few design objects. Only a few tricks are needed to manipulate paint. For example, the eyedropper will allow the user to pick a color from the graphic, which is convenient when you need to match a color. The paint bucket will fill in any enclosed figure, so if you do not have an enclosed shape, the bucket will "spill" onto additional areas of the screen.

Jasc Paint Shop Pro

Paint Shop Pro is a graphic application that is a more greatly developed painting program. It has many features typical to more advanced painting applications. Paint Shop Pro is a program that works with vector graphics. There are tools to create effects on images like "posterizing," which makes an image that would appear with less colors on a poster, and negative effect, which replaces the colors in the image with the opposite colors on the spectrum.

There are tools for creating clones or duplicates, and you can create custom-shaped brushes. Retouch tools allow you to soften, sharpen, emboss, smudge, burn, and lighten in addition to several other options. There is a tool to do color replacements. Picture tubes are like stamps that can be placed anywhere the user wants on the image.

There are also a number of tools for choosing a selected area within a picture. These are easy to work with and also have additional features to them to allow for creating mirror images, rotations, and flipped selections.

Paint Shop Pro also gives the designer the capability of working on an image in layers. The result is that individual layers can be altered and blended in a large variety of ways. Layers can be any combination of rasters or vectors. The layer palette is designed to work with individual levels independently or in conjunction with one another. Pos-

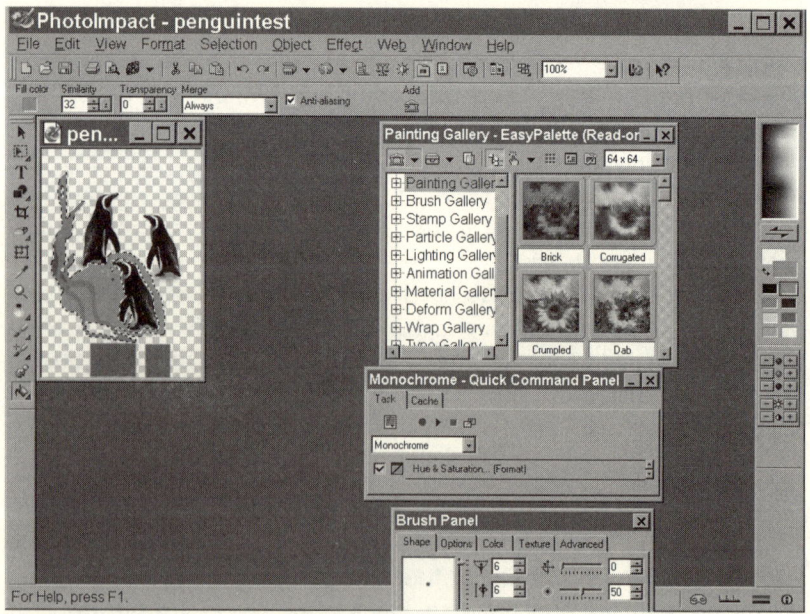

Figure 2.2   Creating an Image with ULead PhotoImpact

sible effects applied to layers include color, dissolve, overlay, light adjustments, and hue and color adjustments.

Masks are applied as a grayscale image to a layer. You can apply masks to hide and display portions of an image. There are even additional effects to add pencil, charcoal, chalk, chrome, neon glow, blinds, weave, and patterned effects.

Many of these same types of features are also available in ULead PhotoImpact. Figure 2.2 shows the desktop for creating an image with the trial version, which is available for download from the ULead website.

Use of Clipart

Clipart are special graphics that have been created by other vendors. Usually they consist of small images or cartoons. In some applications, adding clipart will be a menu option that is presented when adding imagery. You will find that clipart is a very convenient and easy way to jazz up many types of documents and presentations. Remember that most clip art, when inserted, can be adjusted as to its size and location. When you insert a graphic, it will arrive onto your application as an active object. Active objects can generally be identified by the rectangular boxes at the perimeters around the object that would match the major locations on a compass. Remember when you size an object, if you select from the corners, you may make adjustments proportionally, but adjustments from the center will often result in skewing an image in one direction.

If you want more clip art than what is available as part of a package, you can buy clipart on CDs fairly inexpensively or you can also get clipart from many locations on the World Wide Web. Appendix 2 lists several locations that allow use of their images without any additional permission, provided they are used for educational purposes.

There are many graphics tools available. The tools vary from free to rather pricey, with the capabilities varying as well. In the classroom, graphics tools are often met with enthusiasm—perhaps because one of the first forms of play we have when are very young is coloring! Take the time to investigate using the graphics tools in the assignment that follows.

Chapter 2

Activity Sheet 2.1

Painting with a Graphics Tool

Name: _____ Date: _____

1. Open up your paint program and begin a new image. Remember to save your work periodically, so if you have problems or inadvertently mess up your drawing, you can revert back to the previously saved version.
2. Create your own drawing or image and be sure that it includes the following elements.
3. On your graphic, be sure to use the text object tool to put in your name or initials.
4. Use the draw tools to create the following objects on your page:
   - A rectangle
   - An oval
   - An arrow or line
   - At least one additional shape of your choice
5. Use the paint tools to color in your shapes.
6. Use a magnifying tool and paint a fine detail onto your image.
7. Use the paint bucket tool to "fill" at least one of your objects.
8. Use the airbrush tool to paint some color onto your image.
9. Use your paintbrush to paint something freehand onto your image.
10. Change a different size or shape for your paintbrush and paint some additional detail onto your graphic.
11. Print your graphic and turn it in!

3

Word Processing

> We will look at the history of word processing and consider earlier machines that were invented for this purpose. In this chapter we examine different keyboards. Next we go through creating word processing documents. Generally, word processors allow for the creation, editing, extensive formatting, and retrieval of documents.

Word processing is an interesting term that came to us as a result of an advertising campaign. The advertisement was not for a computer, but for a typewriter. Today, many students aren't really sure what a typewriter looks like! The first successful manual typewriter was invented by Christopher Sholes in 1867, and was later marketed by E. Remington and Sons, a then-successful gun dealer. It took about twenty years for the invention to catch on, but eventually the business sector took to it and portable models began to be marketed at the turn of the century.

Thomas Edison patented the first electric typewriter in 1872, but it took about fifty years for a workable model to be introduced. In the 1930s IBM introduced the Electromatic, which was met with much wider acceptance. IBM continued to make advancements and add new features. Then, in 1964, IBM introduced a new electronic model that could store information on a magnetic tape. The advertising campaign for this typewriter coined the phrase "word processing." Following these models, specialized computers that could only perform word processing functions were introduced. These special-purpose machines, called dedicated word processors, were typically large, heavy, and expensive. Many were built into big cabinets or desks that became part of the unit itself. The printer portion was often built into the unit as well and was extremely noisy and slow compared to our modern standards. The components were hard-wired, so upgrading an existing machine was difficult and expensive. Regardless, the dedicated word processors were a huge advancement over the traditional typing pools, where typists were limited in the number of copies they could produce. The Vydec machine, introduced in 1973, was the first machine to use a floppy disk (albeit one the size of a large sheet of paper) for storage. The dedicated word processors were important business tools for about a decade, but when personal computers began to appear on desktops, the dedicated word processors found themselves antiquated by these new machines that could support a word processing application. With the arrival of laser jet printing capabilities, the output of the personal computer was soon far superior to that from earlier equipment.

Word processing applications are a type of program that is often referred to as a software application. These applications are for the purpose of creating documents on a personal computer. Word processing has been the genesis for oodles of computer applications. Prior to the World Wide Web, word processing needs were often the main reason for purchasing a computer. Now most new machines come with at least one, and sometimes more than one, word processing application as a standard package. Most computers have one application that is referred to as a text editor. These text editors allow for the minimum functions required of a word processor. Examples of text editors include Notepad in Windows and Simpletext on a Mac.

Word processors are defined as having five main functions: creating, editing, storing, retrieving, and printing. Many applications extend beyond these functions and introduce all kinds of advanced features.

In *Silicon Snake Oil*, Clifford Stoll (1995) argues that he has not had the need for a new word processor since purchasing his first one. He successfully argues that his word processor from the 1970s suits all of his word processing needs, and as word processing software has progressed and capabilities have expanded, there have been very few additions that are necessary. Certainly as capabilities have changed, manufacturers must convince us we need these new features, or the purchase of new software wouldn't happen. While it is true that earlier versions of word processors have the most necessary features for editing such as cutting, pasting, and copying, most of us have come to depend on what were originally some of the advanced tools and are now seen as our standard requirements.

During the late 1980s, desktop publishing applications were introduced as options for those with personal computers. The desktop publishing applications were typically more expensive than a basic word processing program and far more complicated to learn to use. As word processing packages have advanced and progressed, with typically more and more features being incorporated with each release, the need for desktop publishing has been pushed into a more specialized segment of the computer program market. One of the latest features to be introduced to the word processing programs has been the ability to save documents in an HTML format that can be used as a Web page document. Although these Web pages are somewhat limited, they act as a great foundation for those beginners who are interested in the creation of Web pages.

While the last 100 years has seen such dramatic change in how we create our documents, one thing has remained fairly constant. The keyboard layout common to many of today's electronic devices is the layout that was standard on the early manual models. The QWERTY, named for the top left six keys of the keyboard, still remains fixed in our advanced high-tech lives. In the 1940s, Dvorak researched and created a new keyboard designed to place the most frequently occurring letters in our language in a more efficient layout for our fingers. This design, however, failed to catch on.

LEARNING THE BASIC WORD PROCESSING TOOLS

Whatever word processing application you use, commands by keystroke combinations are vital to all. All applications provide menus and tool bars with many options. Many tasks can be accomplished in one of a few ways: by command through the menus, tool buttons on toolbars, or shortcut keystroke combinations. The best advice in this regard is to memorize the basic key commands that you will need over and over, and seek out the rest through menus and help screens. The keystroke combinations are time-savers, and there is a keystroke combination for all of the five main functions. Check the documentation for your application to identify the combinations.

Open up your word processing application and chances are it will assume that you wish to begin with a new blank document. It will remain named as the system default document (in Microsoft Word, this will be called Document1) until you change it. As you open new documents, they will be named sequentially. Remember, as with all applications, it is important to save and to save often. Even with timed or automatic backups running in the background, it is easier to avoid the problems of restoring documents when you save on your own.

When teaching an introduction to word processing, first open up to a new document. Have the students begin by typing a paragraph. It can be about anything. Alternatively, provide them with a paragraph that has already been prepared. This method requires finding and opening an existing document rather than beginning with a new one. Both skills are imperative to master, and while they sound obvious, they can become barriers to students later on if not carefully mastered.

Saving and Retrieving Documents

There is a subtle difference between the "save" and "save as" commands. If a file has not been previously saved, the "save" option will open up in a window. The most difficult concept here is to be aware of where you are putting your document. Do you want it on the desktop, on a floppy disk, or in a folder on the hard disk? Help your students to identify where you would prefer to store documents in your classroom or library. The most common problem in the class is often the inability to find a document on the second day. Students will swear they stored their document in a particular place and claim it has disappeared. Fortunately, most operating systems have a file find utility that can also be set to search by date. There are versions of the Windows operating system that require the existence of a folder called My Documents. This folder is a good place to save documents, but after a while can become quite full. If you anticipate having a lot of documents, it is a great idea to set up folders within My Documents to make your documents easier to manage. In other operating environments, you can also set up a folder like My Documents for file management.

Once you know where you want your document to be saved, you must decide what to name it. There are a few characters that are not allowed in a file or document name. For example, never use a period in a file name. Also recommend to your students not to use blank spaces in file names, as the blank spaces can be problematic in other procedures (such as attaching a document to an e-mail message). Names that are descriptive are often an advantage later on. The last consideration in saving is the file format or type. Note that the word processing application will normally choose its own file extension to match its kind of file. For example, Word will save as .doc and Claris will save as .cwk. Web pages need to be in an .htm or .html format. The text file extensions .txt and .rtf are the formats most easily used when transferring between programs. Files saved in a text (.txt) or rich text (.rtf) format are saved with many of the particular word processing commands stripped from the document. This is the file type to use if you will be transferring between different applications or operating systems.

Once you have saved your document, the tool button or save options will continue to save over the same file if you do not specify changes that will create a new document. Retrieving a document can be done through menu or tool button options. Again, the trickiest part of retrieving is often locating your document. When you open the window to retrieve a document and the file name does not appear, be sure to also check the file type that is selected. It may be necessary to switch between showing all file types and showing only your specific application format to find your file.

Editing a Document

The insertion point can be identified by the blinking cursor on the document page. The insertion point will move as you type. It is important to understand that, with a word processor, as you type your words will flow onto the document and automatically scroll to the next line. This flow is called word wrap. You should not use the enter or return key at the end of the line. Rather, the word processor will automatically determine what can and can't fit and will send the cursor to the next line as needed. A soft return indicating the end of the line will be inserted automatically by the word processor and will automatically adjust as the amount of text is altered. Many novice users try to determine the lines themselves and place breaks by pressing the enter key when they are near the end of a line. These returns leave what is called a hard return in the document, which will wreak havoc later if you begin to add or delete words and text; the alignment of the sentences will change, yet the hard returns will not adjust and will result in the lines looking jumbled. Resist the temptation to put in these hard returns unless you are doing some specialized type of entry like a poem, in which case the returns become an important element in formatting the document.

Generally, word processors have two editing modes. The first is insertion, which results in text being added as you type. The second mode is overtype. In overtype, typing will result in replacing or typing over the text on the document.

Type in a few sentences on your new document. When you are finished, you may now try to cut out sentence three and insert it to become sentence two. Note that the difference between cutting and copying is that a copy command will duplicate some highlighted text to be inserted to another point. When you cut a section of text from a document, you remove it. The removed text is temporarily stored to an area called a clipboard. This text will stay in the clipboard until overwritten by another cut or copied item. Some versions of word processors and operating systems allow for multiple layers or clipboards to temporarily hold text or fragments. Microsoft Word and Windows 98 limit the user to one clipboard area. The best advice here is to test your application to find out which is your version. Obviously, having multiple clipboard areas is a tremendous advantage when moving around text and paragraphs within a document.

Now return to typing a paragraph or two on your desktop. Essential skills for editing are learning to cut, copy, and paste text. Some interesting methods for accomplishing this task are to type a few sentences or perhaps copy a page from a popular book. Next try to scramble or unscramble the text and practice moving words, sentences and even a whole paragraph. Determining text selection is important in cutting and pasting. In general, clicking the mouse, holding down the mouse, and dragging the mouse over the desired text is an efficient way to highlight text. Alternatively there are key combinations that can highlight text. The highlighted text is the selected text and can contain a space, letter, word, phrase, paragraph, paragraphs, or even a whole document.

Pasting will bring in the highlighted text that was cut or copied and place it at the location of the insertion point, or cursor.

Formatting a Document

Before going any farther, the most useful keystroke to learn in your word processor is the undo command. Undoing can forgive a multitude of goof-ups. When you change a margin in a strange way or apply fonts that only a sharpshooter could read, apply the undo command and save a lot of headaches. When students create a mess and get lost or confused, the best advice is to hit the undo key and get back to a point or comfort level that suits them. If you only memorize one keystroke combination, Ctrl-Z is a good bet.

Most word processing programs have a number of toolbars. In Microsoft Word, the standard toolbar and the formatting toolbar are usually set to appear at the top of the page when you open the program. When they are not present, you can activate them by going to view on the main menu, then to toolbars, and highlight the desired toolbar. Note that all the toolbars can be "torn" from the top of the page and moved to any spot convenient for the user.

So, what are the standard tools? Standard tools help you carry out basic processes such as opening, saving, and printing. Note that the printer icon will send a current document directly to a printer. The printer selected will be the default printer. If you want to change the printer if you have more than one installed, you will need to go to the print option under the file menu. This will allow you to select your printer, choose your range of pages, and choose the number of copies to be printed. The additional tools include checking the spelling and the cut, copy, and paste options. There is a special tool that looks like a backward looped "P," which stands for "reveal codes." When this option is selected, all the codes in the document will appear on the page, including a small dot that represents blank spaces. This code can be helpful when you are trying to understand unexpected results in your document. Clicking on reveal codes will toggle between turning on and turning off every detail known to the word processor.

The formatting tools are the tools that change the look of a document. The most basic formatting tools allow you to manipulate the font or the look of the letters. Different types of fonts or font faces can dramatically change the tone and feel of a document. The tools for bold, italics, size, and underline can be applied to single letters, words, sentences, paragraphs, or whole documents. The majority of formatting tools can be toggled on or off by clicking on the appropriate tool button. With Microsoft Word, the tool buttons are easy to use, and you have the additional feature of selecting the format options from the format menu selection and choosing a font. The advantage of the extra step of using this window is that it previews your text prior to applying the font options. This is handy, especially when you have many font faces to choose from and you can't necessarily remember what the majority of them look like. Additionally, recently selected fonts will appear at the top of the list of the font face tool button. This is a nice feature when you need to change between fonts over the course of a document.

The tool buttons that change alignment selections affect how the document will line up on the page. Aligning to the left or right margins is pretty obvious. Using the center alignment, the program will automatically place the text, such as a title, in the center of the page. Many times, students will not trust this to happen and will tab or space to about the center of the page and begin typing. The best advice when it comes to formatting is to type and get the ideas down, then go back and perform the formatting later. Using tools like centering text allows the word processor to do a lot of the work for you. The fourth alignment option, justify, will result in stretching the text to meet both the left and right margins. It was the format of choice used in publishing for many years and automatically adjusts the space between letters and words. Only if the sentence reaches beyond a certain "hot spot" (usually about 80 percent of the way to the right margin) will the line of text be "pulled" to the right margin. Otherwise it will appear just like this sentence that occurs as the last line of a paragraph.

Tools such as bullets or numbering for outlines can also be useful features. The style used, as in the shape of the bullet, the numerals, or letters, can all be adjusted through menu selections.

Setting Margins and Indents

In Microsoft Word, there are two rulers available. You can display a side ruler, which shows how far down the page the text appears. The top ruler will reveal the tab and margin settings. The best way to set margins is to perform the formatting after you have typed your document. You can most easily set the margins by highlighting the desired text, then move the indent tool buttons on the horizontal ruler. Within Word, switching to the page layout view puts the rulers on the screen. The first line indent appears as an inverted triangle, and the left indent, which appears as a triangle on the left, can be moved along the ruler as desired. Generally they appear to be connected at first glance. The right indent triangle works in the same fashion. Margin settings can also be adjusted from the file menu, under the page setup option, under the margin tab.

Understand that a margin is the distance between the edge of the page and the text. An indent is the space between the start of the text, like the start of a paragraph and the margin. The default for left and right margins is 1.25 inches. The left and right indents are set at the edge of the margin.

Headers and Footers

Headers and footers are items that appear on every page of a document. They can be placed in automatically when a document is printed. Headers and footers in Microsoft Word can be edited when you select the view menu. Items such as an author's name or page number can then be automatically inserted onto all pages of the document. Pagination is another area in which the user should let the word processor do the work for them. Many students will try to type in a page number by hand. This can work, but if there are editorial changes or changes that affect the soft returns, you can wind up with an unnecessary mess throughout your document. In addition, a header or footer will guarantee that the placement, font, and format are identical on all pages of a multipage document.

Footnotes work in the same fashion. While you can choose to place some text in superscript or subscript and hand-code the footnote information, make changes later and you can have quite a mess on your hands. Let the word processor do the work for you and have the footnote information appear in a uniform and complete manner.

Line Spacing

The default for line spacing is single-spaced. You can adjust the spacing to double, half, and so on from the line spacing options, which can be found with the paragraph format options. Again, highlight your text, then choose the menu option of format, then paragraph, and make the adjustments to line spacing.

There are additional line spacing options to consider. Many of these can be found under the control of the paragraph formatting options. A popular editing feature is controlling against widows and orphans. Widows are the last line of a paragraph appearing at the start of a new page. An orphan is a very short word, or part of a word, which comprises the last line of a paragraph. A page orphan is the opposite of a widow: a first line of a paragraph appearing at the bottom of a page. If you want, you can control widows or orphans from appearing in your documents.

Spelling and Grammar Checking

The tool that has become the most valuable for many word processing users is spell check. Spell checkers, while not considered one of the main features of word processors, have become synonymous with word processing. The argument could be made that it was the ability to spell-check that enticed many of the earlier users. Now, teachers can insist that documents handed in are free from spelling errors, and it is far from an unreasonable expectation. The spell-check features can be interactive, where the document will notify the user if the word is not recognized. Microsoft Word places a jagged red line below the misspelled word. Place the cursor over the misspelled word, right-click your mouse, and Word will give you several spelling suggestions to select and replace.

Spell checking does not eliminate one important point. While a word processor can do many things automatically, it still depends on an author to perform the proofreading of a document. It is important to understand that if a word is spelled properly, the program won't identify it unless it triggers a grammatical error. Consider this sentence: After the visit to the main they stopped off at a popular rest for a spike of lunch. This jumble of sentence won't trigger any errors, but clearly does not express the intent of the author. While tools like grammar checking and spell checking have made the task easier, they have not replaced the requirement for careful proofreading. Librarians and teachers, don't forget to emphasize the importance of proofreading: a skill that is being eroded by our technology.

The Drawing Tools

One area in which word processors have offered some new tools in more recent years and versions is with drawing options. The draw tools can help to create documents that are more artistic. While draw tools can't replace high-quality writing, they can provide some visually appealing documents. Individual draw tools vary by application. Most now provide the ability to insert shapes or figures, as well as to draw lines and arrows.

Pictures, clipart, and word art are also popular additions. It is important to understand that these three types of art are all a bit different and have different editing and formatting features available to them. Some word processors come with clipart that can be inserted, but require a system disk to insert the graphic. Word art are specially predesigned styles and formats that can be applied to text. Many allow the manipulation of settings such as color, size, and highlighting. WordArt in Microsoft Word offers the additional feature of allowing the user to rotate the words so that they can be placed upside down or at various angles.

Importing clipart and word art results in an object being placed on a document. There is no limit to the number of objects that can be put onto a document. It is important to recognize that to edit an object, the user needs to click on it to cause it to be the highlighted object. Highlighted objects can be identified by the rectangles that appear at their perimeters. Once highlighted, objects can be dragged or moved when the cursor appears as a crosshair. When highlighted, a right-click on the mouse (in a Window's environment) will also bring up many editing options, including the grouping and order on the page.

Placing Pictures in Your Document

Many different word processors have various ways to insert pictures. With the Microsoft products, it is important to understand the importance of the insertion point and inserting pictures. Pictures, which exist as files on their own, have the requirement that they be inserted. Many a user has tried to open a picture and discovered that the result is a lot of codes that appear as a document of gibberish. This is because the word processor tries to translate those codes into a word processing document. Instead, it is important to insert a picture into a document. The picture will be inserted into the document at the point that the cursor is blinking. Pictures can then be aligned in the same way as any of the text, although the ability to then move pictures around on the document tends to be limited. One way to overcome this limitation is to place a picture into a text box. The text box can then be easily moved around the document. You can then choose to remove the line around the text box, so the picture will appear to be at any point in the document.

All objects can be made smaller or larger. To adjust the size of an object, grab the corner or little square at the perimeter, and the cursor will change to an arrow. Once the arrow appears, hold down your mouse button and drag the object to the desired size and let go of the mouse button. When resizing objects, consider their proportions. If you grab from the points that would be the top or bottom, you will stretch your object vertically. Grab from the points that are left and right and you will stretch your object horizontally. Grab from the top left or right or from the bottom left or right, and you will stretch your object proportionally. It is important to think about. Consider a picture of a dog. Stretching the dog vertically will make it appear more like a giraffe. Stretching the dog horizontally will result in making it look wider and fatter, more like a basset hound. Choose the resizing points with this idea in mind to wind up with images that reflect your intent. A diagonal resizing object at the corner, on the other hand, will adjust your image proportionally in both height and width.

As with any package, the best way to get to know its capabilities is to work with them. Go experiment with your word processor and push it to bring creative documents to your classroom. Remember, you can get wild without risk because you can always undo!

Activity Sheet 3.1
Word Processing

Name: _____   Date: _____

1. What is a dessert that you really enjoy?
2. Find a recipe for that dessert.
3. Using your word processing program, type up the recipe and be sure it includes the following:
   - A title
   - All ingredients listed separately
   - Measurements that have superscripted and subscripted fractions, like ¾ for three-quarters.
   - A degree mark for the oven temperature
   - Detailed instructions for completion
   - Bullets for either the ingredients or the instructions
   - Where you found the recipe

Activity Sheet 3.2

Word Processing

Name: _____ Date: _____

1. Think of a favorite character from literature or cartoons.
2. Create a single-page résumé for the character that you chose. A résumé lists important facts about a person and is usually used as part of a job application.
3. Be sure this résumé includes the following information:
   - Name
   - Address
   - Phone number
   - Education information, such as schools attended and degrees earned
   - Employment information: list place of employment and include a brief summary of the duties that the job required
   - Hobbies
4. Lay out the information in a pleasing fashion so that it is easy to understand and read. Include formatting options to highlight the various sections of information.

4
Spreadsheets

> In this chapter we will review the importance of spreadsheets in the emergence of the personal computer. We will then design a sample sheet to enter data and create formulas. Next we will look at relative versus absolute addressing as well as a look at some functions.

A killer app, or killer application, is one that affects the course of progress. It was one of these applications in the late seventies that moved the direction of personal computing to a new level. Prior to the invention of the spreadsheet, personal computers were machines that were used for limited purposes. Some people used them for word processing, but at that point the printed quality was often not as good as what you could produce with the conventional electric typewriter. While some applications were used for games, others were used for keeping track of data. It was not until VisiCalc's arrival on the scene in 1979 that the business world began to take notice of the abilities of the computer. This was the program that made them think that they had to have one of these new machines. VisiCalc was the first application written specifically for the needs and requirements of hardware available at that time.

VisiCalc, which stood for Visible Calculator provided the first dynamic ledger page. Suddenly the static ledger sheet, which in the past had to be calculated by hand one computation at a time, became dynamic. The old-fashioned ledger page would be composed of a series of computations, and if you needed to change one of the numbers at the top, you had to redo all of the computations, changing all the successive numbers on the sheet. This could be a very tedious process, especially for complex sheets. Now, for the first time, a machine could dynamically recalculate all of those numbers for you. Seeing a spreadsheet for the first time was really quite a revelation for the business world. Suddenly, all kinds of businesses and folks wanted personal computers of their own. Many people discovered that tasks like managing bank accounts and doing taxes could now be a whole lot easier. Can you think of another killer app that has been so revolutionary to our technology? Consider the World Wide Web. Suddenly, the Internet that had been around for over thirty years became engorged with commercial enterprises and households wanting access. Stop and imagine in your classroom what our next technological revolution could be. That idea from the girl in the back of the library might, indeed, be our next big invention.

WORKING WITH SPREADSHEETS

Spreadsheets are set up as a simple matrix. You have many rows and many columns. The columns are labeled alphabetically, and the rows are labeled numerically. The intersection of a row and column is called a cell, and the address is made up by the name of the column and row put together, such as A1 or Z35. Every cell has an address. This is a very important point. Take this opportunity to open up a spreadsheet and locate the labels for the rows and columns. Also notice that the current cell, the one that can be edited, is highlighted or shaded to set it apart from the other cells. In addition, there is some type of an address bar or cell reference at the top of the screen that identifies the current cursor or cell location. Adjacent to the address bar is a formula bar. A range of cells can consist of one or multiple cells. You can highlight a range of cells by holding down the shift key and selecting additional cells, or by dragging a mouse over a group of cells while depressing the mouse button. Note that the top cell of a range of cells will often appear as if it is in inverse video. Inverse video is when the colors are reversed on the monitor to highlight an area. The best way to determine which cells are highlighted within a range is to check out the perimeter border of the cells selected. A darkened border will show which cells are contained in a range. The range can consist of any set of adjacent rows or columns.

Types of Input

Cells may contain three different types of information: numbers or data, labels or text, or formulas. Numbers and data can be presented in many formats. Labels and pieces of text identify or provide information to the user. Formulas may be simple or complex. Some formulas may utilize functions, which are special formulas that come preprogrammed within the package and are able to be inserted. Think of functions as predefined relations that can cover many categories such as financial, statistical, math and trig, and date and time.

To begin examining the power of a spreadsheet, open up your version and begin to enter some simple information. Consider the information for a bake sale and enter in the following information:

	Quantity
Cupcakes	55
Cookies	250
Muffins	45
Cake slice	36
Cake (whole)	8
Pie slice	16
Fudge square	30
Brownie	67
Donut	96

This information is a good start; however, we might want to find out some other things. For example, we can calculate how many pieces we have to sell. The next obvious step is to begin to set some prices for your items, as shown in figure 4.1.

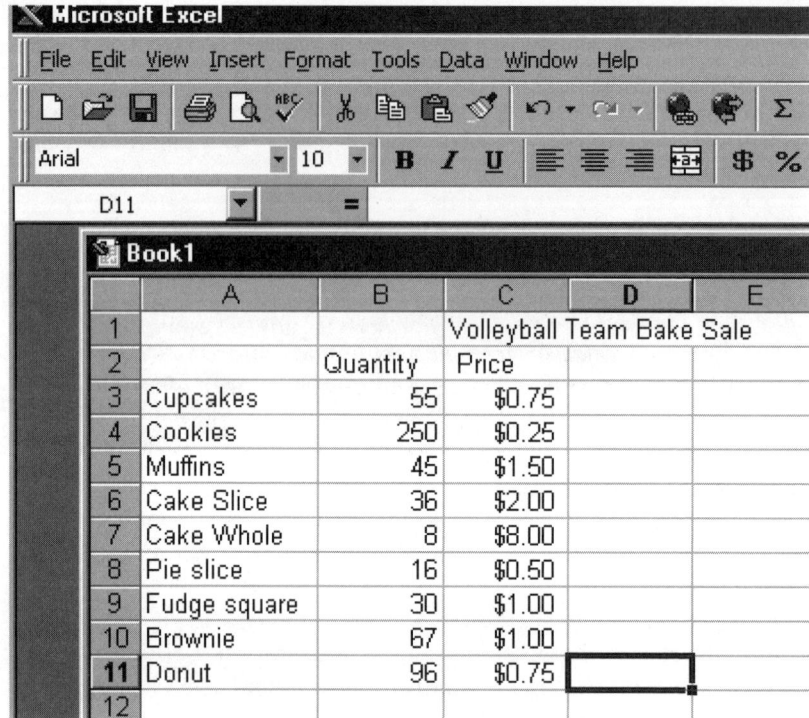

Figure 4.1 Beginning a Spreadsheet

Formatting and Alignment

At this point, you have only numbers and labels. By default, numbers that have been entered will align themselves to the right margin of the cell. The spreadsheet software sets the default, but you have the ability to change the formatting manually by changing the attributes of a cell or group of cells at any time. By contrast, labels or text will, by default, be aligned to the left edge of the cells. To change the alignment, you can highlight the cell and choose the alignment tool button that you need, whether it is left, right, center, or full justification. The alignment of text to the left versus values to the right helps in data entry.

Cell widths are another item that can be controlled by the user. Initially, all columns are set to the same width. To make a column wider or narrower, you can highlight the entire column, move the cursor towards the edge of the cell, and you will see a special cursor change that will allow you to drag the column to the desired size. An alternative method is to set the column width through the menu selection of format, choosing column and then width.

Input a twenty-character label into a cell that contains a column width of twelve characters. If there is no information in the adjacent cell to the right, the contents of that label will appear on the sheet. If, however, there is a value or label in the adjacent cell to the right, the twenty-character label will appear to be truncated at twelve characters on the worksheet. It is important to know that the information was not truncated; merely the display of the information was truncated. If you expand the cell to twenty characters, the twenty characters will still appear in the formula bar as originally entered.

FORMULAS

Adding Formulas

From our sample of the bake sale, you can add some formulas that would allow you to see your profit as you go along. Again, this feature of displaying the numerical changes as you go is what the dynamic nature of spreadsheets is all about. One formula that makes sense is to calculate the total pieces you have to sell. You may begin a formula with a plus or equals sign. The plus sign tells the computer that what follows it is to be a calculation. This can be done in a couple of ways. The formula can be written to determine the amount by typing in each address, such as +B3+B4+B5+B6+B7+B8. A second option is to put the range of cells in a shorthand notation such as +SUM(B3:B8), in which the colon says to include cells B3 through B8. The plus sign that begins this formula tells the worksheet that what follows is a formula. You can also enter an = sign at the beginning. Using an equal sign will result in the spreadsheet prompting you to create a formula interactively, and sometimes, when they are simple, it is easier to enter the formula yourself. After you leave the cell that contains a formula, and return, you will note that you will see an equal sign at the start inside the formula bar This identifies it as

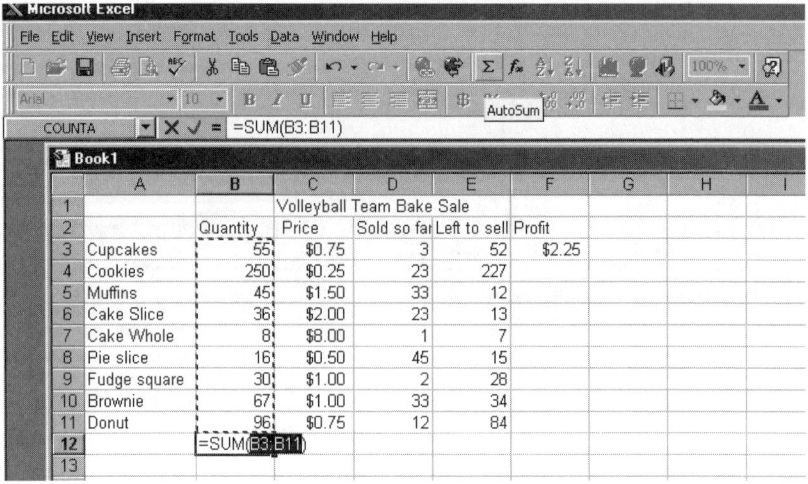

Figure 4.2 Using Formulas in a Spreadsheet

a formula, and not as a label. A third option is to use the AutoSum feature. The AutoSum, abbreviated as Σ, can usually be found on the standard toolbar and will result in highlighting an adjacent row or column when it is entered. You may then highlight more or less cells as necessary and allow the spreadsheet to adjust an AutoSum formula interactively for you.

Relative Addressing

Once you have entered a formula for calculating your profit, you do not need to recreate the formula. You can copy and paste the formula to the cells below it, so that your whole column will be calculated as you go. What you will notice when you copy the formula from cupcakes to cookies is that the address will automatically adjust for the new location. That is to say, the address is copied to suit its relative position. For example, our formula for the profit of cupcakes is =C5*D5, or the price multiplied by how many sold so far. When this formula is copied to the next line, the address will change to =C6*D6, and so on with each following line. That is because the spreadsheet recognizes that the formula is, "Take the cell that is three cells to my left and multiply it by the cell two cells to my left." This formula, therefore, uses relative addressing.

Absolute Addressing

Another type of addressing is absolute addressing. The best thing to remember about absolute addressing is that if you move a formula from one cell to another and it has an absolute address, it absolutely won't change! An address such as =B17-C24 indicates that these addresses will change when copied or moved. To make an address absolute, add a $ sign before the address; now =$B$17-$C$24 will not change when copied or moved to any other location on the worksheet. Note here that both portions of the address, the row and column designation, are made absolutely independent of one another. Remember also that all addresses are made up of a row and column designation. There will be times when you would wish the row to remain constant in a formula, but want the column letter to change as the formula is moved about the sheet. Conversely, you could want the column to remain the same in all cases and want the row numbers to adjust as a formula is moved around the same worksheet. A cell designation of $B17 would represent the column remaining permanent and the row number adjusting when copied to another location.

Formulas Containing Functions

The use of functions in formulas can be accomplished in a number of ways. The most common way to use functions is to allow the worksheet to prompt you for addresses and to build the formula interactively. If you are unsure of the exact syntax for a formula, the interactive option is a good one. You can choose to initiate the interactivity by selecting insert on the menu, and then function. You will then be presented with many choices to fill in and alter. Often, the spreadsheet application has the ability to highlight a piece of the formula and wait for you to either 1) edit it by typing, or 2) edit by clicking on the cell and having that cell's address be placed in the formula automatically. For some formulas, it is easier to type the whole formula yourself. Formulas that are very easy to experiment with are those for descriptive statistics. Try calculating the smallest value contained in a group of cells by using the formula =min(B3:B11).

An advantage to using spreadsheets is the ability to include extensive formatting. You can create very fancy tables to be printed by utilizing all of the formatting options. Placing borders around a cell to draw attention to an ending balance or placing all negative cells representing losses in red ink are just two small examples. Labels can be customized in much the same way as a word processing program can customize documents by allowing the user to set font face, size, and color. You can include your standard formatting techniques such as bold, italics, underline, highlight, and color. In addition, you can place borders and shading to any combination of cells or ranges.

Formatting cells with numbers or data gives the designer a great deal of flexibility. The data cells can be numbers in almost any format including percentages, fractions, currency, accounting, and scientific. Data selections include things like time, date (which has over a dozen formats), and social security numbers. You can preformat the cell by highlighting it and applying a format ahead of time, or you can format it after the data has been entered. Oftentimes beginners will get "strange" data in a cell, and even when they try to delete it and reinput their information, the resulting cell will still appear to have some odd information. Invariably, a cell format has been selected and applied to that cell without the user realizing it. To remove it, just make a new formatting selection that makes sense for the information, and the strange data will disappear.

Advanced Formulas

Every teacher is too familiar with the gradebook. To take a peek at some of the more advanced formulas that you can create and use in a worksheet, let's consider a sample gradebook. The different pieces that make up the formulas used here are referred to as arguments.

Figure 4.3 shows the details for the formulas used to do calculations for a sample gradebook. There are formulas that contain functions to do cell lookups. A common practice for teachers is to drop the lowest grade for a student. This would require logic to determine which score is the lowest. Consider the example where there are two quizzes. If you want to base a formula on a condition, you can do so by saying, "If cell J4 is less than K4, use J4, otherwise use K4." This would translate into a formula that looks like =if(J4<K4,J4,K4). Figure 4.3 also contains a lookup table. There are occasions when you want to create a table within the same spreadsheet, then use that same table to report back val-

Spreadsheets

	A	B	C	D	E	F	G	H	I	J	K
1		test 1	quiz1	quiz2	test2	test3	Reg Avg	which bigger?	weighted	Letter	Pass/Fail
2	Rodman	78	88	100	87	91	89	100	87.43	B+	H
3	Iverson	97	89	99	95	99	96	99	97.29	A+	H
4	Ewing	95	95	95	92	94	94	95	93.86	A	H
5	Jordan	85	74	87	86	88	84	87	86.43	B	P
6	Brown	72	65	90	78	81	77	90	78.86	C+	P
7											
8						=IF(C5>D5,C5,D5)					
9		Grade Lookup Table									
10			0	59	F	I	=((B2*2)+(E2*2)+(F2*2)+H2)/7				
11			60	69	D	I					
12			70	76	C	P	VLOOKUP($I4,$C$10:$F$17,3)				
13			77	79	C+	P					
14			80	86	B	P	VLOOKUP($I6,$C$10:$F$17,4)				
15			87	89	B+	H					
16			90	96	A	H					
17			97	100	A+	H					

Figure 4.3   Using Advanced Formulas in a Spreadsheet

ues based upon where the information falls in the table. The figure above takes numeric grades and changes them to letter designations. To perform this conversion, we use a function called vlookup. The vlookup formula contains three arguments that need to be a part of the formula. If you try to recreate a table like the one in figure 4.3, one of the most important details is to be sure that you enter your table data from the lowest at the top of the table to the highest at the bottom of the table. You will often find in school documentation that letter grades and their corresponding numeric values are listed from highest to lowest. You will need to transpose your data when you place it on a worksheet, otherwise the values returned will be inaccurate. Once the table information is entered, the next piece to understand is the actual vlookup formula. The first formula piece that you need to enter is the cell address that you want to compare against the table. Many students mistake this part as the cell in which they are currently creating the formula. It is important to distinguish between the cell you use to find where it falls in the data table as opposed to the cell where you are developing the formula. The next formula piece, or argument, is the full range of the lookup table. Be sure to start from the top left corner address and include all the cells through the bottom right corner. The last argument is the column designation of the table that you wish the spreadsheet to return. Note that this argument changes between versions of spreadsheet applications and operating systems. The trick here is to know whether, for your software and operating system, the spreadsheet considers the first column in the table to be column zero or column one. Consider the case in figure 4.3, where your table consists of four columns. The first two columns contain the values that your data will need to be within the range. The third column contains the letter grade that you wish to return, and the fourth column contains the pass/fail letter grade. In the case of figure 4.3, the first column that starts with zero and ends with ninety-seven is considered to be column one.

Formatting and Editing Tools

Spreadsheet applications will also include some standard formatting and editing tools. You can highlight a cell or range of cells that you wish to cut, copy, or move. Remember that your anchor, or the first cell in the range, will appear as if in inverse video. You can choose your tools either through shortcut keys, tool buttons, or selections on the menu bar. In addition, you will also have special functions that will appear with the changes of the cursor while highlighting a range. Dragging from the upper right hand corner of the highlighted cell results in a move. Dragging from the lower right hand corner box results in copying the information down or across any additional cells that you may highlight. To make a column or row wider, after highlighting the column or row designation, move your cursor toward the side and it will change to a cross. The cross indicates that you can grow the cells to be either wider or narrower. If you set a cell to be smaller than is required by the data you have entered, the cell will turn into # (pound) signs. To see the data contained, you can move the cursor into that cell and look on the formula bar, or you can make the cell wider to accommodate the data type. For example, a column width for a cell that is set to four, with a format for currency at two decimal places, will require a width of six for the data to be viewed normally. Any setting less than four will result in pound signs (#####) appearing in the cell. Don't panic if you see pound signs. They indicate a column is not wide enough, not that the data has disappeared. Simply adjust the column width and your data will return.

The dynamic nature of spreadsheets make them a great tool for scenario testing. "What if" scenarios that involve calculations have found no better home. The ability to go back and change one value and avoid all subsequent recalculations makes a spreadsheet such a neat tool. What if we charged $1.50 for brownies instead of $1.00? We can instantly see the effect on our bottom line.

It is important to remember that with spreadsheets, the data and results are only as good as the information that is entered. Like any other application, while you can always count on the validity of the results of a formula, you must check to be sure that the information it is using for the calculations is entered correctly! This is a place where "garbage in, garbage out" is the rule. Before we leave this chapter we recall that, as in preparing a text document, we need to remember to check our data to be sure the results are accurate for our purpose.

Activity Sheet 4.1

Learning about Spreadsheets

Name: _____ Date: _____

Task: You will create a spreadsheet that will allow you to keep track of your funds in a checking account.

1. Open a new worksheet and begin by entering the labels in a horizontal row for columns A through G as indicated below:

Check Number	Check Date	Paid To	Cleared	Amount Deducted	Amount Deposited	Total

2. Place your initial balance of $500.00 in cell G2.
3. Format your columns so that you can put dates in the form of dd/mm/yyyy and so that the amount columns are in currency format and show two decimal places.
4. Input the data for the following payments that you have made:
   August 1, number 1000 for $36.75 to the Dog House Supply Store
   August 12, number 1001 for $27.50 to the Linen Loft
   On August 15, you made a deposit for $57.50.
   August 14, number 1002 for $17.59 to the Candy Cupboard
   August 27, number 1003 for $25.80 to the Campus Book Store
   August 30, number 1004 for $73.50 to the Campus Grocery
   September 3, number 1005 for $12.50 to the Candy Cupboard
   September 7, number 1006 for $20.00 to the Gator Magazine
   September 10, number 1007 for $35.80 to the Boosters Club
   September 12, number 1008 for $24.90 to the Cool Groove CD Shop
   On September 15, you made a deposit for $57.50
   September 21, number 1009 for $13.45 to the Subs & Pizza Shop
   September 22, number 1010 for $52.50 to the Campus Book Store

Spreadsheets

September 22, number 1011 for $18.50 to the American Outfits Store
September 23, number 1012 for $119.00 to Cheapo Airline
September 30, number 1013 for $82.50 to the Music Arena Tickets
On October 1, you made a deposit for $240.57
October 2, number 1014 for $63.50 to Bob's Costume Shop

5. Create a formula in G3 to calculate how much money you have remaining in your account. Copy this formula for the additional payments and deposits.
6. Go back to the top of the worksheet and add a new column labeled Bank Shows in cell H1.
7. You have just received your first bank statement. It shows that checks 1000 through 1005 as well as 1008 through 1010 have all cleared. Create a new formula in H3 to calculate what balance the bank is showing at this time. (Hint: You will only reduce your total with the amounts of checks that have cleared.)
8. You have just realized that you did not record the amount to the CD shop correctly. Change your entry to $29.40.

Activity Sheet 4.2

Learning about Spreadsheets

Name: _____   Date: _____

Task: You will create a spreadsheet that will account for the money spent on a shopping spree.

1. Open a new worksheet and begin by entering the labels for address A1 through H2 as indicated below:

		Shopping Budget Sheet				Budget amount	$400.00
Item description	Bought	Store	Amount of item	Tax (if any)	Shipping (if any)	Total this item	

2. Format your columns so that you can have the amount, tax, balance, and shipping columns in currency format, and show two decimal places. Also change the alignment settings for your labels from the format menu so that they are centered and wrap text.
3. Create a formula in G3 to calculate how much money you have spent for the line item, including the tax and shipping. Create an additional formula for cell H3 to calculate the remaining balance. (The remaining balance is how much money you have after this item is deducted from the original budget amount.) Copy this formula down the column so that your remaining balance will be displayed when you enter any new pricing information.
4. Find your data: Identify six people you wish to buy presents for and list them in the "Bought for" column.
5. Search the Web or use advertisements from a newspaper or catalogs. Look for presents to buy for the people you identified in step three. You can look at different stores for clothing, books, toys, electronics, candy, flowers, and many other things. Be sure to note the amounts that you will spend on each individual and place them on the chart.
6. Fill in the additional information for each item in terms of place of purchase, amount, and tax and shipping amounts (if any).

5

Creating Charts and Graphs

> Charting is a wonderful skill and will always add to any presentation. Charting can be thought of as the added bonus to spreadsheet software programs. Today, all spreadsheet applications have charting capabilities. Many include a format that prompts the user step-by-step in the creation of graphical representations of spreadsheet data. This chapter will guide you through choosing your chart type and creating a chart.

Charts can be used for many purposes ranging from basic science fair projects or book reports to complex representations of corporate earnings. Requiring students to create graphs can now be a great addition to many lesson plans. It's important for students to experience the added dimension that a visual display of information can provide. Further, data analysis is often easier with a graphic representation. Spreadsheet software makes charting as easy as pie, if you know a few tricks and take the time to master them.

The basis of any chart is a data set. A data set is a series of information with at least one quality in common that can be represented graphically. When setting out to create a chart, first decide what it is you are trying to show. Do you want to show how one part compares to the other? Do you want to show a trend or a change over time? Do you want to compare before and after in some circumstance? Each scenario has a chart type that will best represent it.

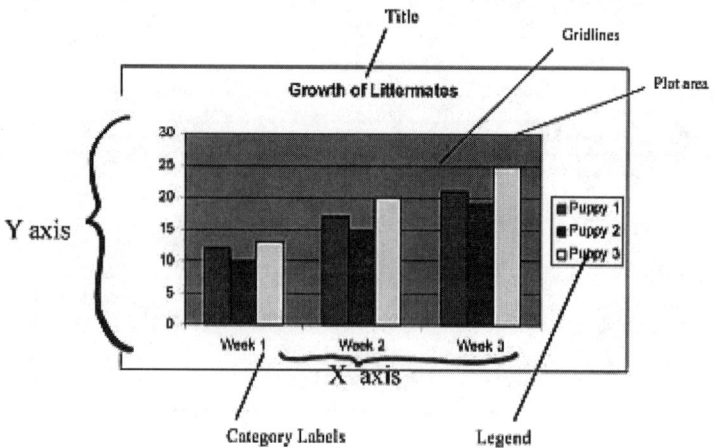

Figure 5.1   Parts of a Spreadsheet Chart

Whatever the chart, the best rule to follow is to keep the chart simple. Simple charts efficiently provide the information. The more complex the chart, the greater the likelihood that the user will misinterpret the data.

To create charts, you must first enter data on your spreadsheet. As the data is entered into the spreadsheet, the descriptions will become data labels and the values or numbers become data points. The more logical you are in setting up your data table, the better. Think about putting variables in rows or columns that will represent your hypothesis. The data points are entered in and become a data series in either a row or columnar format. The charts are a combination of the labels making up the legend and the data points making up a data series. Consider using a different series for each variable. The portions of the chart are labeled in figure 5.1.

THE PARTS OF THE CHART

The chart title should describe in a few words what your chart is representing. It is important that charts always contain titles for the viewers to understand them.

The legend, or key, gives labels to the data that is viewed. Each data set, or variable, appears in the legend as a series, numbered sequentially. If none are specified, the default is series1, series2, etc. You can edit the information at any time in two ways: 1) to cells on the spreadsheet, which will update automatically when changed, or 2) coded into the graph as name.

The perimeters of the chart are called the x-axis for the horizontal axis and the y-axis for the vertical axis. Both of these can contain a scale of values. The scale will be calculated automatically for the user, but can be manipulated by hand to any values the user cares to create. The scale may be represented as numbers or categories.

The plot area is the background area of the chart. In Microsoft Excel, this area can be adjusted as an independent object within the chart. It can then be formatted and adjusted for colors or fill effects that help show the data values most efficiently.

Gridlines are lines across the plot area. These lines are intended to make it easier for the viewer to read the data. Sometimes, especially when data are close, it is hard to determine differences without gridlines, as the objects can present optical illusions. There are times when gridlines seem to add to the clutter, especially in graphs with a large number of values. The user needs to determine when gridlines are appropriate and when they are not.

CHOOSING THE TYPE OF CHART

In general, when you want to show charts that will represent the contribution of different items, or variables, area charts are a good choice. Pie charts show how the parts can make up the whole and are effective in displaying the proportional relationships between data. The most important thing to remember is that all the parts of the pie chart, when added together, need to equal 100 percent of the population being represented. It is a frequent advertising technique to include pie charts that do not represent entire populations, and this is misleading. Consider the following hypothetical example, shown in figure 5.2: You have a group of 100 people choose between four models: Jungle, Park, Mountain, and Cityscape. They choose as follows: Jungle 30, Park 35, Mountain 25, and Cityscape 10.

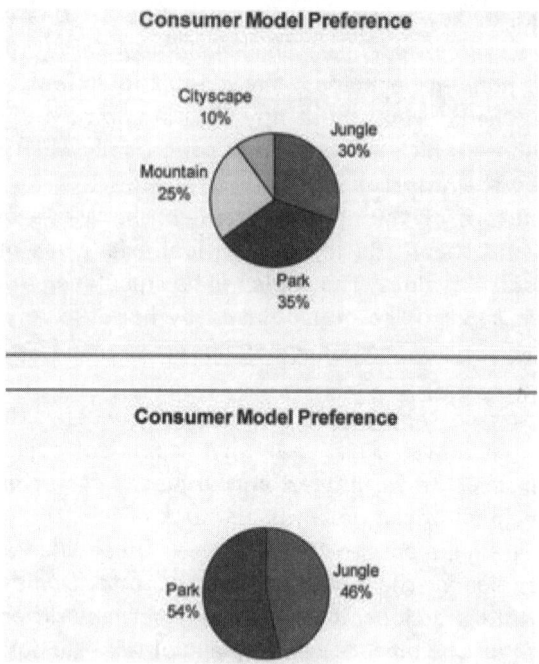

Figure 5.2   Using Pie Charts in Spreadsheets

The first pie chart represents the entire population. The second chart has only used two data points in the series, and still the chart will calculate the values as one hundred percent of the population, so the bottom chart shows a much different representation of the same data. The population for the bottom chart is sixty-five, not 100. This concept is surely something to think about when you review pie charts in advertisements.

Exploded pie charts separate out the slices for emphasis or for highlighting a comparison. Three-dimensional pie charts may also be exploded for emphasis. These choices really do not change the data; rather, they express differences in creative style.

Use bar charts and column charts to show comparisons of items. The comparison is often numeric. Bar charts are preferable to columns when category labels are long because they eliminate the crowding that results below the horizontal or x-axis. These charts also can be shown in three-dimensional versions.

Creating Charts and Graphs

Select line charts when you need to illustrate trends. Line charts work well for showing changes over time. Stacked line charts also show trends, but include the stack to show totals within the variables.

Scatter plots show correlation, or how changing one variable can affect another. When trying to show correlation between two variables, a scatter plot that approaches a perfectly bisecting diagonal line shows an extremely high correlation because as x changes, y changes in the same amount. It is important to remember in analysis, however, that correlation does not imply causation! In other words, the change noted between two variables could be the result of some other variable that has not been evaluated within this model.

When there are multiple data series to be viewed on the same chart, stacked charts are good options. Stacked bars or columns show comparisons between totals while representing proportions of totals within the bars. Choosing these types of charts depends on the message you are trying to deliver. For the charts to make sense, the totals need to be created from data that still makes sense when added together.

One of the most important tricks when creating a chart is to be sure that when you select your data for inclusion, you eliminate any blank rows or columns that may have been added for a table's legibility. These blanks will show up as additional data series and change the representation of your chart or graph. If you are using Excel, you have the ability to switch your chart automatically to consider your data as rows or columns.

When you create a chart in Excel, the chart will automatically be included as part of a worksheet. When you save the worksheet, the chart will automatically be saved as part of the sheet. When the chart is the highlighted object, and print is selected, the chart will be printed to fill the printed page. When the worksheet or a cell is highlighted, and print is selected, the chart will be printed with the corresponding worksheet or cell information in a smaller version. To change the size of the chart on the worksheet, you may select the sizing handles in the highlighted object. (Again, the sizing object appears as little rectangles at the perimeter of the object.) All of the pieces of the chart are treated as additional objects and can be adjusted by highlighting, and then adjusting them when they become the highlighted objects individually.

When using Excel, the chart wizard is the easiest way to create a chart. To invoke the chart wizard, highlight your data range and select either 1) the chart wizard tool button, or 2) insert, then chart from the menu. The chart wizard guides the user through four steps. Step one is the selection of the type of chart. Note that there is a preview available by pressing the view sample button. Step two involves identifying the source data, or data series, for inclusion. Step three allows the adjustment of options like gridlines, legend, labels, titles, and x- and y-axis labels. The final step is to decide if the chart should appear in the current worksheet or as a separate worksheet. Once the chart is created, any of the previous options can be updated or changed. Modifications will be made when you change a chart object. While highlighted, a new menu item selection labeled "chart" will appear on the main menu. The corresponding four steps appear as a menu below the chart option. Highlight and select as needed. As an alternative, you can use the chart toolbar that will allow you to conveniently switch between chart options. Frequently, if the chart isn't correct at the outset, students will attempt to "remake" the chart by going through the chart wizard process repeatedly and will shy away from making alterations through the chart option on the menu. This process is really inefficient in the long run. Encourage chart makers to learn all of the tools available and learn to tweak and adjust the graphic representation using all of the objects and menus that they can select.

CREATING A CHART

The first step in creating a chart is to enter the data onto the spreadsheet. Consider the sample data below. The hardest step can be determining what you want to display in a graph. For the endangered species data, a nice choice would be a column or bar graph that compares endangered with threatened species, and another comparison could be between the foreign and domestic species. Probably the best option is to create a stacked bar to show the picture of what is happening.

In creating a chart, you have to be careful not to include any subtotals or totals in your data set. Doing so results in double-counting data points. If you consider the species lists, and you want to see a

Table 5.1 Creating a Chart

U.S. List of Endangered and Threatened Species

Group	Endangered U.S.	Endangered Foreign	Threatened U.S.	Threatened Foreign	Total listed
Mammal	61	248	8	16	333
Bird	74	178	15	6	273
Reptile	14	65	22	14	115
Amphibian	9	8	8	1	26
Fish	69	11	42	0	122
Snail	18	1	10	0	29
Clam	61	2	8	0	71
Crustacean	17	0	3	0	20
Insect	28	4	9	0	41
Arachnid	5	0	0	0	5

Source: U.S. Fish and Wildlife Service, 1999.

stacked bar representing mammals, your bar for mammals would have four sections, not five. If you make a mistake and include the total, your result will be an additional piece of the bar, column, or pie that contains exactly half of the total data, because you have "doubled" your data and thus half of it will appear in this additional piece. Consider an opinion poll that shows a user preference of pink or blue. If you create a pie you want to see two slices, one for pink and one for blue. If you include the totals as a series in the pie, you will have three slices, and the third slice will be exactly half of the pie: the total of the other two slices.

Excel: Steps to Creating a Chart

Using the data for the species, highlight the cells from group through the last zero in the Arachnid column. Next select the chart wizard on the toolbar, or select insert on the menu and then chart. On the first step window, indicate your choice of chart. At this step you may press the bar to hold and view the sample. This provides a quick check on where your graph is going. Here, choose one of the stacked column selections. The window in step two identifies the series, or adjacent cells, that will make up your columns. For this example our series are in columns. Switching between the series and data range tabs will allow you to make many adjustments. Remember that the name will be the text the user sees in the legend and that the x-axis labels are the ones that appear directly below the columns. Selecting "next" will take you to step three, and here is where you can do much of the formatting—including creating a title and determining whether gridlines will be shown. Note that the default for data labels is none. This is important because data labels can be very important to the information you are trying to display. Pie charts without data labels leave the user trying to guess the size differentials, which can be really difficult when the sections are fairly close. The last step determines whether the chart will be included on the same worksheet, within the object selection, or as a separate page from the new sheet selection.

Once the chart is created, you can make modifications in several ways. The easiest way to make changes is to highlight the portion, or object, needed. Objects can be selected by clicking on them. Some of the objects require the user to double-click to make a selection. For example, if you wanted to change the color of the threatened U.S. species, then click on the small box next to the label in the legend. The second time that it is clicked on, it will be the selected object. A very small box will appear around the perimeter of the little box to the left of the label. Once highlighted, a right-click will allow access to the format legend key. Now the user may choose from colors and fill effects for that piece of the column.

When it is time to print the chart, there are two ways to accomplish this. If the chart is the highlighted object on the spreadsheet, it will print to fill the entire page sent to the printer and will be sized for a standard 8½ by 11-inch sheet of paper. If the chart is not the highlighted object, it will print as it appears on the worksheet. If the chart is sitting on top of the worksheet off to the right of the data, a print command will cause it to be printed in a small format on a page that includes the table information. Basically, remember to keep the chart as the highlighted object and you will be able to print a page-sized chart.

If you want to take your chart and place it into a Word document or PowerPoint presentation, a simple approach is to copy and paste the highlighted chart into the document or presentation. Highlight the chart and initiate a copy command. Copy commands, from the office tools, can be initiated in one of three ways: press the copy button on the toolbar; on the menu, choose edit and then copy; or press the Ctrl and C keys simultaneously. Once you have the chart in the clipboard, minimize Excel and go to the application

Creating Charts and Graphs

where you will be importing the chart. Once you are at the right point in your document or presentation, paste the chart into the document.

When you include all the data points, the resulting chart may not show all of the points along the axis. Rather, it will default and perhaps show every other point. In some instances, this is perfectly reasonable. In others, it is not the desired outcome. To switch these options, you can make several adjustments. First, consider the size of the font and the font face on the axis. Second, consider the angle at which the font is printed along the axis. You can adjust the angle of the text. In Excel, enter the edit axis by highlighting the axis, and a right-mouse click will display the options. The next step is to make adjustments under the alignment tab. Other alternatives are to edit the labels by hand to or change the text in the cell that has been referenced.

Charting is a wonderful tool to provide a pictorial summary for any project or presentation. Many presentation applications will allow you to import a chart created in another program. Take advantage of this and dress up any data with a picture to tell the story graphically. Have fun exploring the activities that follow!

Activity Sheet 5.1
Creating Pie Charts

Name: _____   Date: _____

Chart 1

1. Check through your pockets and backpack, and count the amount of coins that you have. (You may do this in groups or individually.)
2. Indicate the number of:
   - Pennies
   - Nickels
   - Dimes
   - Quarters
   - Half-dollars
   - Other
3. Create a pie chart that shows the distribution of coins. Be sure to include labels on the chart sections as well as an appropriate title for your chart.

Chart 2

1. The following are the modern birthstones for each month. Think about the members of your family. Count how many members have birthdays in each month.
2. For example, you may have two in March, one in April, and seven in May. Use the following grid as a tally sheet. If you have less than three family members, include information for friends so that you will have at least ten people for your chart.

   January—Garnet __   July—Onyx __
   February—Amethyst __   August—Sardonyx __
   March—Aquamarine __   September—Sapphire __
   April—Diamond __   October—Opal __
   May—Emerald __   November—Topaz __
   June—Pearl __   December—Ruby __

3. Create a pie chart showing the representation for the birthstones.
4. Bonus: Adjust the colors on your pie chart so that they represent the stone color for the month.

Creating Charts and Graphs

Activity Sheet 5.2
Creating Bar Charts

Name: _____ Date: _____

Chart 1

Create a bar or column chart that shows the native languages spoken by the most people. (All numbers are in millions.)

Mandarin	885	Portuguese	178
Hindi	375	Russian	165
Spanish	358	Japanese	125
English	347	German	100
Arabic	211	French	77
Bengali	210	Malay-Indonesian	58

Chart 2

Create a bar or column chart that shows the average number of vacation days for some selected countries.

Brazil	34	Japan	25
Canada	26	Korea	25
France	37	United Kingdom	28
Germany	35	United States	13
Italy	42		

Chart 3

Create a column or bar chart that shows advertising expenditures for television and magazines for the following categories in 1998. (Numbers in thousands of dollars.)

	Magazines	Network Television
Automotive	1,702,738	2,401,722
Retail	525,989	1,131,526
Food	646,292	947,716
Liquor	217,256	0
Tobacco	363,683	0
Beer/wine	56,513	468,255

6

Databases

> This chapter will examine the language and culture of databases. It will include an examination of the terminology and an explanation of the different design models. We will then work through developing a very simple sample database using some of the most common applications that users often receive as part of their system software when they purchase a computer.

Databases have become a common word in our everyday language. While many people have a general idea what a database is, very few would be able to define the term. Ask students if they thought they were part of a database. Most often, students don't realize how common databases are, and that information about them is captured in many places. A very savvy student might indicate that their school might keep information about them. Few will conjure up many other examples until you ask them the following questions. Have you ever been to a doctor's office? Has anyone ever picked up medicine for you at a drug store? Have you ever taken a class in art, drama, dance, karate, gymnastics, or a sport? Have you ever subscribed to a magazine? Have you ever filled out a guestbook at a store? Have you ever signed up for a team? Have you ever attended a camp? Have you ever gone on a trip that required an airline reservation? Well, if you answered "yes" to any of these questions, you are part of somebody's database!

Now try this angle. Have you ever used a database? The follow-up questions include: Have you used directory assistance for a phone number? Have you ever asked a clerk if a particular video or book was in stock? Have you ever checked a program listing to see when your favorite program was going to be on television? Chances are if you have done any of these things, you have used a database.

Using databases in the educational arena, at least for students, is usually a difficult topic to comprehend. This is odd, since databases surround our daily existence. Indeed, it often seems the usage of databases is expanding exponentially. Have you been to the dry cleaner lately? Almost anywhere you go, you will find yourself dealing with the end products of databases. However, the only obvious place where databases are a necessity in education is in administrator's offices. Information about student attendance, performance, and course listings lend themselves to easy adaptation into a database environment. The databases at school that students most often utilize are the cataloging systems installed in the library media center. Many cataloguing systems are purchased for the specific needs of these departments, and database logic and design is the core of these systems. The limitations and capabilities of these systems are directly related to the logic and design of the database.

WHAT IS A DATABASE?

Databases have their own language and logic. We are going to examine both language and logic. So far, we have hinted at what a database might be, but now it is time to define one. Think of a database as a computerized collection of structured data that is available through different views. More specifically, a database is a collection of related information that is stored electronically. The stored information can be edited, joined, sorted, and searched through an application program.

Database Terminology

A database is a collection of related information. The related information is contained in records. Records are made up of units that are identified as fields. Fields are the units of information. A key is the component that helps to identify and define a record. A group of records is stored in a collection referred to as a file. So, for example, a database may contain multiple files. For our example, we will have a database of a collection of information about the United States. We can set up records for individual states. If we include every state in our database, we would have fifty records. The fifty records would contain fields, which could be thought of as categories of information. Some samples of fields contained in our state database record may include the capital, the bird, the motto, and the number of representatives the state had in Congress. The key field for each record could be the name of the state. The key field is important to distinguish individual records from one another. Here the state name could serve as the key field because we are sure that each state name in our country is unique. In a database where there is not that distinction, it is important to define a key field that will mandate at least one unique field for a record. Key fields guard against the problems encountered when a database contains duplicate records. Key field uniqueness insures that the integrity of the information can be maintained.

Another way to identify database information is through entities and attributes. Entities, for the example we just described, would be the information about a state or the information contained in a record. Attributes would be the additional information about the capital, the bird, the motto, the population, and the number of representatives to Congress, or the information that is contained in the fields. The nomenclature, or naming, of fields becomes important depending upon the type of database model that is utilized.

Data Definitions

Data definition is the phase in which a database's structure is created. While it is possible to alter most database file structures, it is always a good idea to brainstorm the structure of the file well in advance. A file that is not well-planned will result in poor reporting and hence make the database appear to be faulty. Just as with spreadsheets, the data that comes "out" can only be as good as the data that goes "in." Consider a scenario where you are creating a data file to keep track of the members of student government. Perhaps you define your database to include names, addresses, phone numbers, and locker numbers. For the name field, you might create a fifty-character field. You then take several days to enter the information into the database. At some point several weeks later, you realize you need to create an alphabetized list of the members. Now, some of the names had been entered with the first before the last name, others with the last name before the first name, while still others contain nicknames. Have the system generate your report and you will discover that Anne Ziegler is listed above Nancy Addams. If the data had been entered originally according to separate name fields, one for first name and one for last, creating this alphabetized list would be a snap. Consider also that a few weeks later you discover that you need to keep track of the office that each member holds. While you would be able to modify the record structure and add a field to incorporate this information, you will have to reassess each and every record to update the information. Certainly, it would have been far easier to enter in all the relevant information the first time through each record. These types of situations are examples of why the data definition phase of building a database is so important. Well-designed databases will be far more valuable than poorly-designed ones. While it is true that it is often hard to think of everything ahead of time, you need to try to be as thorough as possible. Time that is spent considering what sort of information will be needed is paramount to creating a good file and recording designs and structures.

Retrieving Information

There are several methods for deriving data from a database. All database management systems (DBMS) allow for the sorting, searching, and reporting of data. However, the methods that are employed for these tasks will vary from system to system. Interface methods include report defining options or specially created forms. The interface methods will vary according to the database management system.

A search is executed when the application looks through the information and, based upon a specific value, provides a listing of information in a predetermined order. A query, which is asking a question of the data, will limit the resulting number of records to be displayed based upon some predetermined criteria that must be met. A sort takes the data and places it in order based upon a value or criteria.

Filters are a way to systematically find out information about the database. Filters allow the user to see things in a particular way without changing any of the information. Filters applied to the database will allow for the creation of reports. In some cases, smaller database files might even be extracted from an original file. Referring back to our example of database records about the states, we could apply a filter that would contain states that had more than four representatives to Congress. Similarly, we could filter states having populations greater than a number of our choosing. There are three parts to setting up a filter. First, determine which field or fields will be used to select records. Next, choose a comparison phrase, which is a phrase like "greater than," or "starting with." Finally, you will need to provide the comparison information, like an amount or a character.

Reports are the outcome of database analysis. Many database applications have report generators. Some report generators are more intuitive than others; however, all are created for the purpose of deriving information from the database. Reports will consist of all or part of the data contained in a database. Generally, it can be decided what type of information or which fields will be listed on a report. From this point, you may have the options to sort and filter information. Grouping might be necessary for the report results. There may be additional calculations, such as totals or subtotals, which can be determined by a report format.

Methods of Accessing the Data

Once you create a database and fill it with information, you will want to be able to easily access the information. Indeed, the motivation to create the database in the first place should be the types of information that the user will later want to extract from the files. There are a number of methods to derive information from a system, and there are several types of interfaces that can be used for data extraction. Think of the interfaces as the dialog methods between the data records and the resulting reports. The following are a few interfaces that are common to databases. Command interface is applying software-specific commands to perform predefined functions for generating information. SQL (structured query language) was developed by the American National Standards Institute with the intention of standardizing the language for conducting queries. At the time SQL was developed, almost every database package had its own proprietary method of analyzing the database and creating reports. With SQL, the attempt was made to standardize the methods of analyzing a database. Natural language performs data manipulation based upon English or language-like commands. QBE (query by example) provides an interface element to be filled out by a user to determine record selection. Forms-based data allows the user to fill out a special "form" that creates the report feature and generates information pretty seamlessly. Application programming interfaces (API) are usually the results of a program or instruction set being custom written and designed by a user.

Database Models

The earliest model of database architecture to be defined was the relational model as defined in 1969 by Edgar Codd. He established essential rules to define the relational model. The relational model can also be referred to as a flat file or tabular database. Set forth by a complex series of rules, the relational model remains the easiest to understand and master. Most database applications available for beginning users subscribe to the relational model.

The hierarchical model is more complex than the relational model. It can best be illustrated in examples like family trees or organizational charts. It is made up of relationships like a parent and child or an employee and a department. While the hierarchical model is easy to understand, it becomes more complex when designing reports and extracting information.

The third model, the networked model, is the most complex. The networked model consists of information at points or nodes, which are then linked in any direction across any level. A networked model is the most complex to design. Linkage between nodes needs to be predetermined and established at the point the database is created. If, at a later point, linkage needs to be reassigned, the linkage has to be totally redeveloped. While this model presents advantages in reporting, is it difficult to manipulate and the hardest to develop.

An important concept in data extraction requires understanding ascending versus descending information. Ascending character data is placed in alphabetical order. If you request ascending information in chronological order, ascending lists will generate results listed from earliest to the latest occurrences. Numerals, sorted in ascending order, will generate information that lists the lowest to the highest.

Security

A log or record of changes may be important for tracking changes to information contained in the database. An audit trail is a detailed record that can be supplied to analyze any changes that have been made to information in a database. Usually the audit trail will track any changes that have been made and will also provide the system with user information—including the identity of the user who made any changes accompanied by time and or date information. Financial databases and any other systems that require a fair amount of security are dependent upon audit trail features to insure the integrity of the system.

Data Integrity

Data integrity is the value of the information contained in a file. As mentioned previously, that data that comes out in a report or query can only be as good as the information that has been stored in the file. Files containing incomplete or inaccurate records will render inaccurate reports. There are different ways to insure data integrity, and many of these methods are incorporated into the design phase of the model. Consider again the student government database. If information about the office held is not entered in a standardized way, reports can be way off the mark. For example, if two individuals enter the data, one may type in "vice president" while another abbreviates the entry and enters "vp." Later a report is generated where the search criterion is "office equal to vice president." The report will only include records entered by the first individual because, to a database, vice president and vp are not equal terms. How can you get around this type of problem? Most database packages provide the capability to provide data validation during entry. You could create a validation that would require all of the entries to be an exact match to a predefined list. In this way you can create a far more robust database. The validity of the report with validation checks will be far superior and will inspire greater confidence in the integrity of the database.

Many people make a distinction between the terms data and information. The raw material stored in the fields is actually the data.

Information is the result of an operation being performed on the database. Information is the end product of a report or query, while the data are the things that you add to the records during the creation of the file.

CREATING A DATABASE

Over the years there have been many popular database packages, including dBase, Clipper, Paradox, and Oracle. Each program had its strengths and features that would be most appropriate in different circumstances. Let us use the example of a database about the states to begin developing a sample database. Remember that the steps used to create a database are consistent among different applications. However, we will create our database using Microsoft Access.

Databases allow the user to view information in two distinct ways. In one method, the information is presented in a format that resembles a spreadsheet. With this method, information is viewed in a table (see figure 6.1). Generally, the records exist within a row, while the fields are listed in columns. The other method is to create a data form. With a form, the information is presented one record at a time. The fields, which have labels identifying what information is to be placed in them, utilize much of the screen at one time. In a form layout, records are input, modified, and reviewed one record at a time.

Designing Your Fields

The first step is to design the fields that will be in our records. In Access, once we go ahead and identify that we want to create a new file, we will see a window that prompts us for information. The default for this program is to begin entry into a spreadsheet-like format to create a new table. The datasheet view presents the familiar spreadsheet layout, and the user can begin entering data immediately. Fields will be labeled as Field1, Field2, etc. At this point, you can rename the fields by clicking directly on the field label, right-clicking your mouse, and selecting the rename option. This method is not intuitive for creating data definitions for the fields in your database, as you can then input different types of information, such

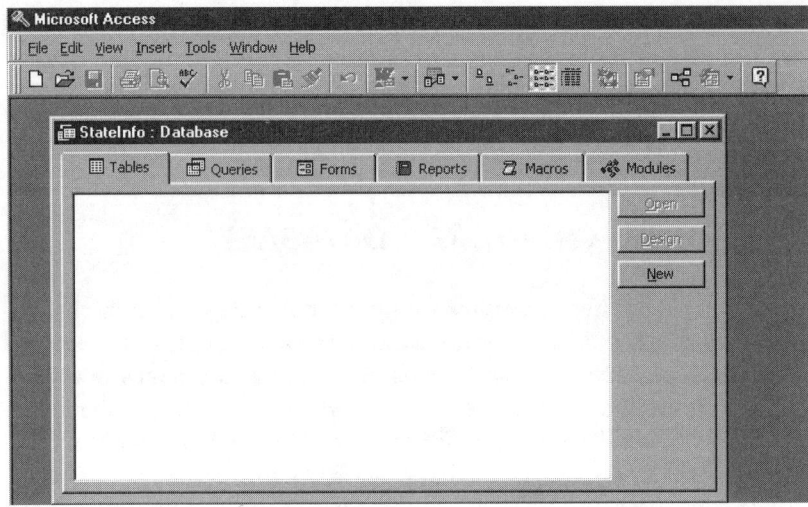

Figure 6.1   Microsoft Access Basics

as character or numbers, in the same fields. This technique, which allows different kinds of data within the same fields, can cause many reporting problems later. The better choice is to create the table with the design view option, found under the table tab. Design view will give you a table like the following. Figure 6.2 shows you a sample for a field. In this diagram you can see that seven fields have been defined, and you can see the data types that have been selected for each. The design view shows you the fields as they are created, and also shows you a table of properties for each field.

Properties are characteristics that you can set, including size, mask, caption, and validation text. Field size determines how many characters will be allowed in the field. When you put any additional characters beyond the length limit, the information will be truncated to fit the size of the field as defined. Format property affects how the field is displayed but does not affect the data that is stored in the field. An input mask is a template that the user will see during data entry. For example, (# # #) could be a mask to assist users to enter their area code. The caption will be the text or label that will be printed instead of the field name. The default value sets a default value that is automatically filled in when you begin creating a record. Validation rules are very specific to limit the data that can be entered into a field. Validation text is the equivalent of an error message when incorrect data is entered. Requiring a field will mean that the record will not be able to close until the information for this field is included. In other words, a required field must have data. Allowing zero length allows for text and memo fields to be empty. An index property will keep an index automatically updated by this field. Indexes presort your information and are important to speed up reporting capabilities in large databases.

The state name has also been defined as the primary key. Remember that you need to define a primary key so that there is no fear of duplication of your records. With Access, the easiest way to define your primary key is to highlight the field you want to be the

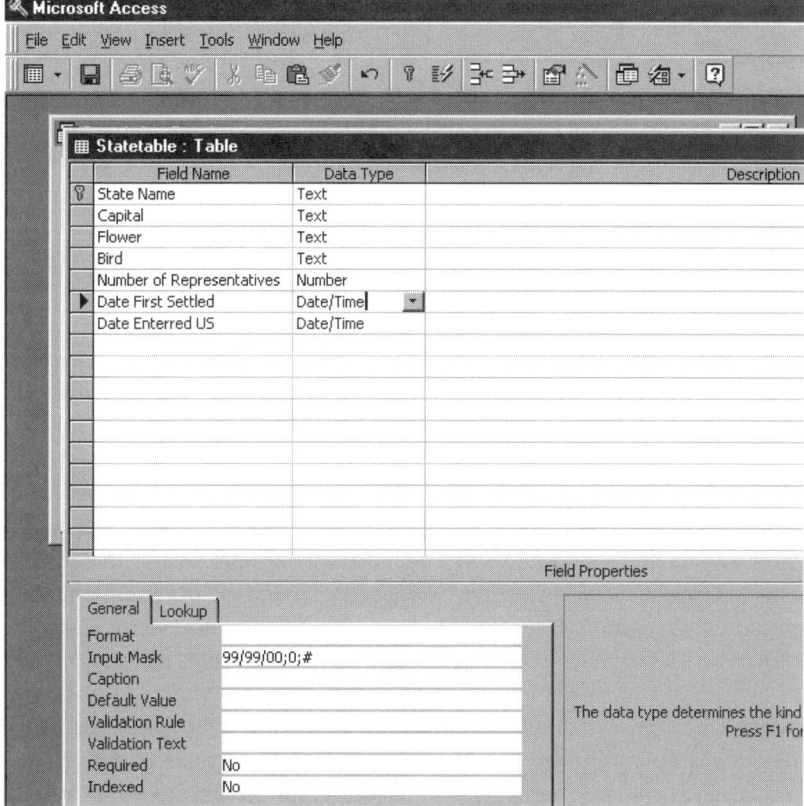

Figure 6.2 Starting a File in Access

key, and then click on the key symbol on the tool bar. If you do not define a primary key, the software will require you to do so, or will generate an "ID" field for you before it allows you to save your information for the first time.

The box toward the bottom of the screen is where you can specify additional field properties. Notice that input masks are being used for the two fields that are capturing dates. The mask will create a space that the user needs to fill out during data entry; again, this is so you can be sure that all the information contained in this field is standardized throughout the database. Once you have finished defining your fields, you will need to save the field information, and that will automatically put the table in the listing that you have in figure 6.2. Field definitions need to include a type for the data contained in the field. Data types vary by product, but for the most part you can choose between text, number, logic (yes or no), and date or memo types. Use numeric fields when you want to perform calculations or use formulas or functions. With Access, an OLE (Object Linking and Embedding) type is used. OLE fields work well for objects like graphics. Each type will have its own requirements to be fulfilled; for example, a date field will require a valid date format.

Create a Form for Data Entry

The second step is to create a form for data entry. There are two views for forms. In form view you can review, modify, and add data. In design view, you can modify the form. Choose the tab that is labeled "forms." Next, choose the "create new form" option. You can choose the design view in which the user has to specifically place fields and labels onto the form. An alternative is to follow the steps of the design wizard and let the system generate a sample form for you. The first step is to choose which fields need to appear on the form. Why wouldn't you want all the fields to automatically be there? Well, you may want to design data entry forms for different people or purposes. If you were designing one form for a user that did not have access to the historical information, it might make sense to leave that field out. In most cases, you will want to include all the fields. Once the form is generated, you can go back at any time to modify the form. To modify the form, highlight it on the table, then click on the design option to the right. You can now click on individual labels and fields, and when they become the highlighted selection (you will see little boxes at the perimeter of the information) you can adjust the sizes, drag the objects around on the form, and perform any of the editorial modifications that make the form easy to fill out for the user.

Once your form is complete, you may use it to view, modify, or enter new data. Access the form by selecting open on the right of the form. Once the form is opened, you will see your information in a format like figure 6.3. At the bottom of the form, you will see an indicator for the record that you are viewing. In this diagram, we are viewing record number two; so far, there are only four records entered into the database. You can continue to enter your data by using either the form or table methods. One feature of Access is that data is saved automatically as it is entered. You do not need to save the file to save the information as you go.

Once you have completed defining your fields and entering your data, it is time to begin to determine what type of information you

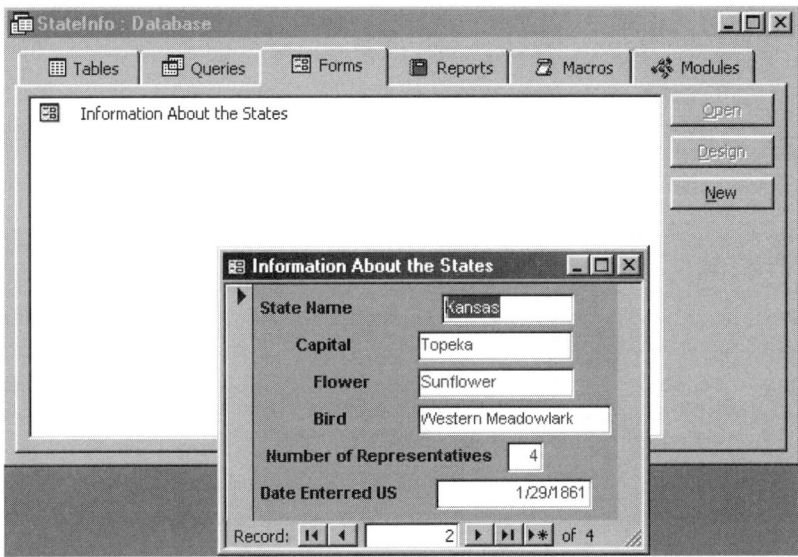

Figure 6.3   Entering Data for Individual Fields

want to derive from your database. One of the questions that is faced at this point is, "Do I want to select a query or a filter?" Queries and filters both have the same effect of (usually) retrieving a subset of records. ("Usually" because there are occasions when the subset can actually contain all the information in the file.) With Access, if you want to view your information temporarily on the screen in a table or form, you should apply a filter.

Reports are the documents that are the result of printing and analyzing the data. You can choose from different report formats. Reports can be vertical or columnar, and they can list all the data contained in the field on a record-by-record basis. Tabular reports present the data in a row rather than a column. Summary reports group the data together and provide information like subtotals.

When applying filters in databases it is important to remember the rules of Boolean logic. Two criteria joined with AND will create a smaller group of information that satisfies both criteria. Two criteria joined with OR will result in every record that meets one or the other of the criteria—usually a larger set than using AND alone. For our state database, if we select flowers with "blossom" and birds with "mockingbird," we would have two records, Arkansas and Florida. The same criteria with OR would result in the records of Arkansas, Florida, Mississippi, Tennessee, Texas, Arizona, and Michigan.

The operators for creating comparisons are as follows: = (equal to), < (less than), > (greater than), ≤ (less than or equal to), ≥ (greater than or equal to), and ≠ (not equal to).

Creating a Query in Access

Begin a query by selecting the query tab in the database table window, as shown in figure 6.1. Once you have selected a new query, you may choose between designing your own in design view or by letting one of the four wizards generate a query for you. With the wizard options, the choices are simple, crosstab, find duplicate, and find unmatched. The Wizards guide you through choosing fields and arriving at a finished product. To create your own query, select the design view option. The first step is to select the table or file to use to extract your data. In our example, we would choose to add the statetable. The next step is to select the fields that you want to see in the results. Look at the example in figure 6.4.

In this figure, you can see that the fields that have been selected are statename, capital, flower, bird, and number of representatives. The results of the query will be sorted by the names of the state capitals. Further, there has been a selection criterion placed on flower. The asterisk in "*nolia" stands for "any characters" or "like" a word ending in "nolia." In addition, there is a criterion of number of reps greater than or equal to seven. Note that this is set up as an OR condition; therefore, my result will be a set containing any records that match either criteria. If you want an AND situation, where both criteria would have to be satisfied for the record to be displayed, then the greater than or equal to seven information would need to be entered on the line above, under "criteria." The criteria line treats all cases as an AND condition. Once the criteria are finished, when you exit, you will be prompted for a name, and then the new query form will be displayed in the box. To run the query while it is the highlighted object, select the open command on the right-hand side. Note that once a query or object is highlighted, the commands to the right apply to that object. If you want to create another new query, be sure that no previously created query is highlighted; otherwise, the query will be created as a subset of the first query.

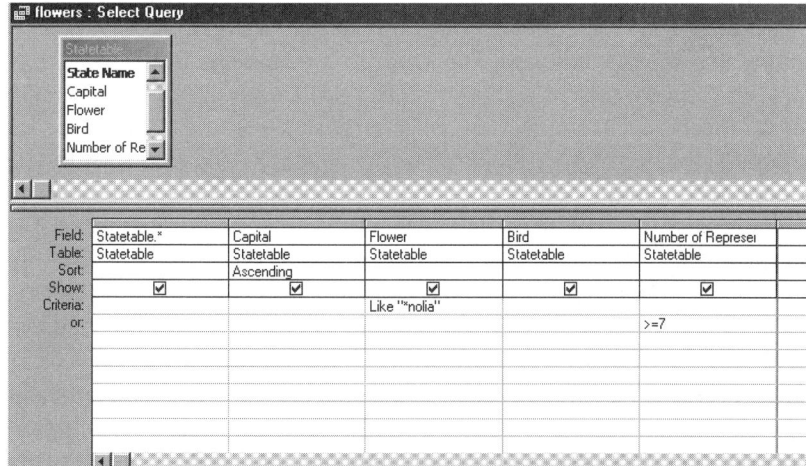

Figure 6.4   Using the Query Function

Creating a Report in Access

Begin a report by selecting the Report tab in the database table window as shown in figure 6.1. Once you have selected a new report, you may choose between designing your own in design view or letting one of the five wizards generate a report for you. With the Wizard options the choices are report, auto report crosstab, auto report tabular, chart wizard, and label wizard. The wizards guide you through choosing the file, specifying individual fields, and arriving at a finished product.

Creating a Database in AppleWorks, ClarisWorks, and FileMaker

Another popular application for creating database files is ClarisWorks by Apple Corporation. ClarisWorks 5.0x has been renamed AppleWorks and was released as part of the software package that is shipped with Apple's iMac and iBook computers. FileMaker, from FileMaker, Inc., is a subsidiary of Apple Computer, Inc. FileMaker is a long-standing database application package that has been popular for quite a few years. While FileMaker is a fairly easy product to understand and to teach, it is not as popular in the classroom at this time because it would have to be purchased for the sole purpose of teaching databases exclusively. It is the rare primary school that has the luxury of purchasing a software application for one purpose, especially when adequate software is shipped gratis, along with many hardware purchases. FileMaker is an excellent database product, but is beyond the scope of this text. However, note that much of its interface, because it is affiliated with the same corporation as ClarisWorks, looks very similar. For example, the flip-pad icon in the upper left corner, identifying which records are being reviewed, is the same. Therefore, the basic skill set from both products is fairly transferable.

To move between records, you have the option of clicking on the icon of the notepad or adjusting the lever at the right of the notepad. The lever acts as a scroll bar through the data records. Defining a database file requires defining database fields. You can begin this process simply by choosing to start a new database by selecting the database option from the starting points when you access the software program. Alternatively, you can specify which kind of file you wish to

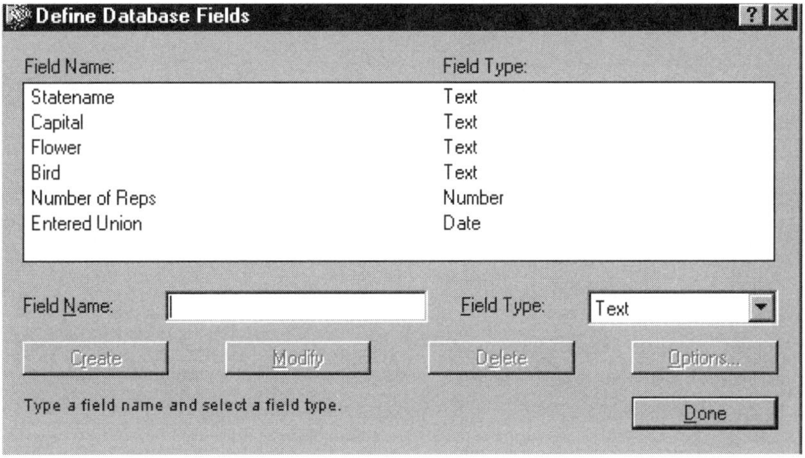

Figure 6.5   Defining Database Fields

begin when you choose file, and then new, from the main menu. As you enter database fields, you will be prompted for a field name and type. To place them into the database, press the create tab. Continue with this process for as many fields as you wish, and then press the done tab when you are finished. You can modify the options of any of the fields you have designed to make the field mandatory or unique or to set a default value (one that the user will see already in the field during data entry, which can be confirmed or overwritten). Review the diagram in figure 6.5 to see where to find the options.

The next phase in accessing data is to create a report layout. With a report layout, you specify what fields you want to appear at specific locations. You can have the system generate a layout for you, or you can work from a blank template. The most important menu option to master is layout. It is here that you will find the mechanisms for many necessary features. The layout view is similar to a form. One essential difference is that the system will default to placing records in succession on the page. The result of a simple layout for our stateinfo database can be reviewed in figure 6.6.

If you want to modify this and view one record at a time, you will need to uncheck the show multiple option on the layout menu. This view is different than reviewing the data in a tabular or single-record form. From the layout option on the menu, you have the capability to switch between the layout and browse options. Browse is for entering,

94   *Chapter 6*

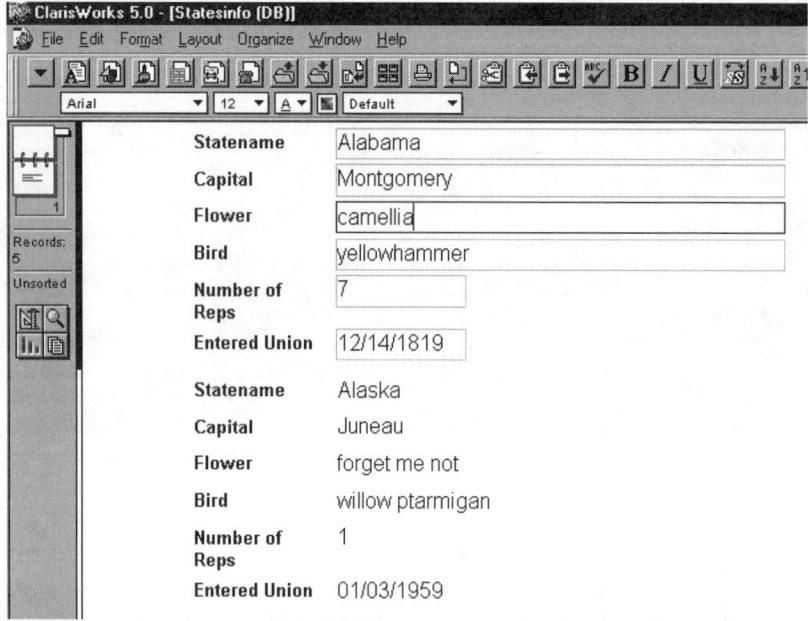

Figure 6.6   Results of a Simple Layout

modifying, and reviewing records. Layout is the option to check for making modifications to a layout.

Modifying a Layout

When layout is checked, the "Insert Field" option will become available on the menu. This is important to know to be able to make modifications and add fields to your layout. In figure 6.7, a data layout for our stateinfo file is being modified. Notice that the screen to modify a layout will present gridlines for adjustments. In this diagram, we have created a layout that only presents the name of the state, the bird, and the flower. The body tag is in the middle of the grid on the left side of the screen. The body tag indicates how large the record will be when it appears. If you were to move the body marker to the bottom of the screen, you would in effect create the equivalent of the form view in other database packages. You can insert graphics and make any modifications to the layout that you desire. When creating a new layout, a pop-up will appear to allow

Databases

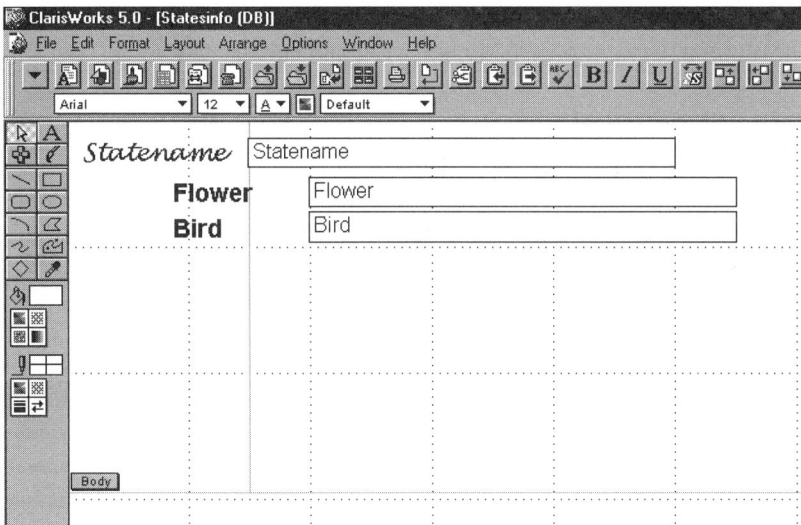

Figure 6.7   Creating Unique Layouts

you to create a name for your layout and make some additional selections. Layout options include standard, duplicate, blank, columnar report, and labels. The edit layout option will allow you to modify existing layouts and to delete layouts that you no longer desire.

When you have more than one layout, it is simple to switch among them. You will find that any existing layout names will appear at the bottom of the layout option on the main menu. The current option that the system is using will be checked and will be at the very bottom of the pull-down menu. To move to a different layout, check the one that is desired.

When a layout is created, the cursor will move to the fields in the order that they are added to the layout. There are occasions where you will want the cursor to move between fields in a different order. To modify the order of the fields during entry, you will need to work with the Tab Order command. The tab order is the order in which the cursor will move during data entry as a result of the user pressing the tab key. One of the most important things to understand with this package is that the enter key will not confirm an entry and move you to the next field. Rather, pressing enter will cause the entry to go to a second row for you to enter additional information. You need to remember to press the tab key to confirm your entries; therefore, movement between the fields is mandated by the "tab order" option.

Finding Information

To find information with the database, you may select the find option under the menu's layout option. The easiest way to search for information is to enter the information directly into the fields in which they occur. For example, if you wanted to find all the states that contained North, you could type North into the statename field box. The result would show the records for North Carolina and North Dakota. If, on the other hand, you wanted to find all the states that had blossom as part of the flower name, under the flower field entry you could place *blossom. You can use the same value operators for searching of <, >, =, and so forth. Additionally, you may use ... to signify a range for dates or times, and an exclamation point (!), which is an abbreviation to search for duplicate information.

ClarisWorks files are saved with an extension of .cwk, whereas Access files as saved with an extension of .wdb. The files that are created in this database may also be saved as other versions of the same software, as well as ASCII text files. Saving the file under the .dbf file type will allow the data to be converted to many other packages. dBase was among the first database applications to use this file extension for database files, and there are other programs that can utilize this format.

Databases are among the most difficult application to incorporate into today's curriculum. The irony is that databases are becoming common in many aspects of our lives. You can even think of a library as one large database where the file is the entire collection and the records are the individual items it contains. Though challenging to bring into the classroom, general knowledge of databases will remain an important technology skill for some time to come. With that thought, it is time to move on and think about the following exercises.

Activity Sheet 6.1
Using and Developing Databases

Name: _____   Date: _____

1. Please answer the following questions:
   What is your name? _____
   What is your favorite color? _____
   What grade are you in? _____
   What is your favorite food? _____
   What is your class section? _____
   What is your favorite TV show? _____
   What is your favorite movie? _____
   What is your favorite holiday? _____
   What is your favorite subject in school? _____
   On average, how many hours do you spend on homework each night? _____ Weekly?___
   What is your favorite book? _____
   What is your favorite sport to watch? _____ To play? _____
   What is your birthday? _____

2. Once you have completed the questions above, think about how you would structure a database file. Would you use all text fields, or would some of the fields require different file types?
3. Create a database file from this information. Be sure to label your fields with field names that are easy to understand.
4. Trade your questionnaire with the other members of your class. Input the answers from your classmates into your database. Once you have entered all of the data, you will need to perform queries or sorts to find the answers to the following questions:

   How many students prefer the color blue? _____
   How many students like to play soccer? _____
   Like to watch basketball? _____
   What are examples of the most favorite TV shows?
   _____
   How many students were born for each month of the year?_____

What is the most popular movie? _____
What is the most popular food? _____
BONUS: How could you calculate the average amount of time students spend studying each night? _____

Databases

Activity Sheet 6.2
Using and Developing Databases

Name: _____ Date: _____

You will need an almanac or encyclopedia to perform this exercise.

1. Have each member of the class select a foreign country.
   Research the answers to the following questions:
   What is the name of this country?
   What is the capital of this country?
   On what continent is this country?
   How many languages are recognized as official languages of this country?
   What is the monetary unit (kind of money, like pesos or francs) used in this country?
   What is the main tourist attraction of this country?
   What is the size of your country?
   What is the population of your country?
   What are the main export items from your country?
2. Once you have completed the questions above, think about how you would structure a database file. Would you use all text fields, or would some of the fields require different field types?
3. Create a database file from this information. Be sure to label your fields with field names that are easy to understand.
4. Trade your questionnaire with the other members of your class. Input the answers from your classmates into your database. Once you have entered all of the data, you will need to perform queries or sorts to find the answers to the following questions?
   Alphabetically, what is the first country in our file? _____
   What is the last? _____
   What country has the largest population? _____
   What continent has the most countries? _____
   What country is the largest? _____ Smallest? _____
   Which countries export fruit? _____
   How many countries have more than one official language? ____
   What are the different kinds of currencies in use? _____

7
Multimedia Presentations

> Media are forms of communication. Multimedia, which is placing more than one form of expression into a project, has allowed us to create presentations that are exciting and appeal to many different styles. When you combine features of sound, video, images, and text, the possibilities are amazing. Today multimedia presentation tools are becoming easier to use. We will take a look at creating the same multimedia project with two popular tools: HyperStudio and PowerPoint.

In the early 1990s, the first commercially manufactured CD-ROMs (CDs) became available. Originally entering the marketplace for music, CDs revolutionized the ability for inexpensive and portable media storage. Typically, media files are large and require more disk space than what is available on a traditional floppy disk. The ability to store these files on an inexpensive medium has created many new opportunities. Once the storage device became available, it did not take long for applications to begin to utilize increased potential.

Multimedia is most often an adjective to describe presentations. Prior to the 1980s, typical media sources included sound, writing, and pictures. Pictures could be still, motion, or animated. It was the arrival of the desktop computer that enabled bringing together these different elements with greater simplicity and much reduced cost.

There were users who quickly found value in creating presentations that incorporated different elements. Software applications to create presentations have evolved, and the preferred presentation applications that are in the market today have become fairly easy to use. Learning the language of a presentation tool can be harder than manipulating the actual software program.

A multimedia project is one that combines more than one type of medium of expression. Simple products combine text and sound together. Others include graphics and simple animations. Adding features of video results in a more advanced multimedia presentation. Any application that could concurrently process more than one form of media was considered to be a multimedia product. Multimedia that is created with the intent of letting the audiences participate is referred to as interactive multimedia.

There are many applications that involve combining media types; some are graphics programs that can be useful, appealing, and fun for children to work. Kidpix is an application that is extremely popular with young children. Kidpix allows the user to paint from palettes, create art freehand, and add sound effects. There is even an option to animate the still images into a special feature called moopies. The artwork can then be saved in a number of formats and imported to a number of other applications.

TYPES OF PRESENTATION SOFTWARE

In general, presentation software is divided into three main types. The first type of presentation is the type that one would use in conjunction with a presenter or speaker. The second type of presentation is the kiosk type. Typically, the kiosk presentation would run for a viewer. It can run on a timer or as a result of a user intervening in some fashion, as with a mouse or key click. The third type of presentation is one that is also viewer-initiated, but exists in a true Web or networked format. The viewer can choose the links presented in this kind of presentation and determine the sequence of the material. The viewer can choose what sections to spend the most time analyzing and in any direction that is of interest. What is most interesting about this type of scenario is that it is possible that two different viewers will experience two totally different presentations.

While there have been several entrants to the presentation software market, the two that seem to be used most often are Microsoft PowerPoint and HyperStudio. HyperStudio has been a popular educational tool and has been effective in the technology-rich classroom. Roger Wagner, who had a background in education, created HyperStudio, which was first made commercially available in 1988 for Apple Computer. The product was created for the educational market and had many advantages for students and teachers. Earlier versions included the author's dog, Addie, on pop-up screens for help. While the product has undergone changes in the industry, the most recent version available is HyperStudio 4 from Knowledge Adventure, Inc.

PowerPoint is a presentation tool from Microsoft Corporation. Many of the applications that are designed by Microsoft are designed to fit the needs of the commercial markets. This is not surprising, as the business market is vast and lucrative. As a business application, PowerPoint has become as basic a tool as the word processor. The business orientation is pervasive in the capabilities the package offers. For example, the templates, which are predesigned forms and patterns that can be incorporated into a project, are often designed to appeal to a business user. Even with these style limitations in mind, PowerPoint can be a powerful tool in the classroom. PowerPoint is so easy to use that you can always think of new ways to apply it to education.

Deciding which tool to use can be the most important question. It is conceivable that your school may not have both products, in which case your decision might be made for you. For our classroom, PowerPoint became a mainstay when it was bundled into the Microsoft educational suite we received on our lab computers. At the outset, many colleagues were skeptical as to the value of this tool in the classroom. However, once we began using it, we have found many ways to have PowerPoint augment our school's curriculum. As a presentation tool, it is obvious that it can add dimension to the traditional lecture classroom. Likewise, it can contribute to a well-polished student report and presentation in the classroom. We have found many nontraditional uses as well, some of which will be explored in the exercises at the end of the chapter. The challenge for a teacher or librarian is to take this tool and expand its capabilities into the classroom.

The educational community enthusiastically embraced HyperStudio, which originally made its appearance as an educational tool. The reaction to the first versions left quite an impression. The earlier versions were a bit daunting to novice computer users, though children seemed to absorb the product fairly rapidly. The end products had so much potential that later releases brought the application much widespread acceptance. What became synonymous with HyperStudio was how effectively the product engaged students. With HyperStudio, the traditional report was now brought together with text, sounds, and images in quite an exciting fashion.

HyperStudio excels at designing presentations that are woven together by the author. While a HyperStudio project can be the end product and presented in a traditional fashion, the product is most outstanding in its ability to help students create a user-centered presentation. With a HyperStudio project, referred to in HyperStudio lingo as a "stack," a user can chart his or her own journey through the author's material. Interestingly, when stacks are fairly complex, it remains very likely that different people accessing the stack will follow it in different directions and have different experiences.

It is true that there is overlap in the types of presentations you can create from both products. It is not surprising that each product has inherent strengths, and to capitalize on these strengths you can make your selection in this way. If you are fortunate to have both products at your disposal and you want a multimedia presentation to accompany your performance, then choose PowerPoint. If you want to create a product that will stand on its own for others to experience interactively, then HyperStudio would be a great choice.

This chapter will describe designing presentations with both products. We will take sample information and build a presentation about lighthouses for each model.

APPLYING HYPERSTUDIO: BUILDING A HYPERSTUDIO STACK

HyperStudio stacks, when saved automatically, get a file extension of .stk. A stack in HyperStudio is a file that contains one or more pages.

Think of a HyperStudio stack as a stack of index cards. Each page in a stack is called a card. A project can refer to a single stack or multiple related stacks. These related stacks could be thought of as chapters in a story. You can create your cards in any order. Know that you can reorder the cards in a stack at any time, so you do not need to worry about creating your cards in any particular order.

With earlier versions of HyperStudio, every time you started up HyperStudio by default you would be placed in the home stack. The latest release brings the user to a screen that requires a choice between the home stack, an existing stack, or creating a new stack. The software will look for stacks in the HyperStudio folder that it created when the program was installed. You have the ability to look anywhere on the desktop by browsing, using the format familiar to your operating system. Note that a stack does not exist until you save it for the first time.

Once you open the application, if you want to begin creating a new stack, make that selection. Otherwise, you may make changes to an existing stack once you found and opened it to the desktop. Leave the home stack for the software to show you samples and present system options. It is a good idea to work with a newly-created stack rather than to make your changes to the home stack. This is especially important when you are sharing resources among class members. You can select the icon for a new stack on the current card, or with older versions, you may choose new stack from the file menu. New cards will always be added to a stack immediately after the current card. The main toolbar for editing your stack can be found under tools on the menu. The tools menu can be "torn" from the menu bar and left at any point the user finds convenient on the screen by holding down the mouse button and dragging the tools palette away from the menu. This same thing is true of the colors palette. It is much easier to work on creating and modifying cards with these two palettes on the desktop.

Painting on a HyperStudio card is very similar to using many of the paint programs and tools that are now standard with the purchase of an operating system. Feel free to experiment with all of the drawing tools, as it is the best way to become familiar with their purpose and charm. The two buttons at the top of the tool palette are the most important to understand. They toggle the user between the two main modes of editing and browsing. You cannot make modifications to a card while in the browse mode. The way to preview a card, as your user will see it, is to be in the browse mode. Changing between these two modes just requires clicking on either the browse or edit tools on the palette. Notice that these modes will result in the cursor changing into either a pointing hand for browse mode or an arrowhead for edit mode. Remember to check which mode you are in if you are trying to make some changes and the card refuses to allow them!

Let's consider creating a sample stack containing information about lighthouses. Some brainstorming is needed before creating a stack. Consider the types of information that you will cover in your project. (A good exercise at this point is to create an idea web, for which Inspirations is an excellent software package.) Decide ahead of time the general format of what you want your stack to look like. Will you want to create one in which the backgrounds will be the same or different on every card? Do you want to create some special artwork for your project? Will you want to import graphics from scanners or cameras to complete your project? All of these elements can be included at any time, but it is helpful to make some design decisions before you begin.

Our lighthouse stack should have a cover, or title card. You have many choices in your design. Note that a stack can be manipulated by using the move command on the menu. Stacks that are going to be created and manipulated by the user should not be dependent on the menu for movement. Rather, a stack should be self-sufficient, and each card should contain the appropriate buttons to move the user from card to card. Most finished stacks are created and presented in a form without menus, which means that the movements through the stacks will rely entirely on the created buttons.

When you begin creating your first card, you can use any of the tools to design something suitable. You can choose to import a background from the file menu selection. You can use a picture, clipart, a scanned image, or basically any graphic to act as your background. You can draw freehand with the draw tools, and you can paint text onto the card. The important thing to know about using the text tool on the tool palette is that this text is for painting purposes only. Once "painted" onto the card, you cannot easily modify the text, such as if you would need to change the spelling. The only way to change painted text is to erase it, repaint it, or paint over it.

If you want to use text that will require editing, you should create a "text object." Text objects can be located below the edit tool on the tool palette, or through objects on the main menu. Text objects can be formatted, edited, and spell checked in an unlimited capacity.

The second card in our lighthouse stack will be an index. It will provide links to other cards based upon a theme or topic. Our look at lighthouses could contain information related to history, location, design, utility, engineering, and lighthouse keepers. You can now create new cards for each of your main topics. Later, you will need to create the links, or buttons, that will take the user elsewhere in the stack. Basically, there are two types of buttons that you can include. One type will consist of a button placed next to the text on the index. The other type will take the text from the card itself and turn it into a button. Both types utilize the same prompts and choice boxes. Once you have the initial text on your card, let's create some buttons. For example, let's create a button that takes the user to the first history card. Select "objects" from the menu and add a button object. The pop-up window allows you to select the shape, color, and icons on the button. You can also select the font face for any text that you place on the button. Once you make these choices and select okay, the button will appear in the center of the card with red dancing ants surrounding it. You can move the button to the place where you want it to appear on the card by dragging it. Clicking on the button will result in bringing up the action selection. The action can be to move the user to another card or to initiate another object such as a sound or video clip. If you choose another card that is not adjacent to the one you are working on, the choice of "another card" will bring up a sorter that will allow you to scroll through all of the cards in the stack. Use the scroll arrows to bring the card you want to link to this button, then click "accept" for the desired outcome. All of the movement selections allow the user to choose the transitional effects to the next location. To turn a graphic into a button, you have the additional step of highlighting the location for the button. Relax; if you make a mistake, you can keep editing the functions and location over and over again. Just be sure you are in the edit mode when you click on the button object, and you can go back into the pop-up menus and change your selections.

The next major component to consider is text objects. Text objects can be thought of as little text windows. The designer can choose to have a text box with or without scroll buttons. Now that most people are familiar with browsers and Web pages, scroll buttons are a fairly obvious concept. In earlier versions of HyperStudio, the scroll buttons were a bit harder to decide upon. Now, most users have a clear idea of how to read beyond the window size provided.

Let's create the card about lighthouse keepers. We can begin by adding a text object from the object selection on the main menu. Immediately, you will see a large box with scroll buttons on the right surrounded by red dancing ants. Clicking inside the box will bring up your options that can be set for the text. Essentially, you can set the appearance, actions, and features of the text box. Appearance is the choice to modify the font face. Actions allow you to associate an action with the text box. Features allow additional choices including your definition of what the cursor should look like while in the text box. The user can choose to make the text box read only. In this case, a user cannot change what appears in the box. If the user does not make the text box read only, a viewer can later alter what is in the text box. This could be useful if you want to create a guestbook-type of feature for a stack. However, for the most part, most text box objects should be of the read only type. Remember to select a font face that is legible and easy for viewers. Be careful in selecting colors that are easy on the viewer's eyes, and don't forget to consider that some viewers may have vision disabilities. Because you have the capability of having a scroll box, you don't have to worry about trying to place all of your text on the card that is viewable.

You can create multiple text boxes on an individual card, which may be appropriate for some cards. Consider our card for location. You may want to include listings by region, so that you could have one card labeled as South Atlantic and then separate text boxes for the South Atlantic states. Label one box as Georgia, containing Tybee Island Light and Sapelo Island Light. Another box for South Carolina would contain Morris Island Light and Charleston Light. The North Carolina text box would contain Currituck Light, Bodie Island Light, Ocracoke Light, and Cape Hatteras Light. The largest box would be Florida, containing Amelia Island Light, St. John's River Light, St. Augustine Light, Ponce de Leon Light, Cape Canaveral Light, Cape Florida Light, Fowey Rocks Light, Key West Light, and Sand West Light.

An additional feature of the text box is the capability of importing text from another source. This allows you to create text in your word processing program and import the text from its document into the text box. Highlighting, then cutting and pasting text into a text box is a fairly easy procedure. When you edit the text box, select get file in the pop-up. The user can then select the file that they wish to import. Note that the only limitation is that you can import .txt or .rtf files. These are the universal file types that all word processing programs have as a saving option. Text editors such as Microsoft Notepad will create .txt files by default and will work well for this purpose. Whatever you choose, be sure to save your text in either of these two text formats for import later. You may use your word processor, call up the document from its original format, and resave it into the proper text file format for import into your presentation.

The last object to consider is a graphic object. HyperStudio is great in that it recognizes many types of image files, including .bmp, .pcx, .gif, .jpg, .tif, .pic, .pct, .tgn, .bif, .wmf, .png, and .psd. To insert an image, you must first open it into a viewer. You also have the capability to preview the image. From that point, you can choose to scale and rotate your image. The scale selection is a great feature that allows you to decide how large you want the image. Once the image is open, you must select what is to be imported onto your card. You can use the rectangle selection tool that is resizable, or the lasso tool. The lasso allows you to trace around the image and is excellent to use when you want to take a piece of a picture. If we had a picture of the Split Rock Lighthouse and three-quarters of the picture was the cliff it sits upon, we could use the lasso to highlight the lighthouse itself, and provide a graphic of just the lighthouse onto the card.

The storyboard tool will bring up all of the cards in the stack as small thumbnails. The cards can then be rearranged by dragging the thumbnails into the desired position within the stack.

As with any application, be sure to save your work. Think about where you place your stack and what you name it so that you can find your work later. Consider working from a hard drive, as HyperStudio stacks get pretty large fairly quickly, and many stacks will not fit on a single floppy disk. This is especially true if you have included a fair number of graphics in your presentation.

The latest version of HyperStudio allows the user to set up a presentation as a slide show. However, much of the functionality would be lost using this option. The fun of a HyperStudio stack can be the results the user gets as they click on various aspects of the presentation and experience the resulting sounds and features. Long text boxes would not be able to be read by the user at their own pace in a slide show. While the ability to use a stack as a slide show may be useful, the true beauty of the application still lies in its appeal to its original audience. The new options exhibited in HyperStudio Version 4 also include the ability to include hypertext links. This feature now allows a presentation to incorporate Web addresses and links into stacks. Although some of the control features would be compromised, it may be extremely useful in many instances of presentation creation.

BUILDING A POWERPOINT PRESENTATION

The PowerPoint vocabulary is fairly simple. Each page is called a slide. Slides can contain any combination of elements including text, graphics, and special effects. When building the presentation, you will work from views.

There are five views that correspond to different stages of development. The slide view is the one in which you may edit individual slides. The slide sorter view provides thumbnails of all the slides in the presentation. Slides can be dragged and dropped into any order the user chooses. The outline view presents the slides in an outline format, with associated text as lists. The notes page view is intended as a place for the speaker to add notes associated with the slide for speaking to an audience. The final view is the slide show view, and it is the one that runs the presentation as it will appear to an audience. Regardless of the view the designer works in, any modifications made are made universally and are reflected in all of the different views. Most presentations are predominantly built between the slide, slide sorter, and slide show views, so these are the ones we will focus on for this chapter.

Before setting out to build a presentation, stop for a moment and consider the audience. When a presentation is created to enhance a speaker's presentation, there are some basic rules to follow.

Of course there are occasions where these presentation rules would not apply, but consider the following:

1. Limit the amount of text on each slide. Slides that contain large amounts of text will cause the audience to sit and "read" the slide, which will draw attention away from the speaker.
2. Choose text that is clear and is free of spelling and grammar errors.
3. Choose font faces and colors that are easy for your viewers. Consider the size of your presentation screen and the distance of your audience.
4. Limit the amount of transitions and your use of audio effects. Noisy presentations will distract an audience.
5. Choose graphics that are easy for your viewers. Again, the size and distance of your presentation screen will affect your audience.

Typically, a PowerPoint presentation for our previous topic, lighthouses, would provide slides to accompany an oral presentation on the topic. It is also possible to create a presentation that would run by itself, in a kiosk mode, but the depth of interactivity as an end-user product is still very different from the project we explored above. Keeping this in mind, it is still possible to do some creative things with PowerPoint that its creators never envisioned.

The wizards and samples created for the user in PowerPoint have a very business-oriented slant. Almost all the designs and samples represent formats that would be common to businesses of all sizes. The AutoLayout for slides will present a slide with templates for text, graphics, charts, and tables. Choosing an AutoLayout will require that the slide contain objects that are predefined. If you use an AutoLayout and later decide that you do not want to keep one of the elements, you will have a difficult time removing them from your slide. For this reason, it is often easier to begin with a blank slide for your presentation.

There are surely many ways to use the slides to augment a curricular experience. You can think of different ways to incorporate slides to provide information. Some of the best educational examples are those that break a process or procedure into its stepwise elements. Slides can easily represent the solving of equations. Each step of the calculations can be shown as individual slides. Stepping through the slide show takes the user from the beginning through to the solution. These types of examples are also ideal for displaying chemical compounds and the result of joining atomic particles. Slides can also be used as worksheets, especially in processes that require multiple worksheets to be completed. The original worksheet can easily be copied as a format to multiple slides, and individual incidents can be analyzed on a slide-by-slide basis. Consider using slides for cost-benefit analysis where each slide can take on one attribute and carefully make an examination.

To begin a PowerPoint presentation, open the application and choose a blank presentation. Once a presentation has been saved, you can access it by choosing "open an existing presentation." The advice when creating any presentation is to save, and save often, to avoid losing your work if some terrible event such as a machine freezing should occur. Note that before you name your presentation, the default will be Presentation1. The next step in preparation is to begin creating the slides. As an aside, previous versions of PowerPoint are not backward compatible: The 97 version can open presentations created in the 95 version, but a 95 application cannot access a presentation created in 97.

Once you begin a new slide, all the elements that are familiar with other Microsoft applications are available, with the same menu and toolbar layouts. It is important to realize that you can only edit a slide from within the slide view. The various view choices appear as five buttons in the lower left-hand corner above the taskbar (if the taskbar is at the default of the bottom of the screen). To move between views, simply click on the button that represents your choice, as illustrated in figure 7.1.

Creating slides can be accomplished by individually adding them when you are ready. Let's revisit our lighthouse example. Suppose you wanted to create a presentation about lighthouses to an audience that did not know very much about lighthouses. Like the HyperStudio example, you would want to create a title or cover slide to highlight the introduction of your presentation. Once editing a slide, you would probably want to show the title centered on the slide in a

Figure 7.1   Viewing Options in Powerpoint

large face. The easiest way to achieve this is to use the WordArt option and enter in your title and author information. The next thing you would most likely want on your first slide is a picture that represents the topic. You can add a graphic image to your slide by selecting insert from the menu, then picture. Once you reach this point, you will be presented with a pull-down menu of options. The most common option to choose is the "picture" and the "from file" or "from clipart" options. The clipart selections come on the system CD, and, unless a full installation of your software was done, you will need to insert the Microsoft CD to access the clips. The pictures from files can be found from any location, including a floppy disk, folder on a hard drive or CD, or any other storage location. If a picture is in the clipboard, then inserting a picture is as easy as choosing paste from the edit menu. This method is convenient in that it does not require you to save an image and take up storage in your computer. You can also select images from a Web page. Right-click on an image and perform a copy command. Now, when you reenter your PowerPoint slide to be edited, you merely have to select the paste tool, or Ctrl-V to insert the graphic.

PowerPoint allows you to choose from many different picture formats, including Picture It, .jpeg, .gif, Windows enhanced metafile, Windows metafile, .png, Paintbrush, CorelDraw, Macintosh .pict, encapsulated postscript, computer graphics metafile, AutoCAD 2-D, .tiff, Targa, Kodak photo CD, Micrografx Designer/Draw, and FlashPix. The default of all types will allow you to see a table of graphics to select from. If you do not see any pictures, yet you are sure that you had saved it inside a given folder, be sure to check that "all file types" is selected. Often users will inadvertently switch types, resulting in mysteriously not being able to find files.

Once you insert a graphic, the image appears as an object with the selection boxes at the perimeter of the object. You can use these boxes to adjust the size of the image. You can dramatically alter the size of the image and make it nearly invisible. Likewise you can stretch your picture to fill the entire screen. In fact, you can spread the image beyond the edges of the slide. Realize that this will result in your image being truncated at the edges when the slide is viewed.

It is fairly easy to move graphics on the slide. Watch for the crosshair cursor to appear when you move your mouse over the highlighted graphic object. When the crosshair appears, you can drag your image with the mouse, or nudge it with the arrow keys (←, ↑, →, and ↓) on the keyboard. Beginner slide show creators often overlook nudging!

Let's return to our lighthouse and begin our second slide. Perhaps the best place to start for this presentation is with the history. To create the next slide, select insert and new slide from the menu, or the keystroke combination of Ctrl-M to initiate a new slide. If you create a new slide, it will always occur following the current slide you are editing. If you are not sure about the location, switch to the sorter view and note where your new slides are placed. Once in the sorter, you may click and drag the slides to the desired locations, so do not worry about where they are created. Reorganizing your slides is a fairly painless process, and you can keep reorganizing even between presentations if you are giving a presentation more than once!

Inserting additional objects like charts and text boxes is a similar process to adding text and WordArt. Note that adding a chart can be a bit daunting. If you choose to insert a chart, PowerPoint will default into a sample chart that you can then alter. This process can be very cumbersome and rather challenging, especially if you want an alternate chart type or have a very different number of variables to be accounted for in your chart. The preferred method would be to open up Excel and create a chart to your satisfaction. Once your chart is complete, while it is the highlighted object, perform a copy command and paste the chart into your slide.

PowerPoint gives you an option to apply a design to your slides. This option is excellent if you want to standardize all of your slides with the same design. However, if you do not want a design on all of your slides, do not make this selection. Once a design is applied, any new slides you add will contain the same design scheme.

You also have the option to choose a color scheme. Color schemes can be altered on individual slides or applied to all of the slides in the presentation. In addition, you can customize the colors by hand for all of the elements such as bullets, titles, shadows, and text. In a similar fashion, you can apply and customize the background of a slide or slides. You can choose to add background colors and effects to individual slides, groups of slides, or an entire presentation. If you want to create a template of your own, PowerPoint allows you to customize your own. To access the templates, go to the slide master from "master" on the view menu. Whatever changes you make to this slide will appear on every slide in your presentation. Once you have created your slide master, the next step is to create the title master. This step is accomplished by choosing the new title master from the toolbar. When complete, choose close and then delete the one blank slide that is contained in your presentation. The last step is to save the master under the file command, and choose template under the "save as file type" option. This is a handy procedure if you want to standardize your slides and include something like a school logo or course information.

The slide sorter is the best place to add the finishing touches to your presentation. As stated previously, reorganizing the slide order is as simple as clicking on a slide and dragging it to the desired location. The number of the slide will appear just below the slide on the right-hand side. You can adjust how much of your slides you can see in the sorter by changing the size of the thumbnail images present. The easiest way to modify how many slides you can preview in the sorter is to change the percentage in the zoom box that appears on the standard toolbar.

You can also add movement to your slides in two ways. You can choose to use animation and transition effects. Animation can be added from the slide show option on the menu. Animation can be either custom or preset. With custom animation, you can decide on events and on the timing of events on your slide. For example, you could animate your slide about lighthouse history. When the slide appears, it has "History" written at the top. You can animate your text so that bulleted items appear as a result of a mouse click or a preset time sequence. The first item might be, "In 1716, a stone tower to attract commerce is built on Little Brewster Island in Boston." You can then animate the next item to say, "In 1718, the first lighthouse keeper George Worthylake drowns on his way back to the lighthouse." In this way, you can build pauses into your presentation and avoid having your audience jump ahead of the points you wish to make.

Transitions are the movements between slides. Transition effects are the way in which one slide disappears and the next slide appears. There are many effects to choose from, and additional items like sounds can be associated with the transitions. Like animations, transitions can be triggered through mouse-clicks or a preset time frame. Transitions can be identified easily in the slide sorter. Transitions will be identified just below the slide thumbnail on the left-hand side. Transitions can be applied to slides individually or universally to an entire presentation.

The slide sorter is also the easiest way to delete entire slides. To delete a slide, highlight it in the sorter. You can identify the highlighted slide by the dark black box that outlines your selection. At this point, the delete key will result in deleting the slide from the presentation. You may choose to hide a slide rather than deleting it outright. With the hide option, your slide still remains in the presentation, but when the show is viewed, any slides labeled as "hidden" will not be presented on the screen. This can come in handy if you had two versions of the same slide and one version might be far more technical or detailed than another. Likewise, you may choose to shorten a presentation to accommodate a time frame, yet maintain the information for the outline that you can choose to hand out to those in attendance.

Printing slides presents you with several options. When you bring up the print menu from the file selection on the menu, pay close attention to two points beyond your printer selection. "Print what" allows you to choose to print slides, notes, outlines, or handouts. The handouts can be further selected as to how many to fit on one page. Here, you can also choose to print any hidden slides or leave them excluded. The other option to pay close attention to is the range. Here you can choose to print all or part of your presentation. This can be very important with large presentations containing a lot of graphics. A fairly simple PowerPoint presentation can rapidly become a daunting print job for many printers.

The final step is to view your presentation. The presentation can be accessed either by the view show button on the toolbar, which is accessed by choosing view show on the pull-down menu below the slide show option on the menu; or by accessing view on the main menu, then slide show. You can scroll through the show by clicking the mouse, striking the enter key, or selecting the arrow cursor keys on the keyboard. The neat thing about the slide show is that it will automatically take to the full screen size and even blank out the taskbar from its location on the screen.

Once you are content with your presentation, you still have some other options to consider. The pack and go wizard allows you to take your presentation and wrap it up into an executable file that can be given to someone else to view. Pack and go is great because it provides you with a way of giving a PowerPoint presentation to someone else to use on his or her computer who possibly does not have a compatible version, or any version, of PowerPoint at all. Created as a final product, the presentation is launched by clicking on the created icon. This file, which is executable without PowerPoint being loaded, will launch the presentation and allow the user to view it in the same format as it appears in the slide show view.

A final option is a fairly easy conversion of a PowerPoint presentation into an HTML presentation. Choosing "save as HTML" from the file option in the main menu triggers the creation of the HTML version. The HTML version can then be easily loaded onto a Web page. What is needed between the presentation and an existing page is a simple link that can trigger the first page of the converted presentation. The individual slides appear as individual Web pages. The transition buttons are automatically inserted onto the Web pages to allow movement through the slides, which are now pages. This feature allows PowerPoint to be used as a Web page creation tool.

Whichever presentation tool you choose, you will find that you have the ability to easily incorporate graphics and images that can provide new dimensions for your viewers. Now let's move on to try some of the exercises that follow.

Activity Sheet 7.1
Using and Developing Multimedia Applications

Name: _____ Date: _____

Creating a Bibliographic Presentation

1. Choose an important figure such as one of the following:

   Leonardo da Vinci   Michelangelo   William Shakespeare
   Galileo   Henry VIII   Martin Luther
   Julius Caesar

   Jot down notes to the following questions, including your sources:

2. What are the important facts about this person's childhood (including place of birth and things about living at that time period that may be important)?
3. What type of education did this person receive?
4. What is this person most famous for doing?
5. What is the significant contribution this person has made to society?
6. What interesting facts are there about this person's life or lifestyle?
7. When did this person die and what were the conditions of his or her death, or what is this person doing at present?
8. With the information you have provided for these questions, design a multimedia presentation that incorporates the biographical information that you have found. Be sure your multimedia presentation contains the following:

   Title page
   Index
   Facts about the life
   At least three pictures or images that represent something about your topic: pictures of the person, his or her work, or anything else that is appropriate
   Bibliography or a list of sources

Activity Sheet 7.2
Multimedia Applications

Name: _____ Date: _____

Presentation 1

1. We will illustrate the life cycle of a plant or animal. For example, if you choose a moth the life cycle consists of:
   - Egg
   - Caterpillar
   - Pupa or Chrysalis
   - Adult moth

(Refer to www.mesc.usgs.gov/butterfly/butterfly-life-cycle.html for sample information.)

2. Create a presentation that represents the stages of development. Be sure to include the following information:
   - Images that represent the stages
   - Information and descriptions about each stage

3. Make your presentation easy for someone new to the topic to understand.

Presentation 2

1. Find a math problem that requires at least five steps to complete.
2. Illustrate the formula, using a presentation so that each step appears as a separate card or slide.
3. Set up your presentation to run by itself so it appears to automatically solve the equation for your viewer.

8

The Internet

> This chapter explains the background behind the Internet and introduces much of the associated terminology. Some common Internet applications—including e-mail, the World Wide Web, listservs, and newsgroups—are introduced.

THE WORLD WIDE WEB AND THE INTERNET

The Internet has become quite a phenomenon in our society. It is funny to hear people who claim not to be knowledgeable about the computer chat about the Internet. What you often find is that they will use the terms Internet and World Wide Web interchangeably when the two are really quite different things. So why are they different? The Internet refers to a collection of connected networks and its corresponding hardware. Telephones, satellites, and high-speed links connect the Internet. The World Wide Web is an application for sharing information that uses the hardware of the Internet. Consider first their history. The Internet, in its earliest form, came into being in the late 1960's. First proposed in 1990, the World Wide Web was not released to the public until 1991.

The Internet refers to the hardware, architecture, and systems that were the dream of the U.S. military community in the 1960s. The Department of Defense (DoD) formed the Advanced Research Projects Agency (ARPA) in 1957. ARPA was established for the purpose of doing research projects in science and technology that were relevant to the military. One area in which the military wanted improvement was communications. Fear of nuclear attack during the Cold War created a need for a communication network that was not dependent on the existing technology of that time. The defense community saw vulnerability in the communications systems that were in place and wanted to develop a new system that would be available to function in pieces. The idea that Washington, D.C., which was considered ground zero—the point at which nothing (or zero) would survive a nuclear attack—was the central point of the communication systems they had at that time. The desire to have a system that could still function if a chunk had been suddenly wiped from the whole picture was a motivator for the development of different types of solutions. ARPA set out to create an alternate means of communication: a means that would allow communication to be broken into its smallest particles, or packets, and then allow the transfer of this information. From 1962 through 1968, ARPA funded many packet-switching networks. The TCP/IP, or Transmission Control Protocol/Internet Protocol (protocol is a set of rules that govern communication between computers or networks), was developed as a way to transfer packets over a variety of media, including satellite connections, wireless radio, and telephone links. One of the goals for the military community was that packet-switching should make eavesdropping more difficult, if not impossible. Therefore, the military sponsored several programs and proposals to make the packet-switching a reality. The earliest transmissions included some of our most prestigious universities, and by Labor Day weekend of 1969, the Internet, or the ARPANET as it was originally called, was born. By 1971, there were twenty-three hosts on the ARPANET, and e-mail, or electronic mail, had been invented. Today many people are surprised to hear that e-mail is over thirty years old.

By 1973, the first transmissions were made globally, and true Internet architecture had become a reality. There were specifications for Ethernet and gateways as well as for file transfer protocol (FTP). This new TCP/IP protocol was key because it would allow communication among different computer networks and give them the ability to communicate. By 1979, the first Usenet news groups were established using Unix. Unix is an operating system developed by AT&T Bell Labs. Unix is still used by many machines today. By the early 1980s, there were additional networks using the Internet, including BITNET (Because It's Time NET work) and CSNET (Computer Science NETwork). In 1981, the National Science Foundation created CSNET as a backbone to allow access for institutions that did not have access to the ARPANET. Later the CSNET would add the NSFNET. By 1982, ARPA establishes TCP/IP as the protocol for the ARPANET, which is one of the first times that the ARPANET was thought of as an Internet, a connected set of networks. The 1980s saw explosive growth of the Internet from 100 nodes in 1977, to over 100,000 in 1989. By 1990, it grew to over 300,000 nodes, or hosts. In the early 1980s, the IP or Internet Protocol was made up of a series of numbers separated by periods. The domain name system (DNS) was devised in 1983 as an easier way to keep track of the IP addresses, which identified which node the user was trying to locate. The DNS created a hierarchy whereby letters or words were used instead of numbers. This system provided a huge advantage because hosts no longer would need to be identified by a series of numbers. By 1990, the original ARPANET lines had been replaced by faster and more efficient lines.

In 1995, the National Science Foundation announced that it would no longer allow direct access to the NSF backbone. The NSF then began contracting with different companies to be providers of access to their backbone. Fees are imposed for the creation of domain names. The internet service providers, or ISPs, make access to the Internet available for fees to their customers.

Through the first twenty years of the Internet, usage was specialized, and users needed to have a certain level of computer expertise to utilize the applications that made use of the multitude of networks. There was one individual who initially had the vision that the Internet needed an outlet for allowing people to easily share information on the structure that was already in place. This vision is what drove Tim Berners-Lee to design the World Wide Web as a point-and-click browser and editor that could work on a client machine by 1990. The World Wide Web program was based on a system that identified anything on the Internet through the use of a URI, or Universal Resource Identifier, upon which the system of URLs or Uniform Resource Locators is built. Early on, he recognized that there was a wealth of information at the various sites on the Internet but no easy way to retrieve it. Berners-Lee understood that there was a need to simplify how different systems could communicate. While working at CERN in Geneva, Switzerland, Berners-Lee identified the need and the potential and was given the opportunity to pursue the creation of a system. Soon, the system was in place; once the potential of the URI system was understood, it continued to grow at an unprecedented rate every year through the 1990s. The incorporation of the hypertext documents application became known as the World Wide Web, and before long additional browser applications became available.

Browsers

The first browser released to the public was Mozilla in October 1994. Browsers are software applications that were designed to allow the user to look at the content on a host site. Browsers are an interface to the Internet and require a physical connection for access. For many, the connection is supplied from an internet service provider, or ISP. ISPs vary in what they provide, as well in as the fees they charge. Many ISPs have sprung up to try and meet the needs of various markets. Initially, the bulk of the commercial ISPs provided access through the use of phone lines and modems, where the modems inside the computer provided the physical connection to the ISP. Technology has been advancing very rapidly, and now there are additional choices for connecting to the Internet. One choice that is increasing in popularity includes wireless technology that works much like cell phones and radios, as well as permanent cable connections that are a significant improvement over using the preexisting phone line structures. It is important to remember that as the Internet has been advancing, so have capabilities of the cables that we use to carry the packets of information to their destinations.

World Wide Web

The arrival of the World Wide Web ushered in a true revolution. In 1993, The National Science Foundation (NSF) created the InterNIC to provide specific Internet services, for now the number of hosts had reached over 2 million. At the start of 1993, the World Wide Web had approximately 600 sites, and by the end of the year that number surpassed 300,000. By 1995, the Internet had 6.5 million hosts and over 100,000 WWW sites.

Interestingly, throughout its development, the Web has been a truly global endeavor. While various agencies have been in charge of different technical and hardware aspects of the Internet, there has not been any one organization in charge of its content. This legacy is still with us today. While commerce and commercial endeavors continue to flood the Internet, there remains no central body to monitor or control the content. This lack of control of content has many implications for education, especially in your classroom. One of the largest implications is the idea that there is no central body responsible for the content of anything posted on the Web. Therefore, it is up to the viewer of the content to determine the legitimacy and accuracy of the website. This is an important fact and one that cannot be taught lightly. While children are known for the ability to adapt to new technologies, they are also at risk from those who at the very least are masquerading with misinformation and at the very worst are true predators. Therefore, one of the most important lessons about the Internet is how to evaluate a website.

Usually the first introduction to a website is through its address or URL. Addresses conform to standards that provide you with information. The first part to the address tells the protocol used. Some initial URL locations include: file:// for ftp sites, gopher:// for gopher sites, news:// for newsgroups, and http:// for hypertext pages. The URL is truly a place where you can learn a good bit of information from a name. The first protocol portion is terminated with :// symbols. Additional slashes in an address indicate other distinct sections. The second piece, from the :// through the first single slash of /, contains the domain name. The domain or host for a particular website tells you a great deal of information. The portions of a domain name are separated with periods, referred to as "dots." The last two parts of the domain name indicate the kind of entity that you are dealing with as well as its location. In the case of many United States websites, .us is often not added to the domain names, but most of the other countries hosting websites fortunately do comply with the two-letter country designation code at the end of their domain names. There are several abbreviations used in domain names, and some of them can be seen in table 8.1. Country designations are available in table 8.2. Any Web address or URL, no matter how long, contains a domain name. After the domain name, you get at more specific information of where the "page" or

Table 8.1 Domain Extension Abbreviations Indicating Type of Host

.com	commercial
.net	network
.edu	education
.mil	military
.gov	government
.k12	K-12 school
.org	organization
.int	international
.store	retail store
.web	Web-related business
.rec	recreational activity or facility
.firm	business
.nom	users desiring personal nomenclature (naming)
.info	informational
.aero	aviation industry
.info	general information
.biz	businesses
.coop	business cooperatives
.museum	museums
.name	individuals
.pro	professional

document can be found on the host server, which is the computer on which the Web page lives. Information can include directory and file name information that tells the visitor its exact location on the host computer. Finally, the last part is often an exact document or page name. Usually an address ends in .htm or .html, which is short for hypertext markup language, the format of the Web page.

The HTML codes are what create a Web page. Web pages in their HTML state can be a bit daunting to read. To resolve this, enter the browser. Browsers are a software application written for one main purpose: they allow the viewer to see the pages on the WWW as the creator of the page intended them to be seen. Browsers take and translate all those hypertext codes in a seamless fashion for the user. The first commercial browser available to the public was Mosaic, which later became Netscape. While there are different browsers available to the public, it is somewhat ironic that browsers do not all interpret the HTML codes or tags in the exact same way. For instance, colors are not the same in all browsers. For example, different

Table 8.2   Country Designation Codes

Code	Country	Code	Country
.ae	United Arab Emirates	.gh	Ghana
.af	Afghanistan	.gi	Gibraltar
.ai	Anguilla	.gr	Greece
.al	Albania	.gu	Guam
.ao	Angola	.gt	Guatemala
.aq	Antarctica	.hk	Hong Kong
.ar	Argentina	.hn	Honduras
.au	Australia	.hr	Croatia
.ba	Bosnia and Herzegovina	.ht	Haiti
.bb	Barbados	.hu	Hungary
.be	Belgium	.ie	Ireland
.bg	Bulgaria	.il	Israel
.bm	Bermuda	.in	India
.bn	Brunei	.iq	Iraq
.bo	Bolivia	.ir	Iran
.br	Brazil	.is	Iceland
.bw	Botswana	.it	Italy
.ca	Canada	.jm	Jamaica
.cg	Congo	.jo	Jordan
.ch	Switzerland	.jp	Japan
.ck	Cook Islands	.ke	Kenya
.cl	Chile	.kh	Cambodia
.cm	Cameroon	.kp	North Korea
.cn	China	.kr	South Korea
.co	Colombia	.kw	Kuwait
.cr	Costa Rica	.ky	Cayman Islands
.cy	Cyprus	.lb	Lebanon
.cz	Czech Republic	.lr	Liberia
.de	Germany	.ly	Libya
.dk	Denmark	.ma	Morocco
.do	Dominican Republic	.mc	Monaco
.dz	Algeria	.mx	Mexico
.ec	Ecuador	.my	Malaysia
.ee	Estonia	.ni	Nicaragua
.eg	Egypt	.nl	Netherlands
.es	Spain	.no	Norway
.et	Ethiopia	.nz	New Zealand
.fi	Finland	.pa	Panama
.fj	Fiji	.pe	Peru
.fk	Falkland Islands	.ph	Philippines
.fr	France	.pk	Pakistan
.ga	Gabon	.pl	Poland

(continued)

Table 8.2 Country Designation Code (continued)

.pr	Puerto Rico	.sy	Syria
.pt	Portugal	.td	Chad
.ro	Romania	.tn	Tunisia
.ru	Russia	.tw	Taiwan
.rw	Rwanda	.uk	United Kingdom
.sa	Saudi Arabia	.va	Holy See (Vatican City)
.sd	Sudan	.ve	Venezuela
.se	Sweden	.za	South Africa
.sg	Singapore	.zm	Zambia
.sv	El Salvador	.zw	Zimbabwe

browsers interpret codes for color names slightly differently. Software vendors agreeing on open standards for the Web will hopefully eventually resolve this situation, but you can never be sure what legacy the newer generations of software will have in store. In the meantime, the World Wide Web Consortium (www.w3c.org) "develops interoperable technologies (specifications, guidelines, software, and tools) to lead the Web to its full potential as a forum for information, commerce, communication, and collective understanding."

Internet FAQs

A common Internet acronym is the FAQ, or Frequently Asked Questions. FAQs have become very common in many of the Internet applications. FAQs provide guidance by answering the users' most common questions. You will often hear these pages referred to as "facts" pages. If you are looking for a help page, chances are it will be identified as a FAQ page!

Search Engines

Search engines and search repositories are terms that represent tools that are used to find information on the WWW. The search tools allow users to find locations that contain whatever type of information they are looking for. Search engines work by looking for key terms, or keywords. Search engines allow you to narrow in your focus and find lots of information at your fingertips. Search engines and repositories are often confused as being the same thing, but they are actually a bit different. Repositories are usually designed in a way where the user can start with very general categories or topics and continue through a matrix to narrow down a search. Repositories, which can also be called subject trees, provide a structure and a framework in which to look for pages. Repositories are maintained and catalogued, usually by a fairly large staff, to allow the user to find information. They are typically huge and contain minimal restrictions upon what gets included. Some repositories also allow keyword searching based upon the indexing scheme.

The key to remember is that the user starts with something very general and can continue moving to something far more specific. Repositories will generally list general categories from which the user may choose. For instance, some general categories might include plants, animals, planets, and geology. A person looking for information about black lab puppies might follow the trail through animals, domestic animals, pets, dogs, veterinarians, puppies, and breeds, and eventually find more precise information that they are looking for. Repositories can be a great advantage when you don't know ahead of time exactly what you would like information about, as you can usually find lots of interesting information along the way. However, when you have something specific in mind, a search engine is a better way to try to find your information. Specific examples about how to use the different types of search engines are presented in the chapter about the World Wide Web.

Not all search engines were created equal. Some provide rankings while others offer additional information. One of the most frequently asked questions for teachers and librarians is, "What search engines do you use?" The best answer to give is that the one that works best is the one that you find yourself most comfortable in using.

Boolean logic is often applied to areas of computer science. Reports that are created for database systems almost always involve Boolean logic. Programming languages and search engines alike rely upon Boolean logic. Boolean logic is used in creating all kinds of data reports. The Boolean operator AND (intersection) retains the elements of two or more sets that are common to all of the sets. The Boolean operator OR (union) combines all the elements of the different sets into a larger set. The third Boolean operator NOT (complement) retains only those elements that are not specified. The best way to describe Boolean logic is with an example, such as

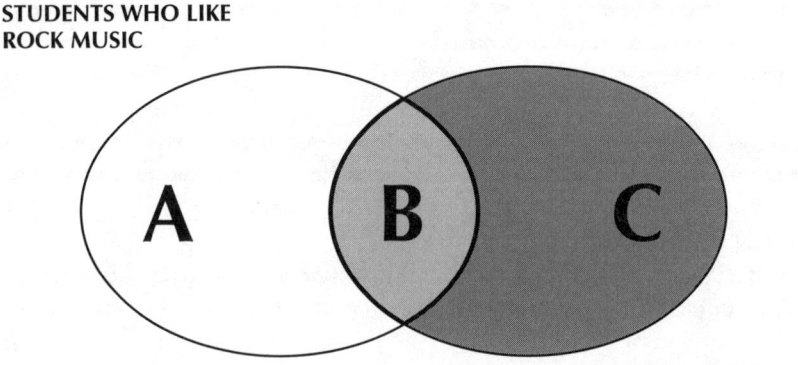

Figure 8.1   An Example of Boolean Logic

the Venn diagram in figure 8.1. If you have two populations that like different things, then they may overlap.

If circle one shows you all of the students in the sixth grade that like rock music (section A), and circle two shows you all of the students in the sixth grade that like country music (section C), section B is the area that is common to both of the original sets. If you apply Boolean logic and want to know which students like country OR rock, the result would be sections A, B, and C. If you want to know which students like country AND rock, the result would be section B. For those who like rock and not country, your result would be A, and for those who like country and not rock, the result would be C.

As you apply this logic to a search engine, it can have dramatic results. When you enter key terms, if the connection between the terms is an OR scenario, you will wind up with far many more documents than you may have originally intended to find. Using the operator AND, you will usually significantly cut down on the number of pages or results that you find. The websites that are returned to you in your search are often referred to as hits. Using OR will almost always dramatically increase the number of hits that will be available to you after your search.

While all search engines allow for Boolean terms, there is no standardization in how they are executed. One search engine might use a combination of a plus sign (+) and a blank space to indicate an AND, while another might call those same characters an OR. Fortunately, most search engines provide a help screen or template that you can review to determine how the terms are interpreted. In addition, there is often an "advanced" search strategy that will allow the user to specify whether or not they want to include the keywords in which type of scenario. The advanced tools will often help you fine-tune your search so that you can significantly narrow down the number of hits that you may have had in your initial results. Good search strategies take practice and intuition on the part of the user. Don't be frustrated when experimenting with a new search engine if you keep winding up with thousands and thousands of hits. The best advice might be to learn and focus on just a couple of search engines and their search strategies. In this way, you can memorize the way the engine uses its codes and commands so that you don't need to reinvent the wheel each time you go in and begin a search.

Electronic Mail or E-Mail

E-mail, or electronic mail, is another frequently used application on the Internet. E-mail is mail that is transmitted between computers. Soon the capability to transfer e-mail messages between cellular telephones and other digital handheld devices will become more commonplace. The Internet has given all kinds of folks the ability to send messages anytime, to anyone, for less money than it would typically cost to send a letter or make a phone call. In one sense, e-mail can be thought of as an electronic letter or message. Messages sent via the Internet are delivered quickly, and in many cases, the time lapse between sending and receiving seems almost instantaneous. E-mail has allowed us to find an inexpensive means of communication over great distances. E-mail messages can take the place of more expensive telephone and fax communications. When you want to make an overseas phone call, you have to take a few things into consideration. First, what is the time difference with the country you are calling? Second, what are the calling rates for that period? Calls during the business day are more expensive than those placed in the wee hours of the morning or on the weekend. In contrast, e-mail messages all cost the same regardless of location, and are delivered at any time of the day or night with no fluctuating costs.

There are different kinds of e-mail services available. Some e-mail packages are considered to be private and are loaded on one network, usually within one organization, school, or business. Others are web-based and are offered as an additional service from a website.

You must have Internet access to utilize mail from this type of service, whereas the private services may allow the receipt of mail through a network and do not necessarily have to provide Internet access for the delivery of mail. Regardless of the type, all messages are broken into their packets and use Internet hardware to get from the sender to the recipient.

All e-mail requires an e-mail client. The client is software that lives on a users' computer and handles the functions of the mail. The mailbox and address book can be stored here. There are numerous types of clients available, and all have their own conventions and structures. Usually all stick to the standard metaphors of a mailbox, address book, and the like.

E-mail is like the old-fashioned mail in that you must address it, compose the messages in the body of the document, and send it. What people generally need to do with e-mail is to send it, read it, reply to it, manage a mailbox that houses it, and manage their addresses in some form of address book. The details of how to do these activities vary with different mail packages.

A common feature for e-mail applications is the ability to create distribution lists. Most packages have the facility to allow you to create your own bulk mail. Distribution lists allow you the capability of sending one written message to multiple recipients at the same time. The traditional mail would have required that an individual copy be printed and then sent to each recipient. With e-mail you can send one message to a group, all with one click of a send button. Further, mailing lists can be abbreviated for personal use once so created; they will automatically pull the exact address information needed. It is the equivalent of creating an alias for a friend in an old-fashioned address book. Now, whenever you need to mail something to the friend, you only need to remember the alias, and you do not need to look up the entire address every time you wish to send them some mail.

Distribution lists create a situation unique to e-mail. You need to understand the difference between a simple reply and reply sender. When responding to a group address, a simple reply will be sent to everyone named on the list, not just the person who initiated the original message. Reply sender, on the other hand, will send a reply only to the individual who initiated the original message. E-mail users often get annoyed when other users don't understand the difference between the two forms of replying. The situation that arises is that mailboxes begin to fill up with unnecessary junk mail of additional responses that are of no interest to the other folks on the distribution lists. This situation has caught many an e-mail participant in an embarrassing situation.

In general, there are three parts to an e-mail message that are discernable to the user. The first part is the header, which tells information about where it was going and who sent it, as well as the time and date it was sent. The second part is the body, which contains the actual message as composed by the sender. Finally, the signature is the part where senders can personalize their messages and provide additional information about themselves. Oftentimes the types of information that are useful in the signature are the equivalent of the items you would find on letterhead or on stationary of an organization.

E-mail addresses are made up of two basic parts. The first part is an alias, and is usually selected by the user or assigned to the user by a system administrator. The second part is the domain name of the recipient location. The two halves of the address are joined together by the @ sign. The inventor of this standard felt that it was appropriate because the person was "at" the location named.

E-mail attachments are documents or files of different types that you can send "attached," or linked, to a traditional e-mail message. Attachments can vary from images or pictures to fairly complex word processing documents. Here it can be a bit tricky because people will sometimes send an attachment without being aware of the kind of software the receiver has on the other end. This will sometimes result in attachments that the recipient will not be able to open or view properly. Sometimes the recipient can open it, but it looks like a bunch of coded gibberish and is not discernable. It is important that if you are interested in sending attachments, you should check about what kind of system the receiver is using. Otherwise, choose to send standard file formats that are common to all kinds of systems. For images, file types that are common are .jpg or .gif files. For documents, .rtf (rich text format) is usually allowed in all word processors. Otherwise, check to see what software packages you have in common. If you don't know, send an e-mail message and ask them. Nothing is more frustrating than getting an e-mail attachment and not being able to open it!

E-mail Attachments and Viruses

A potential threat to using e-mail is the transmission of viruses. To date, one of the most common ways that malicious viruses are spread to computers is through e-mail attachments. Computer viruses need to find a way to infect a new host machine. One of the most common types of entry has been to disguise a virus as an e-mail attachment and then send it with a message. While most virus attacks are only a nuisance, there are some that are highly destructive. As a general rule, don't ever open an e-mail message that has an attachment from a source you do not know. Further, be wary of any messages containing a subject line that you don't understand.

Many have criticized that as e-mail usage expands, people are becoming far more informal in their written communications. People

Table 8.3   Emoticons!

:-)	happy	}:-)	devil		
:-(	sad	:-l:-l	dumb question		
;-)	wink	<:)	dunce		
:-P	stick out tongue	<:-O	eeek!		
:>	very happy	}-)	evil		
8-)	happy with glasses	l<:-)	graduate		
:-{	frustrated	:-)(-:	just married		
:<	very sad	(-:	left-handed		
:/	confused	X:-)	little kid		
:-O	surprised	<:3)~~~~	rat		
:-D	laughing	:-*	oops!		
:'-(	crying	:-]	obnoxious		
:-C	really upset	:-o	oh		
:-X	sworn to secrecy	=l:-)	Abe Lincoln		
:-( )	shouting	O:-)	saint		
}:-<	cat	M:-)	saluting		
:-l	hmmm	:-y	say it with a smile		
C=:-)	chef	:+(	scared		
l:-)	thick eyebrows	:-@	screaming		
*:o)	clown	:-Z	sleeping		
3:-)	cow	/\oo/\	spider or bat		
X-)	cross-eyed	:-v	talking		
:-[	critical	l:-)	teacher		
:-t	angry	(:>-<	thief		

tend to use e-mail for those quick messages and pay less attention to spelling, grammar, and style. In fact, there are several acronyms that are now commonly used, as well as special faces called emoticons. To see what the emoticon is trying to represent, turn the picture at a 90° degree angle and the symbols will look like a face. See table 8.3 for some popular examples.

You may see some additional acronyms associated with e-mail messages. POP or POP-3, which stands for post office protocol, is the standard that clients use to handle the incoming e-mail they are receiving. Another type is SMTP or simple mail transport protocol, which defines how the host computer transfers the mail. Basically, with SMTP the host machine asks permission for the mail to be sent at a specified time and waits for a signal that it has been received. SMTP handles the outgoing process. MIME or Multipurpose Internet Mail Extensions handles the delivery of attachments from one mail location to another.

Newsgroups

Newsgroups are discussion groups that have sprung up from Usenet (the Users Network). Usenet was originally launched at Duke University in 1979. At that time, one of the best sources for electronically sharing information was through electronic bulletin boards. Essentially the bulletin board allowed the users to post messages that could be viewed by all of the participants. Newsgroups are divided by topics.

Many of the newsgroups are moderated. A moderator is a real person watching the postings by the participants, so that if anyone in the group misbehaves they can be expelled from the group. Often the lines of the conversations, also called threads, can be challenging, so these are not necessarily the best places for children to participate on the Internet. As the conversations and usage expanded, the only way to find information was to go back and review all the messages involved. While the application was very popular, the interface was not all that wonderful, so in 1995, a new interface called Deja News was created at www.dejanews.com to allow a far more user-friendly approach.

Most browsers provide a feature to allow you to look at the postings in the group. Some of these software applications include Newsreader in Netscape Navigator and the Mail and News menu item in Microsoft Explorer. If you are interested in participating in a newsgroup, this software can save you time and potential embarrassment. Newsgroups are notorious for their disdain of new participants, referred to as newbies. For example, presenting a message in all capital letters is the equivalent of being in a room with someone and screaming at them. If you need to add emphasis to something in your message, you are expected to surround that portion with the asterisk (*) symbol.

Gopher

Gopher is an information retrieval system based upon a menu interface rather than images. It was developed at the University of Minnesota, home of the Golden Gophers. It is easy to think of a gopher as a way to "go for" information. Selecting and retrieving are accomplished by double-clicking or by selecting a menu item number. The search tool for the gopher clients is called Veronica. The traditional gopher address was made up by combining the elements of type, host, path, port, and name in a sequence that is similar to that of the URI.

Listservs

A Listserv is an electronic conference. Listservs can be described as a blend of electronic bulletin boards and e-mail. A group or conference is formed, usually with a common focus. What happens is that a group is hosted on a computer or server somewhere. Correspondence with the group is done via e-mail to that location. Since communication is through e-mail, participants can be at any location around the globe. Often, there are moderators who review messages before they are mailed to the members of the group.

Commands (like correspondence) are sent to the host computer via an e-mail message. Usually, commands to join or leave a list are sent to a listserv server account, while posting messages to the group is done to a specific conference address. This is a necessary distinction, otherwise the group members would be seeing messages about folks coming or going from the list, rather than messages about the topics.

In summary, the Internet is a growing place that is increasing the flow of information and communication in our society. The next chapter will focus in more detail on the fastest growing portion, the World Wide Web.

Activity Sheet 8.1

The Internet

Name: _____ Date: _____

Answer the following questions:

1. Why are the Internet and the World Wide Web not the same thing?
2. What does FAQ stand for?
3. Find a website that has a FAQ section. What types of things do they offer?
4. What are some of the advantages of using e-mail?
5. Why should you not open an e-mail when you do not know the sender?
6. For the following populations (there are 250 people in the survey), please determine the following:

   - 185 people enjoy eating french fries
   - 27 people like french fries with salt
   - 52 people like french fries with ketchup, but not with salt
   - 15 people like french fries with ketchup and salt
   - 25 people like to eat their french fries with a soda
   - 100 people like to eat their french fries with a hamburger
   - 200 people enjoy a soda now and then
   - 56 people enjoy a soda with a hamburger

   Draw a Venn diagram that shows what you know about the people in the survey.

9
The World Wide Web

> This chapter will focus exclusively on the World Wide Web. It will discuss how to evaluate information from websites, focusing on the verifiability, authorship, and currency of the information. Informational websites often provide knowledge of other sources and provide links to them. We will look at tips for getting the most out of your browser software. This chapter will also provide additional information about search engines. Finally, we will provide some explanations of the most common errors encountered while using the World Wide Web.

The World Wide Web is an interactive application that represents the set of information that is connected by computers and networks. It is based on millions of hypertext documents that can deliver text, graphics, sound, and video. The hypertext documents have their own built-in capabilities that are manipulated by browser software. The idea of surfing comes from the analogy that there is an ocean full of documents, or pages, and a user can browse or "surf" through them. A web server is a computer that stays connected to the Internet and allows users to visit, or access, the documents that reside on it: it is a computer that is acting as a host for users visiting the pages.

The key to moving about on a Web page is to be aware of any changes on screen that affect the cursor. When a standard cursor, such as an arrow, changes to that of a pointing hand, it indicates that the position is linked to some other place. The link can be within the same page, to another page on the same server, or to yet another page at an entirely different location. When the cursor changes, the user can launch movement to the linked location by a click of the mouse or by striking the enter key. Interacting with Web pages in this fashion is also referred to as point-and-click.

It is important to remember that because Web pages live on host computers at millions of different locations, there is no one central repository. Just as there is no central location or agency in charge of the Web, the Web provides us with new challenges in evaluating the validity of what we see. Since there is no one authority in charge, there is no moderator; likewise, there is no one in charge of content. Anyone who knows how to create a hypertext document can post information to the Web. This situation presents many new challenges to individuals searching for information and not understanding the ramifications of the way the Web is constructed.

Creating a Web page, or HTML document, can be a very simple process. Most word processing applications make provisions for saving any document as an HTML document. Of course, pages that provide high levels of interactivity require additional programming. Many of the pages that provide very specialized interactions utilize a scripting language such as Java in addition to the HTML codes. The vast abundance of great content and information available on the Web should override our fears about the source. A reader will have to make judgments as to the validity of the information and be able to act as a bit of a detective in deciding when to trust the facts and figures as presented.

The lack of authority or control over content makes the Web a very unique place. Never before has any society seen so open a resource that can be accessible by so many. Of course accessibility is limited to those with electronic resources and know-how. While the Web can serve to bring individuals together, it is also resulting in an ever-widening gap between some members of societies. Never has a medium contributed to so great a divide between those of differing economic backgrounds. Think about a poor third world country. Consider a nation that is struggling to feed and house its population. In places like this, citizens do not have phones, let alone computers.

How is the Internet contributing to further the divide between the people of these nations and those of wealthy nations? Government and special programs are trying to address the inequalities between those with and those without access. Programs have been launched to bring the Internet to many locations. Public libraries provide a free point of access. However, when we stop to consider what the Web really requires, there are two essential ingredients: the Web requires connectivity and the ability to read.

Literacy rates can be scary statistics. At this point, members of our society who do not read will not reap the benefits of the Internet. The digital divide has been identified as a real phenomenon and one that, hopefully, societies will begin to address. Remember, too, that the digital divide is not just an economic divide. The digital divide can be gender-based, and the digital divide can be generation-based. As adults struggle to catch up to the computer skills of their children, so do senior members of our society get pushed further away.

WEBSITE EVALUATION

Anyone can become an author on the World Wide Web. If you go into the reference section at a library, you can feel fairly confident that the materials you pull from the shelves will be reliable and verifiable. It is important to realize that not all of the traditional printed resources are of equal value. Printed references are improved by the work of publishers and editors. Bibliographies from printed reference material should lead to sources of similar authority. Often bibliographies on Web pages take the form of lists of links. Sometimes authors review pages they link to, but not always. Sometimes an author can review a page and link to it, then its creator can later update the page. Now the second author may be linking to content that is no longer acceptable or up to their standards. The idea here is that Web pages can be dynamic. What appears at one session may not be there the next. It's much trickier than a published book, where the words will remain long after the author has gone. For these types of reasons, the ability to evaluate a website is an important research skill.

Website evaluation is an important skill. The evaluation form in figure 9.1 provides a sample form that can be used in evaluating a website. The

Website Evaluation Form	
ADDRESS (URL)	
Category ☐ Advocacy ☐ Business/marketing ☐ Reference/information ☐ Personal ☐ Entertainment ☐ News ☐ Other	Sponsoring Body or Group Author Webmaster
Purpose and Audience? Does the information seem to be accurate? Can you verify the accuracy? Are there references to other works? Is there knowledge of other sources? Are there links to other works on the same topic?	
Can you detect a point of view (or bias)? ___ Yes ___ No	
Date of last page update?	
Date you accessed the page	
Page relationship to sponsor?	Provide snail mail address? Phone information? Fax information?
General Impression and Comments:	

Figure 9.1   Website Evaluation Form

form was developed to help students break apart the parts of the website that they can see. Unlike other printed media, anyone can publish his or her work on the Internet. There is no editorial body in charge of reviewing information that is placed online. This lack of content control creates a whole new climate for education. In the past, our students have been taught that, for the most part, the printed words they find in their books are factual. Enter a whole new media, where anyone with an opinion or an agenda can post pretty much anything. One of the most difficult skills to teach is the idea that you can, and sometimes should, question the material that you read. Teach Web users to question the authority of their sources. Endless possibilities are now available for students on the Internet.

A generation ago, students were limited by the physical structure of their libraries. Today, libraries reach outside of their walls and into other locations. Sometimes those other locations are additional libraries nearby or across the globe. Sometimes those other locations are research laboratories, and other times those locations can be less trustworthy. While the Web can provide access to information at varying levels of complexity, students need to learn what sources they can trust.

Website evaluation begins with the URL (Uniform Resource Locator) or Web address. The domain name, which appears between the double slash and the single slash (// through /) at the beginning of the address is the first place to begin. The domain name indicates the type of category that the sponsor is designated as, such as a school, government, or organization. (Review table 8.1 for a list of domain name abbreviations.) When an address is lengthy, you can often break out the domain name portion to view the home page of the sponsor. The home page can often be illuminating as to the sponsor's legitimacy. Breaking apart a Web address and seeking out the home page of the sponsor is a good first step in evaluating materials. The next step is to identify the kind of sponsor.

Verifiability

When you are unsure of a sponsor, you can usually determine the sponsoring body by going to the domain in the URL. Again, look to the section between the double slash and the first single slash of the address to determine the sponsor. If you eliminate the additional parts of the address after the first single slash, in most instances you will go to the home page for the address. Generally, home pages are the first page or front page that is presented at a website, and sometimes they contain the types of information that you would equate with a table of contents or index to the site. The home page generally contains descriptive information about the sponsoring organization or presents a link to an additional page where this information can be determined. Often the home page contains information about the physical location of the sponsor as well as webmaster contacts and dates of updates. Look into your Web page to see if there is identification information such as locations and phone and fax numbers. Physical address information can be a key factor in feeling that your information can be traced to a legitimate source. Of course, this still does not mean the information is accurate, but it gives you a starting point.

Authorship

A Web page or document will often have more than one person involved in its creation. The page can have an author or authors and a webmaster or webmasters. Who are webmasters? Webmasters are the individuals responsible for the creation and layout of information on a website. You can think of webmasters as the artists behind the page. Webmasters are not necessarily the individuals responsible for the contents of a Web page. Sometimes there are authors listed on a page, but more often than not, authorship is not included in the information. It is fairly common to see a webmaster listing on a home page, or at least an e-mail address to contact the webmaster's organization.

Of course, it is also possible to have one person act as the author and webmaster. In these cases, is your page the creation of a webmaster who has expertise in the subject matter? Authorship for books is taken for granted because it's so easy to identify them. Not so with Web pages.

Tilde Symbol

Sometimes, the tilde symbol (~) can be seen within an URL. The original context for a tilde was to indicate a directory belonging to an individual. The tilde was a convention that went unnoticed by many outside of the educational arena and has somewhat fallen by the wayside. The tilde is of great use in website evaluation because its original intention was to indicate content that was the opinion of the author and not necessarily that of the sponsoring organization. For example, www.highu.edu/~jones/war.htm would indicate an educational facility fictitiously called Higher University. The tilde would indicate that the document named "war" was published by Jones. Therefore, the document contained in war.htm was the work and opinion of Jones, and not necessarily that of Higher University.

Let's consider the different categories of sponsors. The category can indicate more than an affiliation. Is the sponsor a branch of government or the military? Is the sponsor a commercial location? The most important thing to remember about commercial establishments is that their bottom line is almost always making money. Though a commercial site may sponsor outstanding information, there might be advertisements running in a separate area or banner on their page. Sometimes, the information is highly credible and well documented. Consider, for example, the websites for newspapers or news broadcast networks. Remember, not all newspapers were created equal. Some have high editorial standards, while others are more concerned with selling newspapers and not necessarily stopping to check the validity of what they publish.

Bias or Point of View

This leads us to the hardest type of organizations to understand, the "dot-orgs." Organizations, or .org domain names, are allocated to nonprofit organizations. Nonprofit organizations are often not concerned with using their websites to make money. They do, however, have a very powerful motivator that can be quite different from that of a commercial enterprise. Their bias or orientation usually fuels the motivation for organizations. It is important to think about what an organization stands for when considering the information that is available on their website. Consider the hypothetical organization www.gohunting.org. This fictitious organization was formed to promote hunting wildlife in remote forests. Would you expect that this type of organization would be biased toward allowing people to own firearms? You could almost guarantee that this organization would have a bias. Consider an organization for the protection of endangered species. Would you expect that they would have a bias when it came to allowing for the expansion of a shopping mall development in an area rich in wildlife? The idea that a bias could affect the slant on the information posted is a very important point. Sometimes a bias is easy to discern; other times it can be very subtle. Being an educated viewer is the best solution.

Currency

Many pages contain information indicating the date of their original posting, or their last updates. There are cases when timeliness is important. Consider the nature of the information you are looking for and whether or not it is time-sensitive material. Although all pages do not have posting dates, many home pages do.

References and Knowledge of Other Sources

Another thing to look for in evaluating Web pages is the nature and amount of references. Research pages that represent the traditional types of papers will contain references. Do the references provided point to books, journals, and traditional printed media? Are the references provided in the form of links to other Web sources containing similar types of information? Web links are valuable and helpful. Has the page you are evaluating shown that it is aware of the other sources in its subject area by providing good, clear links? Links can provide extensive URL information, or the author can create them without extensive information. For example, a link to the National Air and Space Museum can be printed on the page as "National Air and Space Museum" or the link may be vague or cute, perhaps something like "More Planes" or "My Favorite Museum!" Clearly, knowledge of other sources is important for a reference material, and the same should hold true for an electronic Web page.

Getting the Most from Your Browser

Once connected to the Internet, the software application that you use to translate the computer codes into pages that you can read is called a browser. To date, the two most popular browsers are Netscape Navigator and Microsoft Internet Explorer. Both browsers have some features in common. Both have toolbars with common functions. The tool buttons include both forward and back buttons.

Clicking on these will move you between locations that you have visited, or surfed. The stop button will cause any action to cease. This can be useful, for example, when you have requested a Web page that has internal errors that will cause your browser to appear to be stuck. The stop button will halt the loading of that faulty page and return control to the user. The home button will take the user back to the page the user has specified to greet him or her. The home page is the one that the browser, by default, will always open to when the browser application is launched. Both browsers let the user set the home page address. Both browsers also have a history feature that allows the user to backtrack between other past sessions. How far back the history goes depends upon the settings that the user chooses. The default for history in Internet Explorer is twenty days. All Web page access will cause some information to be stored on the user's computer. The graphics and text from pages are stored in temporary folders upon access. The length of time for saving storage or temporary folders will depend upon an individual's system setting. Saving history can eventually have an impact, as it will use up disk space. Storage implications are something to consider when setting the length of the history settings.

To set the home page in Netscape, choose "options—general preferences" and type the URL into the home page location box. To set the home page in Internet Explorer, go to tools on the menu, then to "Internet options–general" and type the URL into the box that has the picture of a house and is labeled "address." The Netscape reload tool displays and updates the current Web page you are visiting. For Internet Explorer, refresh does the same thing. The Netscape images tool button will allow you to change whether a Web page loads with or without its associated images. The main advantage of loading without images is that a page that has a lot of graphics, or has graphics that are compressed at a high resolution, will have a slow loading time. Loading with text only will always be faster. To achieve this in Explorer, go to tools on the menu, then Internet options, then click on advanced. In the multimedia area, clear one or more of the "show pictures." You can then choose to view the pictures individually by right-clicking on the icon that holds the place of where the image would appear.

Another feature the browsers share is the ability to store preferred Web addresses. Netscape referred to these saved special locations as bookmarks. Internet Explorer refers to them as favorites. This saves time, especially with sites you want to return to again and again. Bookmarks or favorites allow you to save having to retype the URL when you want to return. Additionally, you can give the address a name that gives you an additional clue about why you saved the address. This shortcut allows the user to just click on the selection rather than retyping the address.

One of the neat features of a browser is the ability to capture images from a Web page. Here, the way to capture the images depends not on your browser, but on which operating system your computer is running. With a Mac OS, you would move your mouse so that the cursor is over the image you wish to capture, then click the mouse button and follow the onscreen prompts, such as copy or save image. With a Windows OS, you would move your mouse over the image you desire, then press the right mouse button, then choose either copy or "save picture as." In addition, you can turn the image into the background on the desktop by choosing "set as wallpaper."

To actually go to a Web page, you can type the address that you want to visit. With Netscape, the "go to" prompt presents a bar where you can type the address or URL. With Internet Explorer, you have a bar that is labeled "address." Just like in Netscape, type in the URL. To launch your entry you can either press the enter key or click the mouse.

There is one point that is vital no matter what browser you use. You must be accurate when you type in your URLs. Most times in your classroom when a student can't find a Web page, it turns out that he or she has mistyped some of the information in the address.

Let's type in some addresses and look at some interesting sites. While there are thousands, if not millions, of excellent websites to look at, there are several that can be very illustrative of the different kinds of organizations as well as the types of information you can find.

The first address to take a look into is http://lcweb.loc.gov/homepage/ichp.html, which is the address of the Library of Congress. Careful identification of the domain name tells you immediately that it is a government website. There is indeed a wealth of information available from the LOC. Fortunately, we are beginning to see more and more pages and content designed specifically with children in mind. Pages that are designed for kids can present information with language that is easier for children to understand. Indeed, many times information can be so technical that the kids' page can be a better alternative for nontechnical adults. Try these two kids' pages and see what you think: At www.niehs.nih.gov/kids/home.htm there is a kids' version of the National Institute of Environmental Health Sciences. The Department of Agriculture at www.usda.gov/nass/nasskids/nasskids.htm is another excellent example. Try www.odci.gov/cia/ciakids/, the CIA's homepage for kids, or http://dhr.dos.state.fl.us/kids/ for the page sponsored by the state of Florida.

The following is a location that is the home to some of the most exciting technology research in the country: http://pubweb.parc.xerox.com While a commercial site, it is a research branch of a corporation, and often has some of the most exciting Web pages presented in great formats.

An international example, http://mistral.culture.fr/louvre/louvre.htm, is a more challenging domain name to decipher. The .fr tells us it is from France, and it is the home page of one of the most famous museums in the world. This page has another great feature, in that it is available entirely in English or French. Sites that offer multilingual features usually provide the user with a spot or "flag" that the user can click to change the default language setting.

There are numerous examples from domain names ending in .edu. Educational sponsors have long led the way in presenting information and research online. Take a look at www.geom.umn.edu/apps/gallery.html to work with the Gallery of Interactive Geometry. The only tricky things that can sometimes happen on a site sponsored by a college or university can be when the page exhibited reflects the opinion or beliefs of a member of that community and does not necessarily represent the views or research of the sponsoring institution. One of the best examples of this was the site of a professor at a major Midwest institution. On his page, he had pages of information that he claimed were absolute proof that the Holocaust had never taken place and that the Holocaust had been nothing more than a great hoax played on nations and people. To an untrained observer or a young child who had never studied the Holocaust, it would look like a major university was promoting the notion that the Holocaust never took place. The same university provided very careful wording on their home page, indicating that the works of individuals did not necessarily represent the opinions of the school. However, they had to respect all members of their community in their beliefs and allow access to everyone. They did, in the near future, remove all of the personal pages onto a separate server with a different domain name, so that in time it became more obvious that the page represented the opinions of one individual professor and not that of the institution. Regardless, you still need to be careful, because not all examples are as clear. Sometimes information can be very carefully disguised or even presented in a subliminal format. The best advice is to challenge everything, even information that comes from an educational source. Remember, no one is acting as big brother when it comes to information posted on the Internet.

The last example to take a look at is www.avma.org, which is the home page of the American Veterinary Medical Association. The AVMA has a home page that is a real good example of what a home page should look like. They provide great menus to guide the user through the features of their site. They have clear information that helps the user understand exactly what their organization is about, as well as extensive information as to their location and how to reach them. The AVMA is an organization whose mission is clear. They are there to see to it that animals get the best possible care from their humans. One feature of this website is the Electronic Zoo. This was assembled initially by a single veterinarian, Dr. Ken Boschert at Washington University, who has created an outstanding repository of animal-related websites. They are broken apart by categories and subdivided several times. Whatever animal is your interest or favorite, you are almost guaranteed to find information links to it here. The Zoo is comprehensive and of value to veterinarians and folks who just want to learn more about animals.

Links are one of the best parts of the World Wide Web. Most links are displayed or created in a page so that the user easily identifies them. Again, links can lead the user to another location on the same page, another page on the same host, or completely off to another website on another host out on the electronic waves. Links are usually coded so that they are offset within the text in another color. The most common is a shade of royal blue. When the cursor is moved over the link, the icon will change to that of a pointing hand, hence pointing the user to another location. You do not need to know an address to follow a link. To follow a link, all you need to do is click on it, and the browser will take you to the next location. This is where it is important to remember that a ← key or clicking on the back tool button will return you to the previous page. Once returned, the link will usually appear in a third color relative to the text that surrounds it. This color indicates that it is a link that has been followed, and the user has previously visited that page within the session.

SEARCH ENGINES

Once you become comfortable with accessing Web pages by typing in known addresses, the next step is to conquer using search engines and repositories. There are many search engines to choose from on the Web. One of the ways to judge a search engine is by its interface. Search engine pages can go to the extremes in complexity. Another thing to consider is the amount of space devoted to advertising. It will sometimes seem like advertisers don't play fair. There are some less scrupulous engines that allow their advertisers to place content or pictures that are not well suited for younger viewers in their advertising space. Sometimes these advertisements can also be confusing in their content and trick people who are trying to find something totally unrelated into checking out what has been advertised. Truly annoying in the classroom is the advertisement that makes the student think they have a real error message. Many search engines make money by allowing other companies to advertise their products on a part of their page. Still others make suggestions of places for you to link to where they can make money by selling their wares. The most annoying of all are pop-up ads that launch in new windows upon page access.

Most search engines provide an online help feature. It is important to check out the specifications of how the engine you have selected interprets the way you type in your selection. It is the case that different engines will treat the same code quite differently. One engine might interpret a blank space as an OR condition, while a plus sign indicates an AND. If you enter two terms with a space and plus sign, you will have an entirely different result than if you enter two terms with no spaces and plus sign between.

While there are no strategies common to everyone, there are some conventions that seem to be a safe bet. In general, all proper names should be capitalized. Use quotation marks around phrases or fragments that you want included together. Searching for information about "children's literature" together in quotation marks would be more specific than gathering results about children and all types of literature.

Search for proper names and titles by separating them with a comma. Using "Sally Ride, Astronaut" would be more useful than "Sally Ride Astronaut."

You can search for words or phrases that appear together on the same page by using the AND combination, but you can narrow your scope to look for words that appear within a short distance on the page by adding [brackets] to your specification.

Asterisks after a fraction of a word will result in finding all instances that contain the first characters. For example, "lab*" would render sites containing Labrador, laboratory, and labor, to name just a few. This technique can be most useful when you are unsure about proper spelling. Not surprisingly, spelling is vital in searching. Just as URLs need to be entered in perfectly to locate a website, a search term has to be exact to render useful results.

Choosing a Search Engine

Remember that different search engines use different commands. Don't try to be an expert in all of them. Do try and master the techniques for the ones that you are most comfortable using.

There are search engines that return evaluative information with your search. The results screen for Lycos will rank the sites it returns. The ranking is based upon the occurrence of your search terms in the title, heading, links, and keywords of a page. It will then post a percentage of the match of the terms. In addition, the results with the highest percentages are listed at the top and the lower percentages are below.

Search engines all create an index that is compiled by a computer program. The way in which these indexes are created can affect their capabilities. Search engines can differ in how they perform their search and in the size of their index, the frequency that they update, the speed in which they return results, and the presentation of their results. Some search engines are built to search other preexisting search engines.

Engine Warning

While you can be very methodical and choose an engine that works best for you, you can still get results that don't seem to match what you are looking for. Remember that search engines are based upon keyword searching. The words can be embedded in many parts of the document. Sometimes, you can wind up with documents that seem to be unrelated to what you were looking for. Worse, the results can be sites that are inappropriate for children. Why can that happen? Easy: those who are unscrupulous in nature know how search strategies work, too. They can embed common terms that students might go searching for, like "science fair" or "periodic table of elements," onto a pornographic page.

Pesky Problems while Surfing

Sometimes, the Web pages you want to visit will seem stubborn and not want to come up in your browser. As a result, you may receive a somewhat cryptic message as to why the page can't or won't be displayed. One annoying message is a message that the server you are trying to connect to may be busy, or is not accepting connections. In this case, the problem is pretty much as it was stated. There is not enough bandwidth for you to visit that location. Much like getting a busy signal when you are making a phone call, sometimes you might get through if you try back again a few seconds later, or perhaps minutes, hours, or days later.

The error message that says it is unable to locate the named server, or an error related to a DNS, indicates most often that a URL has been placed in the address field that does not exist. If you think you know for sure that the address exists, check your spelling again, and you will almost always find that you have mistyped the entry. If you try to make an educated guess and type in what you think sounds like a reasonable address, and it comes back with this message, the guess you made is not valid, and the domain name has not been registered as you have imagined. Also, a 404 Not Found error indicates that there is a misspelling, or that the page that was formerly there has been removed from that server.

Of course, if all of the address information is correct, check to be sure you have not lost your connection to your internet service provider and that your connection is still functioning properly. Many times a connection to the Internet can be lost in the midst of a session, and suddenly the browser seems to be throwing up error messages left and right. That's always a good indication that it is time to check your connection.

The 403 Forbidden error occurs when you try to access a page for which you have not been assigned access privileges. A system administrator can place restrictions at the page level, so although you may be able access parts of a website, other parts can be forbidden.

Messages related to socket information usually indicate that there was a problem in transmission. Oftentimes, like the old-fashioned telephone busy signal, trying again a few minutes later will solve the problem.

Another message, which can be somewhat pesky, is one stating that the information you have submitted is not secure. This means that the information passed to this server may be vulnerable to being intercepted and read by other sources. This is not a problem as long as you are not submitting anything that you consider to be top secret, such as your credit card information. Sites wanting credit card information will usually have some sort of encryption or higher security levels in place that you will be made aware of before you send this type of information. Likewise, if there is no higher-level security measures installed, think long and hard before submitting vital personal information that you may not want shared or rerouted.

The last frequent error message is related to a site moving. Messages like "site has moved" or "these pages have been moved" indicate just that. Sometimes, the user will be rerouted automatically after a few seconds. Once you reach the new address be sure to update your favorites if you want to keep it handy for later access. If the address is not rerouted automatically, there will often be a link to click on to launch the new address. Again, remember to update any lists you have that keep this URL. If, indeed, the page has been removed, you are out of luck because the page is no longer viewable through your browser.

WEB QUESTS

Web quests are exercises that are created as an adventure in surfing. Rather than leaving students to sift through the results of searching, quests can provide guided, pre-screened information. Some students think of Web quests as treasure hunts. There are library sites that provide some on their pages on different topics. Sometimes, content is so plentiful on the Web that searching becomes too distracting. Web quests provide an opportunity to turn down the volume and focus on what the quest developer had in mind. Start a room full of people searching on a topic on their own, and you will quickly discover they will all surf through many different locations and wind up in very different places. It is rare that even two of them will have the same surfing experience. Quests provide a way for an instructor to be confident of the content that the students will see.

In summary, the World Wide Web can provide many educational opportunities in your classroom. The following activities are tied to websites that were great resources at the time this text went to print. Be advised that if these result in error messages, there are sure to be many more that could be substituted. Please check them before copying and distributing to your class!

Activity Sheet 9.1

The World Wide Web

Name: _____ Date: _____

1. For the following addresses, indicate whether the websites are educational, commercial, government, military, or organization.

   www.columbia.edu/~jns16/monet_html/monet.html _____
   www.gsh.org/crossroads/ _____
   www.stonecarver.com/gargoyle.html _____
   www.ipl.org/exhibit/mushist/ _____
   www.anagramfun.com/cgi-bin/anagrams.cgi _____
   www.kings.k12.ca.us/math/real.world.html _____
   http://lcweb.loc.gov/exhibits/1492/ _____
   http://tycho.usno.navy.mil/what.html _____

2. What is the orientation, or bias, for the following organizations?

   www.avma.org/_____
   www.pantheon.org/mythica/ _____
   www.decision.org/ _____
   http://chestnut.acf.org/ _____

3. In what countries are the following sites located?

   www.nobel.se/_____
   http://mistral.culture.fr/louvre/louvre.htm_____
   www.ausport.gov.au/squash/sqasafe.html _____
   www.bbc.co.uk/_____

4. In what states are the following sites located?

   www.hcc.hawaii.edu/dino/dinos.html_____
   http://wombat.cusd.chico.k12.ca.us/_____
   http://avatar.lib.usm.edu/~degrum/authill.htm _____

5. Who is the domain, sponsor, or host for the following?

   www.ausport.gov.au/squash/sqasafe.html _____
   http://quest.arc.nasa.gov/activities/webcasts/index.html____
   http://forum.swarthmore.edu/dr.math/tocs/puzzle.high.html
   www.mta.nyc.ny.us/nyct/subway/index.html _____

Activity Sheet 9.2

The World Wide Web

Name: _____ Date: _____

1. Choose one of the following websites. Complete the evaluation form (figure 9.1) for the one that you pick!

   http://natzoo.si.edu/zooview/exhibits/greatcat/guide.htm
   www.cbc4kids.com/
   http://cccturtle.org/contents.htm
   www.oncolink.upenn.edu/images/child/gallery3.html
   www.droodles.com/drwhat.htm
   www.frbsf.org/currency/index.html

2. One of the wonderful things about the Internet is the number of museums that have provided virtual tours and exhibits. Identify the full name and location of the following museums:

   www.ummz.lsa.umich.edu/
   www.bishop.hawaii.org/
   www.moma.org/
   www.miamisci.org/
   www.hocm.org/
   www.deutsches-museum.de/e_index.htm
   http://mfah.org/
   www.nysm.nysed.gov/womenshistory/index.html
   www.clemusart.com/
   www.imj.org.il/
   www.austmus.gov.au/
   www.aviation.nmstc.ca/
   www.ethno-museum.ac.at/en/museum.html
   www.kyohaku.go.jp/
   www.museum-london.org.uk/

3. Now go back to one of the museums listed above. Choose a virtual exhibit to explore. Once you have viewed the exhibit, answer the following:
   - Which museum did you choose?
   - What exhibit did you look at?
   - What did you find the most interesting about it?

Activity Sheet 9.3

The World Wide Web

Name: _____   Date: _____

1. Please visit the following website to find out about mammals: www.mammalsociety.org/aboutmammals/index.html
2. What are three characteristics that make mammals different from other animals?
   1.
   2.
   3.

3. You may use the following websites to look up information about mammals and answer the questions that follow:

   www.cws-scf.ec.gc.ca/hww-fap/eng_ind.html
   http://natzoo.si.edu/
   www.naturalia.org/ZOO/indexing.html
   www.perthzoo.wa.gov.au/wildlife.html
   www.rhrwildlife.com/animal.htm
   www.abdn.ac.uk/mammal/facts.htm
   www.seaworld.org/AnimalBytes/animal_bytes.html
   http://sln.fi.edu/tfi/hotlists/animals.html
   www.birminghamzoo.com/search/

   -A is for anteater. How many insects does an average anteater consume in one day?
   -B is for badger. What has a sett got to do with a badger?
   -C is for camel. What does the camel store in its hump?
   -D is for dolphins. Dolphin family groups are based around what member of the pod?
   -E is for elephant. What is the gestation period for an elephant?
   -F is for ferret. Is a ferret a good pet for a child?
   -G is for giraffe. What happened in Paris in 1827 when a reticulated giraffe was placed on display?
   -H is for hippopotamus. What does a hippo do for sunscreen?
   -I is for impala. Impalas are diurnal; what does this mean?

- J is for side-striped jackal. What does this animal do during the day?
- K is for klippspringer. What do klippspringers like to eat?
- L is for llama. Why are llamas not accustomed to being touched?
- M is for pine marten. What are pine martens often mistaken for?
- N is for Nubian goat. Whose company do Nubian goats enjoy?
- O is for otter. What do otters like to eat in the spring?
- P is for pronghorn. What kind of an animal is this?
- Q is for quagga. This animal is now extinct. Who did it most closely resemble?
- R is for white rhinoceros. What is the horn of the rhino made of?
- S is for snow leopard. Why has the snow leopard become endangered?
- T is for tiger. How many subspecies of tigers are there?
- U is for transcaspian urial. How do these sheep communicate with each other?
- V is for vervet monkey. How long do these monkeys typically live?
- W is for wallaroo. In what country would you expect to find wallaroos?
- X is for extinction. What does "extinct" mean?
- Y is for yellow mongoose. Where would you expect to find a yellow mongoose?
- Z is for grevy's zebra. Is it true that a zebra is a horse in striped pajamas?

10

Creating Web Pages Using HTML

This chapter will look at the coding that goes into creating a page to be viewed on the World Wide Web. HTML, the coding that is used to turn text files into Web pages, is fairly easy to understand. This chapter will guide the user through creating their own Web page using HTML. It is important to understand that while Web pages can become extremely complex and varied, the coding language behind them is consistent. By creating some simple pages, you can gain appreciation for the work of others. First we will learn what HTML is all about, and then we will build a sample page that can be seen within a browser.

UNDERSTANDING HTML

HTML stands for hypertext markup language. The markup can be thought of as special tags that get inserted into the text of a document. The tags contain instructions that the browser then interprets. Browsers translate the inserted tags, and the result is the output readily seen by the viewer. To the Web surfer, the page appears as a page in a book or magazine does. The tags are "removed" by the browser according to the instructions to the browser program and are not a part of what the user needs to see. Browsers, the programs that are used to view the pages, and webmasters, the people who write and design the pages, have grown in their sophistication and capabilities. In addition, the HTML language has grown, and there are additional languages and plug-ins that can now be used in the creation of far more elaborate Web pages.

The first international standards were created in 1988 for sharing document-based information. These standards were called SGML, and they associated the document content with its structure together as one item. The earliest version of HTML was based on SGML. The group that has overseen the growth and development of HTML is the World Wide Web Consortium, which can be found at www.w3c.org. Their website contains information about the history, as well as the technical standards, of the World Wide Web. The most recent version (which in this case isn't so much a version, but a group of agreed-upon standards for usage) of HTML is HTML 4.01. The consortium is now working on standards for XHTML, which will be the next generation of HTML. It is the reformulation of HTML 4.01 in XML. XML, or Extensible Markup Language, is designed to be an extremely simple dialect of SGML. As standards evolve, a basic understanding of HTML—a language that is presented through the use of "tags"—will be beneficial for any Web page designer. Since the foundation for Web pages has been HTML, a working knowledge of HTML can be useful in developing an understanding of page development.

Text Files

The starting point for every Web page is a basic text file. A text file is one that contains only the printable letters, numbers, and symbols from the keyboard. These characters are all represented in the ASCII character chart. The ASCII, or American Standard Code for Information Interchange, table standardized codes used for all the characters and control codes that are possible sources of input for a processor. There are twenty-eight possibilities that are represented in values of zero through 127. The ASCII chart contains the decimal and hexadecimal equivalents so that the decimal equivalent of an "A" is sixty-five, while the decimal equivalent of "a" is ninety-seven. Text files do not contain any special or formatting codes embedded into them. With HTML, you place the formatting codes for the browser into tags that are embedded into the text file. The browser then reads the tags, performs whatever is indicated in the tag, and your page appears as you intended it to look to a viewer.

Text files are simple files. Entering text via a keyboard creates them. Text files have the advantage in that they are simple and can be understood by many operating systems, including Macintosh and Windows. Text files are fairly simple to construct and can be created using many applications. Most operating systems provide a text file editor. In Windows, the most common application for creating text files is Notepad. Apple Computer systems come with SimpleText as a text editor. Additional options include word processing applications that give you the option to save a file as a text file. In the earlier days of programming, programmers would choose fairly spiffed-up text editors to write their programs. You can find text editing programs that are rich in features and shortcut keys. The main limitation to working with the simple editors like Notepad or SimpleText is in the size of the files that it can handle. Complex Web pages can be quite large text files and exceed the capacity of a simple editor. Fortunately for most beginner purposes, Notepad or SimpleText will work just fine.

What turns a text document into a file that can be interpreted by a browser is a naming convention. It is important that when the document is saved, it is saved with an extension of .htm or .html. This convention remains from earlier Microsoft operating systems that mandated file names of not more than eight characters and an extension of period and three characters that identified the source of the file. While no longer limited to eight characters with three character extensions, the convention of identifying a text document intended for Web viewing with an .htm or .html extension remains. So, to turn your SimpleText or Notepad file into a Web page, when saving be sure to name the document with .htm at the end of it. Some text editors let you choose the file type under "save as." In those cases, select HTML files upon saving. With Notepad, be sure to name your file in the .htm convention, and when you later open the file, it should default and open into a browser.

Here it is important to mention that once a text file is saved as an HTML file, clicking or opening the file will cause it open in a browser window. This is the method you would use to preview how the page would appear inside a browser. Since opening the document at this point will lead you to the browser, it leaves a question about how you can go back to edit the original source code. To return to the editor, one option is to open the text file from the editor. Another option is to select the file and drag it onto the icon for the editor you are using. A third choice, if you are working in a Windows environment, is to right-click (the alternate menu for the item) on the text file and select the edit option. The default HTML editor will open at this juncture.

The hardest concept to understand about Web pages is that the Web page is really only made up of the text file. The other items that can be part of the page, like the pictures, audio, or video clips, really don't live inside the file as part of the page. The text file contains the locations where the browser can find those other objects, like pictures. The browser then imports the other pieces and makes it look as though the page were made up of all the combined elements. This is a strange concept for many to understand, and may account for why there are so many pages on the Web that contain markers for missing pictures or images. Generally, when a browser cannot find a graphic in the directory where it expects it, the browser will display a box with a red X in the upper left-hand corner.

HTML tags can be easily identified within a text file. All HTML tags are enclosed in the angle brackets < and > without the need for any blank spaces. In addition, HTML tags act as a switch to make something happen. To turn off the switch, the tag is repeated with a slash (/) inserted first. So, for example, the code to place a sentence in italics would begin with <I>, and everything that follows the tag would appear in italics until the browser encountered the tag of </I> to stop the italicizing. Like everything in life, there are some exceptions, and the HTML exceptions are some tags that do not require being "switched off" to stop. These exceptions are called standalone tags. Examples of standalone tags are the
 (line break), <HR> (horizontal rule), and <IMG> (image) tags. Some tags have implied stop tags that, if left off, will not affect the display of the text. Examples of these include <P> (paragraph) and <TR> (table row).

Typically, Web pages are divided into head and body sections. The head contains information about the document, and it can contain special instructions and other elements. The majority of the observed document will be contained in the body.

Let's begin creating a Web page. Start by opening up a text editor. For now, we will assume your editor is Notepad. The first tag that should be placed in the document is <HTML>, this tag says to the browser, "here comes a web page." Not surprisingly, the final tag at the bottom of the document should be </HTML> to stop the page.

At this point, it may be helpful to know that the HTML tags are not case-sensitive. Often you will find that tags are created using all capital letters. While this is not a requirement, it can be very helpful. The capital letters help to offset the tags from the text contained in the file. Sometimes when trying to find the mates for tags, it helps if the tags stand out just a bit more from the text of the page. At any point in the document you can include comments. The browser will never display comments; in fact, any tags contained within a comment will be ignored.

Let's continue with our example of lighthouses by creating a general informational page about lighthouses. We begin our page with <HTML> <HEAD>. Next let's create our title, <TITLE> All about Lighthouses... </TITLE>. This might be the only element we want in our head, so we will stop </HEAD> and begin with our <BODY>. A tag for a title will tell the browser what to place in the title bar at the very top of the browser window. (Note that this is not a title at the top of the page that would appear just below the menus and toolbars; rather, it is the title that will appear in the title bar just after the icon and before the name of the browser application.)

The body should contain all of the content that the user will see in the browser. The text can appear in six different sizes in a browser. The size of the text is determined by the setting of a tag called a header. The tag for header is an H followed by the size, which is declared by the digits one through six. The smallest of the heading sizes is six, which is a little counterintuitive, while the largest is one. Let's create some headings for our document. You can begin a paragraph with <P>.

<H1> This page is about Lighthouses. </H1><H2> Historical highlights </H2> <P> The first lighthouse built in the United States was sponsored by a group of merchants who wanted to attract commerce to Boston. The stone tower on Little Brewster Island dates back to 1716. </P>

The next paragraph will begin to discuss the first lighthouse keeper.

<P>The first person to be hired by the merchants to keep tallow candles burning in the tower was George Worthylake. Maintaining the candles proved a very difficult task, and Worthylake had very little time to actually help guide ships into the harbor. </P>

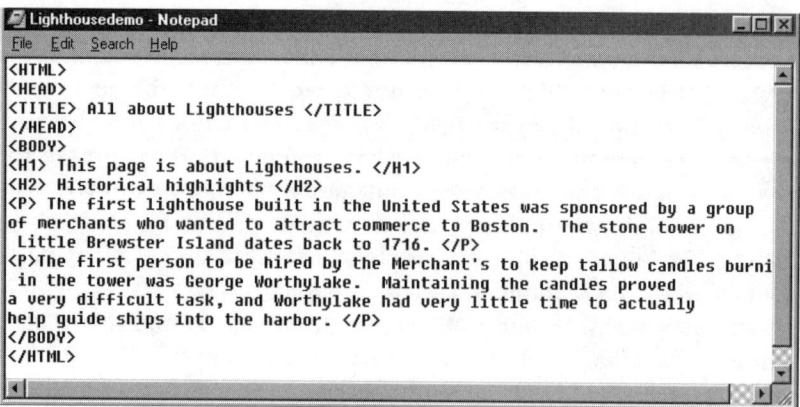

Figure 10.1   HTML Basics

At this point, let's take a look at a sample text file with the pieces we have used. You can see the text as it looks in the editor in figure 10.1.

Once you have saved the text file, in this case as lighthousedemo.htm, you can load it into your browser. You may access it by opening the lighthousedemo file, or you may first open your browser, then select the file and open command and browse to the location of the file. Your sample should now look somewhat like figure 10.2, but notice that the amount of text displayed on each line will be influenced by the size of your browser window.

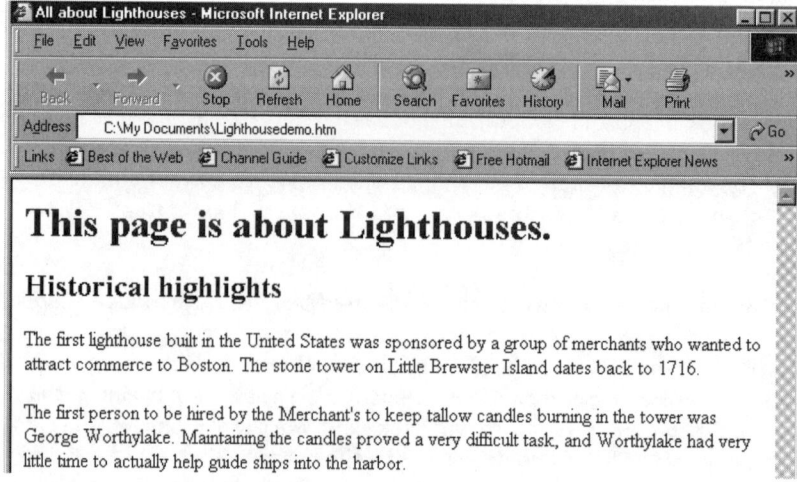

Figure 10.2   A Basic Web Page Formatted with HTML

Like a word processor, a browser will automatically wrap text at the end of a line. This feature is to accommodate the window size of a browser. There is no way to know in advance how large a window the user will allow for their browser. To accommodate, the browser will automatically scroll the text to the next line. There is no need to enter return or carriage codes to cause the text to go down to the next line. Again, the browser will perform this task automatically. In addition, the browser will ignore blank spaces and compress a group of blank spaces into a single blank space. Let's say you place your sentences below each other in your text editor as follows:

A lighthouse was placed as a sentinel against the darkness.
Lighthouses were placed to warn ships of dangerous shoals.
Lighthouse keepers are often referred to as wickies.
The nickname wickies comes from the tallow candles they kept lit.

When a browser displays these four sentences they will appear in paragraph form, not as single line items. The occurrence of a <P>, or paragraph tag, will cause the browser to move the text to begin a new paragraph. Another option to force the browser to move to the next line is a break tag or <BR>. Placing the break tag at the end of each of the four sentences above will result in them being displayed as they appear above.

Conversely, if you do not want a line break to occur, you can prevent one with a no break or <NOBR> tag. There are some circumstances when you may wish to prevent the cursor from moving to the next line. One situation would be a series of graphics, such as the items in a menu, so that they will all remain on the same line.

There are generally three ways to align text. Left alignment is the default. Centering text is as simple as <CENTER>, ending with </CENTER>. You can also specify the alignment within a paragraph tag such as <P ALIGN="left">.

By now you are probably wondering how to cause formatting changes to your text. This is done with tags such as <U> for underline, which is stopped with </U>. Check out the effects of the following tags:

<U> Lighthouses of the North Atlantic </U>
<EM> Lighthouses </EM> that capture the imagination.
The lighthouse at <I> Littler Brewster Island </I> is the oldest in the U.S.

Chapter 10

Compare the following text effects:

The lens that is _{the best known} is the Fresnel Lens.
The lens that is the best known is the <BIG> Fresnel Lens </BIG>.
The lens that is the best known is the <B> Fresnel Lens. </B>
The lens that is the best known is the <BLINK> Fresnel Lens </BLINK>.
The lens that is the best known is the <SMALL> Fresnel Lens. </SMALL>
The lens that is ^{the best known} is the Fresnel Lens.
The lens that is the best known is the <Q> Fresnel Lens. </Q>
The lens that is the best known is the <S> Fruslan </S> Fresnel Lens.

The equivalents for the tags are as follows:

<SUB>—subscript
<SUP>—superscript

```
<HTML>
<HEAD>
<TITLE> All about Lighthouses </TITLE>
</HEAD>
<BODY>
<H1> This page is about Lighthouses. </H1>
<H2> Historical highlights </H2>
<P> The first lighthouse built in the United States was sponsored by a group
of merchants who wanted to attract commerce to Boston. The stone tower on
Little Brewster Island dates back to 1716. </P>
<P>The first person to be hired by the Merchant's to keep tallow candles burning
in the tower was George Worthylake. Maintaining the candles proved
a very difficult task, and Worthylake had very little time to actually
help guide ships into the harbor. </P>
<CENTER><U> Lighthouses of the North Atlantic </U><P>
<EM> Lighthouses </EM> that capture the imagination.</CENTER>
<P>The lighthouse at <I> Littler Brewster Island </I> is the oldest in the U.S.
The lens that is <SUB> the most well known </SUB> is the Fresnel Lens. <BR>
The lens that is the most well known is the  <BIG> Fresnel Lens </BIG>.<BR>
The lens that is the most well known is the <B> Fresnel Lens. </B><BR>
The lens that is the most well known is the <SMALL> Fresnel Lens. </SMALL><BR>
The lens that is <SUP> the most well known </SUP> is the Fresnel Lens.<BR>
The lens that is the most well known is the <Q> Fresnel Lens. </Q><BR>
The lens that is the most well known is the <S> Fruslan </S>  Fresnel Lens.
</BODY>
</HTML>
```

Figure 10.3   Coding for Special Effects

Creating Web Pages Using HTML 165

<B>—bold
<BLINK>—text to blink off and on
<SMALL>—current font size minus one
<Q>—short quotation
<S>—strike-through
<BIG>—current font size plus one

Let's take a look at the source code and the resulting page in the browser. Look at the results in figures 10.3 and 10.4. If you want to add more than one effect, place your tags next to each other. For example, if you wanted to place Little Brewster Island in bold and in italics, you would place your tags into your text such as,

<B><I> Little Brewster Island </I></B>

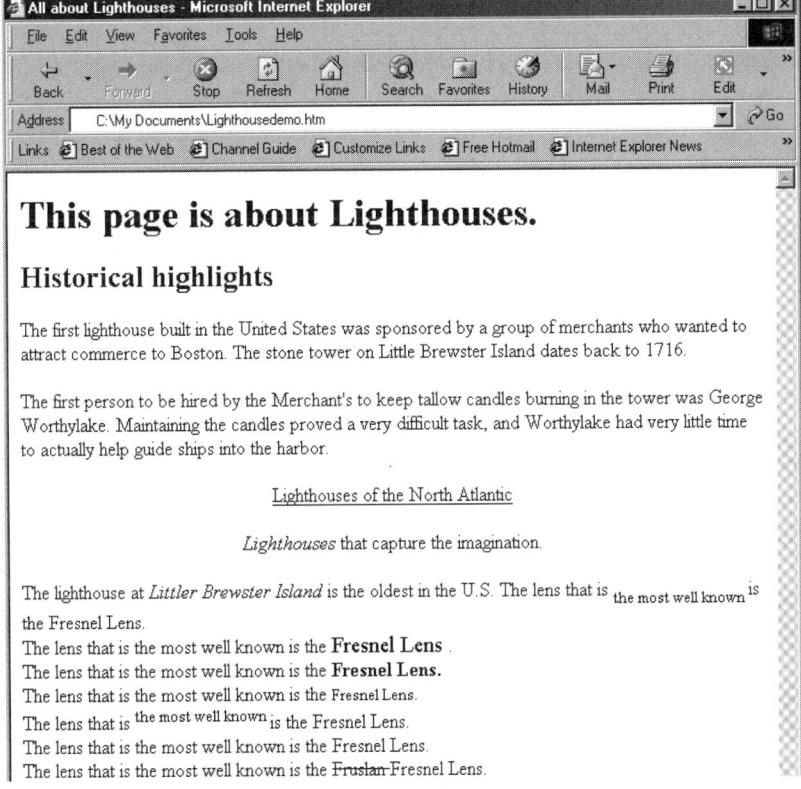

Figure 10.4 Formatting Special Text in HTML

It is also a good technique to stop your tags in the reverse order. Here we have two tags that we have begun; when it is time to turn off each of the effects, turn off the last command first, from the inside working out. So, in the example above, we stopped the italics and then the bold, rather than stopping them in the order that they were initialized. This becomes a more important habit when coding grows more sophisticated.

There are also tags that allow you to make selections about the attributes for the command. Associated values to a named command are referred to as attributes. Formatting options are often included as attributes or options within a command. Attributes occur in the tag separated by a space from the initial command. Regardless of any attributes, the corresponding stop tag does not contain the attribute information. For example, you may want to choose a size for your font for your text. The default size for the browser is three. You can begin a size such as <FONT SIZE=3> and end with </FONT>. Sometimes the values for attributes need to be placed inside quotation marks. For the most part, attributes, which contain a single word, number, period, or hyphen, do not need quotation marks around them. Attributes that contain more than one word are separated by periods or a comma or contain special characters that need to be contained in quotation marks. Be careful that you include both a start and end quotation mark, as the browser will ignore commands until it encounters the second, or closing, quotation marks.

If you wanted to switch the color for your font, you can add an attribute for color. Color brings us to an interesting point. Different browsers contain different definitions for individual colors. Until the World Wide Web Consortium worked on making HTML standards, different browsers developed their own conventions. Interestingly, when creating a page, attributes and even entire tags can exist in one browser and not in another. This has been a development nightmare for webmasters for several years. However, many of the conventions appear to be standardizing a bit more. There are many books and sources available that will identify, in a dictionary type of reference, which features are available by browser and browser version. As browser versions advance, you find that there is more commonality to the code definitions. A prime example of the discrepancies is the way browsers interpret colors. The color "names" are not consistent

Table 10.1 The Sixteen Basic HTML Color Names

Aqua	Black	Blue	Fuchsia
Gray	Green	Lime	Maroon
Navy	Olive	Purple	Red
Silver	Teal	White	Yellow

Note: Colors in italics are nondithering. Cyan and magenta, not included on this list, are also nondithering.

among different browsers. While you can choose to use the name of a color, realize that it may not appear the same when interpreted by different browsers. In the case where a browser doesn't have a definition for a color, the attribute will be ignored. There is an alternative to work around this inconsistency among browsers. Colors can be specified by identifying them by their color "triplet." The triplets tell the browser how much of the red, green, and blue (RGB) to mix in creating a color. (Refer to chapter 2 for additional details). While there are 140 color names, only 16 of them are standard among the majority of browsers.

Of the 16 colors listed in table 10.1, only 8 are nondithering, which means that they will look the same on different monitors and settings. There are a total of 10 nondithering colors. The remaining 130 will shift to the nearest equivalent color available for that system. In some cases, the difference is only slight. In other cases, especially with pastel colors, the difference can be dramatic. Regardless of using the color name or triplet, examples for some font colors are listed below:

<FONT COLOR="RED"> or <FONT COLOR="#FF0000">
<FONT COLOR="LIME"> or <FONT COLOR="#00FF00">
<FONT COLOR="PURPLE"> or <FONT COLOR="#980098">

There are numerous resources available on the Web for finding the color name charts and triplets. Some will even allow you to sample your font and background colors. Regardless, color choices can often reflect the designer's sense of style and personality. It is important to remember that the design choices have implications for those who may choose to view your page. Remember that not all viewers will have excellent eyesight. Choose colors and font faces that complement each other rather than clash. Be aware that there are a number of Web surfers who cannot distinguish all colors and may in fact be colorblind.

If you want to control the size and color, you would place both attributes in the tag and end it as follows:

<FONT COLOR="RED" SIZE=4> This text would be red. </FONT>

The legacy of having browsers ignore blank spaces is that there is no easy way to indent with HTML. There are little methods to get around this. When teaching touch-typing years ago, there were two standard rules that you were to begin a paragraph with an indent, and always include two spaces after a period. The irony is that in HTML, you cannot easily indent your paragraph, and even if you leave two spaces after a period, the browser will only display one! There are a few options that will simulate having an indented area. Browsers will insert white or blank space to offset a quote. The tags for block quotes are <BLOCKQUOTE> and </BLOCKQUOTE>.

Creating Lists

One way to work around the lack of indent capabilities is to create lists. Lists, by definition, will automatically provide indents and adjust spacing. The tags for creating ordered (numbered) lists and unordered (bulleted) lists are very similar. The list tags are convenient in that you do not need to control the line spacing. Creating a new item for a list will automatically result in the text dropping to the next line. Begin your ordered and unordered lists with <OL> and <UL>; both lists are stopped with </OL> and </UL>. The list items are identified with an <LI> tag. With unordered lists you may have an attribute for "compact," to display the block as small as possible, and options for disc, circle, or square bullets. Consider the following lists:

```
<UL type=disc>Lighthouses of Lake Huron
<LI> St. Helena Island Light
<LI> Grand Traverse Light
<LI> Grosse Point Light
<LI> Chicago Harbor Light
</UL>
```

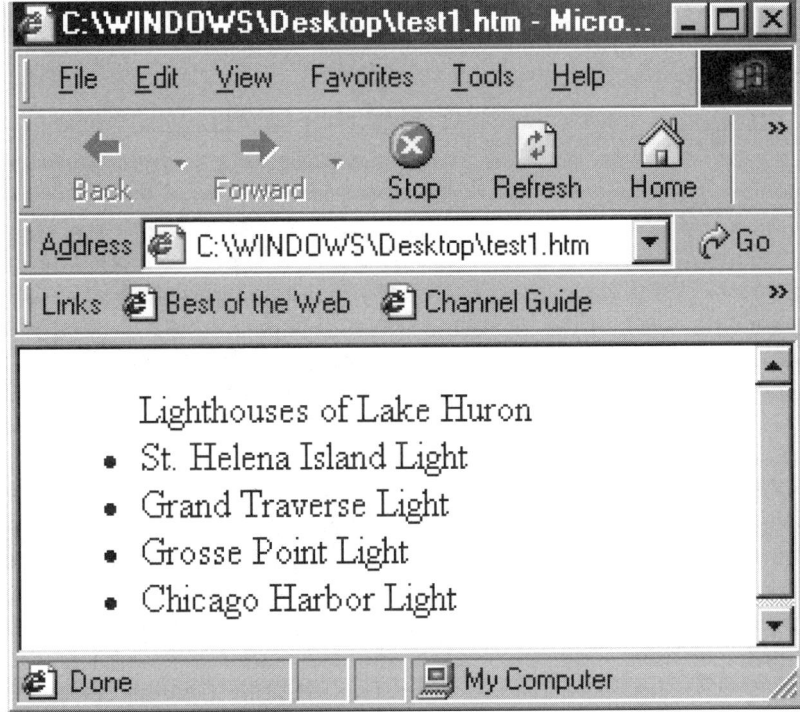

Figure 10.5 Formatting a Bulleted List

The next example shows a nest of lists. They have been indented to identify the two separate lists but do not actually need to be indented in the text document.

```
<OL type="A"> Famous Lighthouse Keepers
<LI>Lime Rock Lighthouse, Ida Lewis, rescuer
<LI>Point Pinos Lighthouse, Francis Gibbons, socialite
<LI> Little Brewster Island
   <OL type="i">
   <LI> George Worthylake, drowned
   <LI> Robert Saunders, drowned
   </OL>
</OL>
```

Ordered lists also have the compact attribute, and start by indicating the starting number or letter (here the default is 1). Style options include a type attribute of Arabic numerals (1), uppercase letters (A), lowercase letters (a), uppercase Roman numerals (I), and lowercase Roman numerals (i).

Creating Tables

The last formatting feature we will examine here is the creation of a table. Tables have many attributes associated with them. When starting out with tables, keep them simple until you have the hang of them, because tables can become difficult to design. The considerations that make them harder to design are usually tables containing blank cells and when you want your data to span the column or columns to accommodate blank spaces. In addition, you have many options for alignment within cells. The cells can be centered, left, or right, and can be aligned vertically as well as horizontally. Further, you can control the width and spacing between and around cells to make the bars appear thicker or in different colors with the cell padding identified in the border options

For now, let's keep things simple and develop a small table. The most crucial tags are <TABLE> to define a table, <TR> for table row to identify a row, and <TD> for table data to place information into a cell. The HTML 4.0 specifications have begun to discourage the use of tables in Web pages. The evolving standard for defining tables is through Cascading Style Sheets (CSS). At this point, not all browsers support CSS, so many webmasters still rely on creating their own tables.

Tables can be defined with a width attribute. The width attribute can contain an absolute or relative value, which will affect the display in the browser window. The absolute value will make the table width a defined number of pixels, regardless of the browser window setting. The relative value will adjust to incorporate a percentage of the screen, regardless of the setting. An absolute value of <TABLE WIDTH=540> would make the table 540 pixels wide. A relative value of <TABLE WIDTH=50%> would make the screen half of the current screen width. There are attribute settings for border, cell spacing, and cell padding. Borders provide shaded dimension around the table. Higher numbers will create fatter padding in the appearance around the edges of the table. Cell spacing refers to the number of spaces between cells and affects what looks like the shaded border around cells. Cell padding refers to the number of spaces between the border and the data; i is the buffer space around the data within the cell. The default value for cell padding is 1, and the default value for cell spacing is 2. The column span attribute is placed within a table data to indicate that a cell should extend into additional columns, such as <TD COLSPAN=2>

Let's create a table now to see the format of the table tags:

<TABLE border=3 colspacing=3 cellpadding=5><CAPTION> Lighthouse Locations </CAPTION>
<TR>
    <TD colspan=5>North Atlantic</TD> </TR>
<TR>
    <TD>Maine </TD>
    <TD> Massachusetts </TD>
    <TD> Rhode Island </TD>
    <TD> New York </TD>
    <TD> New Jersey </TD></TR>
<TR>
    <TD colspan=5>South Atlantic</TD></TR>
<TR>
    <TD> Maryland </TD>
    <TD> Virginia </TD>
    <TD> North Carolina </TD>
    <TD> South Carolina </TD>
    <TD> Georgia </TD></TR>
</TABLE>

Lighthouse Locations

North Atlantic				
Maine	Massachusetts	Rhode Island	New York	New Jersey
South Atlantic				
Maryland	Virginia	North Carolina	South Carolina	Georgia

Figure 10.6 Creating a Table in HTML

Inserting Images

By now, you are probably anxious to begin inserting graphics into your Web pages. Remember that the graphic needs to be identified to the browser because it does not really reside inside of the text file. The text file merely contains a pointer that tells the browser where it can find the image and instructions on how to display the image. The easiest way to set up the text files and their graphic pointers is to be sure that the text file and images are all coming from the same location. If you have created a folder on your computer for your text files, be sure that the images reside there as well. Then, when it is time to load your Web page onto a server, you will need to be sure that not only the text file gets transferred, but that the images get placed onto the server as well. A common error is to tell the browser where to find the image on your hard drive. Later, after loading the page to a Web server, when the page goes "live," it will look in the original location for the image. If the image is not on the same place on the Web server as it was defined when you created the file, the server will not find or display the image. The easiest way to insure that you don't lose your images is to place the images into the same directory as the text file. Don't layer their location in the image definition, and you won't have to worry about those same layers existing on the hosting Web server.

Browsers support mostly two types of image file formats that were discussed in greater detail in chapter 2. Remember that the two formats that browsers use most are .jpg for photos and .gif for simple images and animations. There is a third .png format that is still not as common. The three-letter graphic format designation dates back to the days of the older Microsoft operating systems, which required that file names contain a three-character file type designation. Regardless of the format, the method for insertion is the same.

The image tag is <IMG> and it also has attributes associated with it. The basic image tag is <IMG SRC="nameofgraphic.gif">, where SRC stands for source and the portion in quotes is the name of the image file. As a general rule, image tags do not break the text and can be placed within it. By default the bottom of the image will align to the bottom of the line of text. If the image is larger vertically, the line of text will appear to drop down to accommodate the height of the image.

It is important to remember that adding objects to a Web page causes the page to load more slowly. The more that is added, the slower the page will load. For this reason, many users choose to set their browsers to not load images automatically. Instead, they will choose to load the images only when they want to view them, and instead they see a generic place card where the image is intended. For this reason, many Web designers place "alternative" tags on their images. Alternative tags will provide a description of what the image is supposed to be in the event that the user has turned the images off in their browser. An example would be <IMG SRC="Lighthouse3.gif" ALT="St. Helena Lighthouse" >, so that a user would see the text identifying the lighthouse if the images were turned off.

The vertical alignment attributes will override the default of placing the image in alignment with the bottom of the line of text it appears in. Horizontal alignment values are left and right. The text will wrap around images automatically if they are specified to align to the left or to the right. Once the text has wrapped by the image, you may want to increase the white space around the image. Vspace will add white space above and below the image, while hspace will add space to the left and right of the image.

Creating Links

We have finally arrived at the instructions for creating links, the object that has made the Web as popular as it is. In general, you can create three types of links. The first link is a link that takes you to another location on the same page. In this scenario, you would press on the hyperlink and it would quickly jump you to an alternate location on the same page. You sometimes see this in large documents, or in documents that have lots of headings. Consider a very long page that contained short blurbs about thirty different lighthouses. You could create an index at the top of the page for all thirty, and clicking on any one of them would result in the user going straight to the associated blurb of text for that entry.

The second type of link is one that takes you to an alternate page, but in this case, the alternate page resides on the same host. Think of these links as the ones between different documents without leaving the website. The third type of link is the one that jumps you from one website to an entirely different location. This type of link is the type where you are reading information at one location, in our example about the information of lighthouses. Now the link that is provided to the user takes the user to lighthouse information posted at an entirely different location, like the Coast Guard. In this case, the user has gone from one Web server to an entirely different one. If, however, the link is broken—that is to say the location intended is not available—the user will get an error message in the browser and not leave the original location.

Let's begin to analyze the structure of a link. The first part of the tag is <A> and concludes with </A>. The A in this case stands for anchor. Think of the analogy of a boat throwing out an anchor, and the user going ashore. Hopefully when the user returns after their adventure elsewhere, the boat will still be there upon their return. In the case of a hyperlink, the user leaves the original location and goes off to another. Later, when and if they choose to return, they can get there quickly by using the browser shortcut of the back button or the backspace key on the keyboard.

The easiest link to create is an external link, and we will begin with that one first. Typically, you will see a list of links on a Web page. They contain text on the document. When the user moves the cursor over the link, which is offset by a different color and underlined text, the cursor will change to a pointed hand, and the links location will appear at the bottom of the browser window in the bottom left-hand corner. Insert the address as an attribute with the anchor tag creates a link. Consider the following fictitious example: <A HREF="http://www.aboutlights.org/locations/atlantic.htm"> A List of Atlantic Lighthouses </A>. Clicking on the text in the document that reads "A List of Atlantic Lighthouses" would take the user to a document called atlantic, in a directory called locations, on another Web server whose domain name is aboutlights. The most important thing to remember here is that the URL must be exactly correct, and the hosting Web server must be available for the link to work. Just like when you type an address into a browser window, if you do not get that address absolutely perfect, you will not be able to access the page at the intended location.

Creating a link to another document on the same server is basically the same. However, instead of including the protocol and domain name identifiers, you can simply include the name of the document. These types of links are fairly straightforward. A link of <A HREF="greatlakes.htm"> Great Lakes </A> would take the user from the current page to another page in the same location called greatlakes.htm.

The hardest part for beginners in creating links is to remember that the text that occurs between the <A> and the </A> tags will be displayed as the link on the Web page. Sometimes, the text and the reference will be the same thing. The actual location is listed as the text on the page as well as the definition for the browser. Even in this case, the text needs to be written out as well as the reference. If no text were provided between the two anchor tags, the user would not have anything on their document on which to click. The link could still be there and be active, but it would take a fluke for the user to find it and use it. Conversely, beginners often forget to turn the link off. In this case, everything that comes after the definition of the link becomes part of the link, usually resulting in lines of text that are highlighted and underlined!

Creating a link to an internal location, one on the same page as the current document, will require an additional step than the other two links. With internal links, you will have to name the link. You will need to provide the name in the anchor tag, and you will need to identify the point in the document that the name is referencing. Pretend that we have a long document that contains a list of thirty lighthouses, and under each lighthouse name there is a paragraph or two about each one. We could provide a list of links to all of them at the top of the document. To create one on the list, we would create a link like <A HREF="#light24"> Thomas Point </A>. The next step would be to "name" the point in the text that we want to identify as Thomas Point. We would then drop down to our twenty-fourth listing, and before the lighthouse name and corresponding text we need to include <A NAME=light24> Thomas Point </A>.

There are many additional tags that have not been discussed here. What this chapter has attempted to do is to create an overview of how to create a very basic beginner's Web page. There are numerous books and sources, both online and printed, which are dedicated solely to the purpose of designing pages in HTML. At this point, we will leave advanced Web design as being beyond the scope of this book of essentials. Not surprisingly, there are new products and tools developing all the time. In some ways, it is fun to design your own Web page from scratch to understand how the pieces fit together.

Regardless of the development tools, browsers give users the opportunity to look at the HTML code behind any page. Find the option on your browser menu that will allow you the view source option to look at the code. Pick a simple page to preview, as the really elaborate professionally developed pages most likely will overwhelm you. Gradually work up in complexity. What can be fun is that for most pages, you can take a look and see "how they did that."

There are other Web page elements that should be discussed to round out the current state of Web page development. It is important that when you create a Web page, you understand that that page has to be posted on a Web server before it becomes active and live on the Web to be viewed by outsiders. Posting the pages requires a host. The host can be internal in your organization, or you can choose an outside source to host your pages. There are many ISPs that provide space to subscribers to host Web pages. If cost is a consideration, there are numerous websites that provide free Web page hosting. Many of my students have posted their own pages on www.angelfire.com. While sites for Web hosting vary, there are a few sources that provide free hosting for educators.

Form elements in HTML are very straightforward. Forms contain objects like radio buttons (a circle that is allowed to be selected by a user). However, creating the process between the collected information and the location it needs to be sent to for interpretation is an advanced skill. There are applications that allow you to collect the information and download the data to a specified location, such as an e-mail message. These types of applications require working with a Web server to direct the information. There are a number of alternatives for carrying out this type of activity, which is referred to as scripting. Scripting languages provide the link between the data that is collected on the form and distributing that data to another file or program. The common gateway interface (CGI) is a method that allows interaction between a Web server and Web-based applications. Perl is one of the most popular languages for writing CGI programs or scripts, which are invoked by the Web server when a user makes a request. Perl needs to be installed onto the computer where you will be creating your scripts as well as downloading the Perl language onto your server. One advantage to a language like Perl is that it is developed by programmers and distributed openly for free. To learn more about downloading Perl, visit the Perl website at www.perl.com. An alternative to a scripting language is to use an application that can intercept and transfer information. In the Microsoft environment, active server pages (ASP) was developed for this type of information control and transfer.

Interactive Web Pages

How to create an interactive Web page is the next point of interest. Web pages that are interactive and that provide the user with some type of feedback are also created by using scripts. Scripts can be thought of as mini-programs that are created in another language. In these cases, the language structure and design more closely approximates a programming language than we have seen by creating tags. A common scripting language used in Web pages is Javascript, which has some similarity to the Java language. Another scripting language is VBScript that is based on the Visual Basic (and before that, the Basic programming language). Scripts can do many types of tasks. A typical task may provide the user with the time or date on a page. Another task may ask the user for color preferences, and then adjust the page to color settings. Still other scripts can be used to perform mathematical calculations or serve as interactive quizzes.

Emerging Trends

An emerging form of HTML is Dynamic HTML. With Dynamic HTML, you begin to see a separation between the structure and content of the page elements. Cascading Style Sheets (CSS) allow you to keep your formatting elements separated from the structure of your document. This separation makes Web page construction and modification much easier. An example would be to set the style for the largest heading tag, <H1>. You could create a style sheet for the heading tag so that whenever it is encountered, the color will be green and a font-family will be one of your choice.

Dynamic HTML also allows for the creation of events. An example of an event would be a rollover effect. With a rollover effect, you could change one graphic to a totally different image when the cursor comes into contact with, or "rolls over," the original. Dynamic HTML also includes the capability to include events in the forms of transitions and filters.

XML, or Extensible Markup Language, is the HTML that has been created for carrying out electronic commerce. Commerce has security and encryption needs that are well beyond the scope of traditional HTML. Enter XML to fill that gap for the commercial Web market. XML allows for the creation of user-defined tags. In this scenario, users can define tags for items like prices and quantities.

HTML is growing and changing almost every day. As the Web grows up and expands its seemingly limitless horizons, languages and ways to tackle new needs and preferences will emerge. So much development has happened with HTML in so short a time that it will be exciting to see where the language of the Web evolves in the future.

Activity Sheet 10.1
Creating Web Pages with HTML

Name: _____ Date: _____

Design a poetry Web page using what you have learned in HTML. Your page should contain the following items:

1. A poem that you have written
2. At least one illustration for the poem
3. Links to some poetry by your favorite authors

Chapter 10

Activity Sheet 10.2
Creating Web Pages with HTML

Name: _____ Date: _____

The following is a list of prefixes that are often used in science:

anti- against	herb- pertaining to plants
arth- joint	hetero- different
auto- self	homeo- same
bio- related to life	macro- large
chloro- green	micro- small
cyto- cell	multi- consisting of many
di- double	osteo- bones
epi- above	photo- pertaining to light
exo- outer	plasm- forming substance
gastro- stomach	proto- first
hemo- blood	

The following is a list of suffixes that are often used in science:

-cyst pouch
-derm skin, layer
-gen producing
-itis inflammation
-logy study
-meter measurement
-osis condition, disease
-phage stage
-phase stage
-pod foot
-stasis stationary condition

Now, using the information above, create an HTML document that will put the prefixes and suffixes into a table format. Be sure to include titles or headings before your table.

11
Developing Web Pages

> Now that you have a basic understanding of what HTML is, and how it is created, we shall take a look at some of the alternatives to writing HTML code by hand. There are a number of programs that will perform the task of taking your text document and automatically creating the necessary tags to turn your document into a Web page that is suitable for viewing by a browser. This chapter will focus on building a Web page about lighthouses, but will use different applications as the building blocks. We will take a look at a couple of the applications and build a sample page together. Finally, we will take a look at a useful diagramming tool, Inspiration.

Writing HTML code from scratch, while rewarding enough on its own, admittedly can get rather tedious. Fortunately there are several applications that will allow the user to make selections from a menu and generate the appropriate tags to perform the desired effect. Not surprisingly, the Web page generation software varies greatly in ease of use and complexity. We shall begin by building an HTML document using a word processing application.

There are a number of Web page builder application packages to choose from at the present time. What is amazing is that the capabilities built into these packages are expanding as the use of scripting languages and the HTML options expand. Choosing a tool can be a very difficult process. Not surprisingly, there are many price tags to go along with those options. Fortunately, most of the Web page building packages on the market have made allowances for educational or reduced pricing. Be sure to ask the vendors or resellers about any discounts for educational use that would apply to your classroom or library. You can even find free or shareware (really inexpensive) packages that can be downloaded off the Web. Some are trial versions of Web applications, and others are full-scale applications. You will need to experiment and do some research to see which one is right for your classroom. Providing a table of your options in the scope of this text would not prove very worthwhile, as the options are continuously changing. Instead we will investigate some of the more common resources available today.

Most of the word processing packages now come with resources for creating Web pages. Most of these are basic page options. They are great for creating illustrative or informational pages. They allow the creation of tables and most of the general formatting options. However, creating any type of dynamic resource is usually beyond the capability of these programs. These dynamic resources and advanced Web page creation techniques require a more sophisticated Web page creation program.

Some of the Web page program options come installed with the software on a new computer. For a while, Windows-based machines were being shipped with an Express version of Microsoft FrontPage. In many cases, users were not even aware that Express was present because perusing the programs options from the task bar did not reveal that the program was there. Rather, you might find it if you downloaded an HTML document and attempted to edit the page, and FrontPage would load! (The other way to check to see if it is there is to go to the find command from the start programs task bar and do a search for FrontPage.)

FrontPage is Microsoft's offering for a full-blown Web page builder. Adobe Systems Incorporated, an industry leader in desktop publishing for many years, has had a few programs for Web page design. Among the packages that they offered was Pagemill. Pagemill was an easy program to learn and was available for both Macintosh and Windows operating systems. Adobe has moved on to another product, GoLive. Macromedia, Inc., is another vendor that is actively pursuing the Web construction market. They offer a suite of products to design just about anything you can think of for the Web right now.

The Web page construction tool from the Macromedia lineup at this time is called Dreamweaver.

BUILDING A WEB PAGE IN MICROSOFT WORD

Using Word to prepare a Web document is a fairly easy task. The software does not assume that you understand anything about HTML or about the conventions used on the World Wide Web. With Word you essentially have two choices. You can first create a document, and then when it is almost complete you can save it as an HTML file. This option exists on its own under the file option on the menu as "Save as HTML," or can be accessed when saving the file by manipulating the file type to be an HTML document. The other option is to do a save command just as soon as you begin creating a new document and selecting the file type to be HTML. Really the two methods are the same, but one initialized much earlier on in the process. Initializing it as HTML early has a distinct advantage. The advantage is that the menu options will change to reflect the options available in a Web page. What exactly does that mean? Consider the formatting toolbar. While working on a Word document, the tools will include the font face, alignment, bullets, highlighting, and font color. Once saved as an HTML document, this toolbar will look different. The tool bar will no longer have a font size, but rather a large and small letter "a" with a tiny triangle pointing up or down, a horizontal ruler line will appear on the toolbar, and the highlighter will no longer be present. Likewise the format pull-down menu will change to only include formatting options that are valid for a Web document. Of course, exactly what tools appear will depend upon your version of Word and how you have the toolbars set up to look. Toolbars can be customized as the user wants, so that toolbar references may not always be exact. For the most part, you should see new toolbar options that represent the valid options and selections for viewing on a Web page.

Let's examine what tools are available for creating your Web page. Remember that a browser cannot interpret font sizes. Rather it has six relative font sizes. In Word these font sizes can be manipulated directly. Pressing either the increase or decrease font size buttons will result in a change.

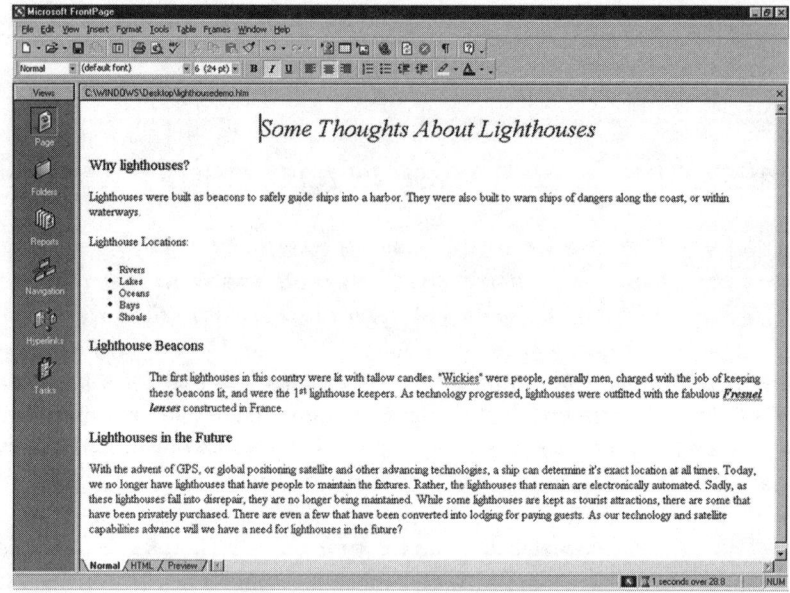

Figure 11.1   Lighthouse Page

Take a look at figure 11.1, and you will see that the majority of formatting options appear on the toolbars and can easily be used on the page. This example shows the changes of font size, use of bold, use of italics, changes in alignment, as well as the use of bullets. Notice that you cannot indent a paragraph. When you attempt to do so, the whole paragraph will be indented to appear like a block quote. This is because browsers cannot view blank spaces. They only interpret tags and wrap the text into the window for display, ignoring all blank spaces. It does not matter if you place more spaces between words; the browser will overwrite that and interpret the multiple blank spaces as a single space.

One nice feature is that you can switch from your document to view the source code. The source code is your document, plus the tags that have to be included for the browser to interpret your commands. The source code can be viewed by selecting view from the main menu and then choosing HTML source. The source code for the page in figure 11.1 is represented here in figure 11.2.

Developing Web Pages 185

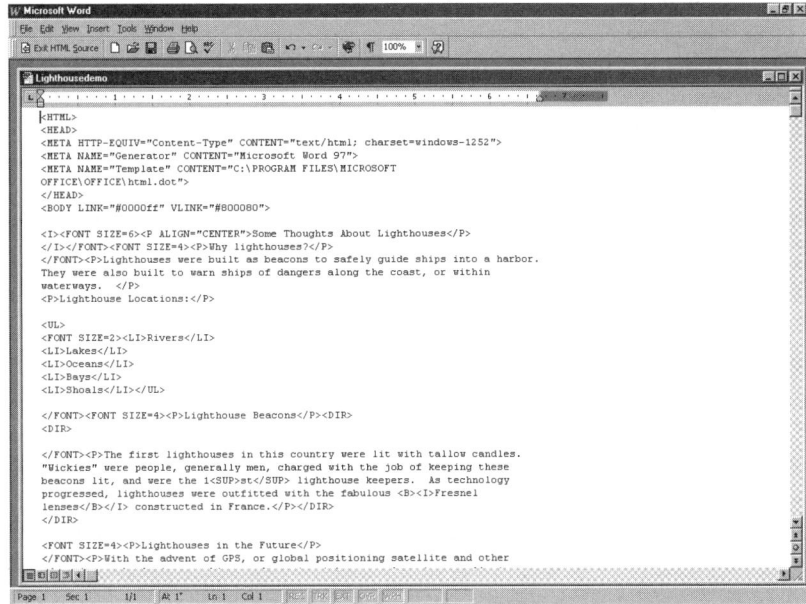

Figure 11.2 Source Code for Lighthouse Page

Notice that you can exit from the source code through the menu at the top of the page labeled "exit HTML source." This is also a useful way to learn how to write the tags on your own, as was done in chapter 10. You can experiment with your document with the items on the tool bars, and then look at the source code to determine how to include similar coding sequences on your own.

Most of the formatting codes are fairly easy to figure out. The best way to find out about them is to experiment with them. Remember that while working in Word, you can always undo the last steps in sequence, so it is fairly easy to recover from mistakes. Experiment with the formatting options and develop a nifty page of your own.

Our page so far has been made up only of text. One of the first advanced steps that you need to learn is how to put in a picture. Remember that pictures don't actually reside in the document in which they are viewed. Images exist as files in their own right. The graphic file formats that can be used on a Web page include .jpg, .gif, and .png. What the Web page actually has embedded into it is a location that points to an image. Once the browser finds the image, it is then imported directly into that location on the page, still existing as an entirely separate entity.

To begin the process of placing in a graphic, select Insert-> Picture-> from File, then browse and locate the graphic file you wish to include. In this example, we have inserted a lighthouse.gif that was created in paint and saved as a .gif image. You must remember that the default location will be coded into your page. When it is time to post this page to a Web server, you must include the graphic files as well as this page file. It is also extremely important to remember to place the HTML document and the graphic file in the same folder. As long as they are in the same folder and posted from the same folder, you will not have any problems. If, however, they are placed in different folder, the result will be a box bearing an icon that indicates an image that cannot be found. For simplicity's sake, the best advice is to always place your graphic files and your HTML documents in the same folder on your disk. That way, when it is time to move them, you will not need to worry about broken links.

Another key to remember in working with this application is that you may not "open" your graphic file. Doing so will cause the word processor to try to translate the image into its coded version. It is important to remember that while working with Microsoft applications, you will need to insert your images.

The next important addition to your HTML document will be the creation of a link. The simplest way to insert the hyperlink is to go to the location on the document where you want the link to appear; while the cursor is in that location, press on the insert hyperlink tool button. You may also use insert, then hyperlink on the main menu. If you want your hyperlink to be based on text, you will need to highlight that text before selecting the insert hyperlink. Once the text is highlighted, the procedure is the same.

Once you have requested an insertion, you will see a box that looks like figure 11.3. Enter in the Web address that you wish to link to in the first box. Be sure to include all of the parts of the address, including the protocol, or http:// portion, of the address.

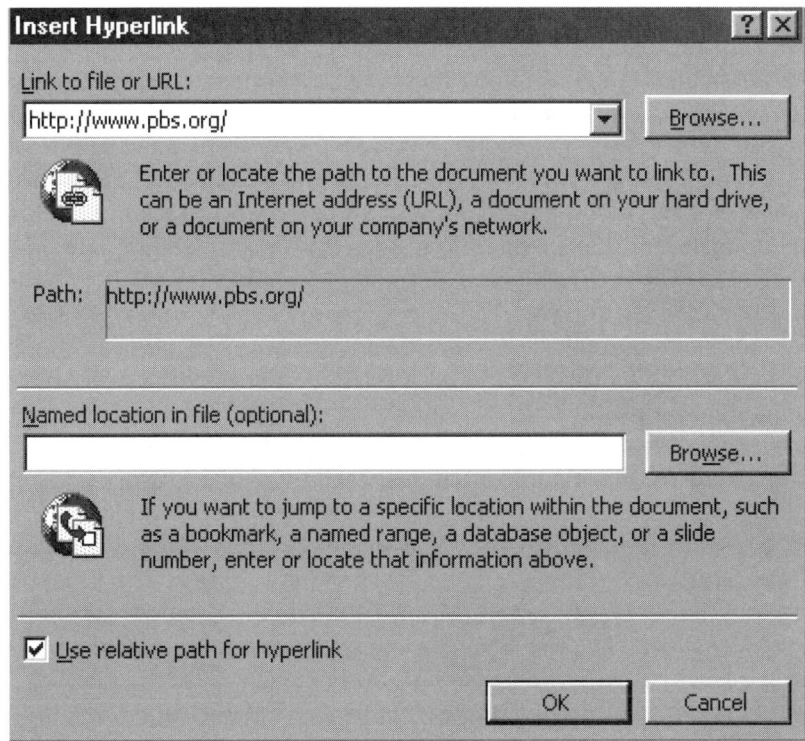

Figure 11.3   Creating a Hyperlink in Word

At any time during or after the construction of the HTML document, you can preview what the page will look like when posted online by selecting the Web page preview tool. The icon for the Web page preview is a blank sheet with a globe in the center and a magnifying glass askew on the right. If you are not sure which tool it is, remember to pause your cursor over the tool button and allow the help to display the name of the icon. (This is true of all of the tool buttons at any time during your word processing session.)

USING FRONT PAGE

Launch FrontPage, and you will enter a screen to create a new HTML document. What is important to understand is that all of the documents, files, graphics, clips, etc., that are going to be a part of this application will be understood as a part of a web. A web contains many different files and components, and it can exist within its own hierarchy of settings and folders. The main web is the default web called the root web. Think of it as the top level in a family tree. All the webs you create will be at a level below, like children. Any of the created webs can be linked together, or exist separately and be displayed as separate units. One of the nice features of FrontPage is the amount of templates that it has already packaged for you. You can access them by starting "new" under file then selecting page. Selecting Web is a more difficult process. This method would be wise if you were going to be posting your Web pages to a Web server by yourself. However, the creation of a Web server is beyond the scope of this text. Some of the pages in the wizards that are available include the creation of a bibliography page or a search page. For now, we will just work with a normal page like you have when you open the application. Note that rather than a simple "document1" name at the top, the default name is new_page_1.htm. Additional pages will be numbered sequentially. This is in keeping with the nomenclature for an entire website. When you are ready to post your web, the software will help you to move all the components and position your files on a Web server.

At this point, we will use the same document that we created in our lighthousewpdemo. The tool buttons and menus at the top of the screen are just about identical to those of our word processing application. You can experiment with those as you see fit. Figure 11.4 shows our page as it is typed onto a FrontPage document.

The biggest change on the desktop is the toolbar that is to the left of the desktop area, as well as the tabs at the bottom of the screen. The tools to the left allow access to various views, and they include:

Page—This is the editor and where we type our text and create our page. Most of the work will be completed in this view.
Reports—Displays reports that contain information about individual files contained in the Web.
Folders—Lists all of the files for file management contained in this web.
Navigation—Shows how visitors will be able to move throughout this web.
Hyperlinks—Gives a bird's-eye view of all of the links that exist in a tree format.

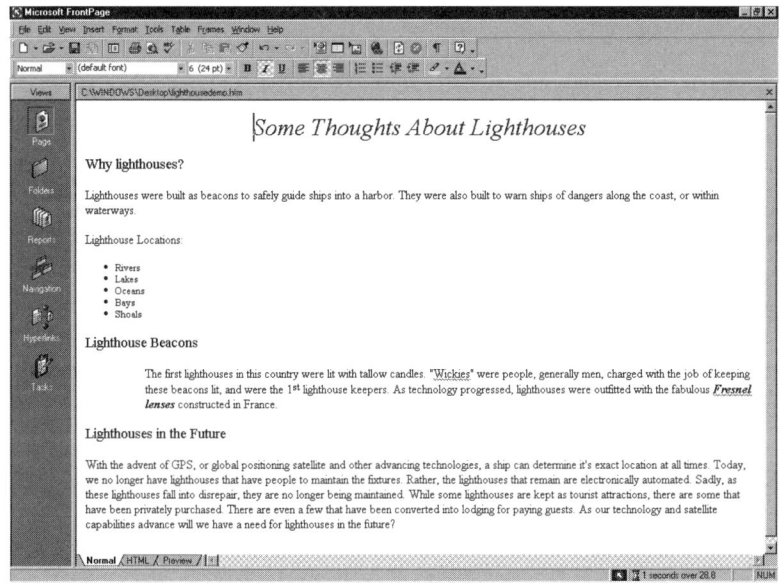

Figure 11.4   A FrontPage Document

Tasks—Maintains a list of items that need to occur as the site is constructed.

The next important tabs appear at the bottom of the window: normal, HTML, and preview. Normal is the editor for the page. HTML is where you would click to view the source code for the page. Preview presents a preview of how the page will appear when viewed through a browser.

Inserting an Image

To insert an image, you follow a process similar to that in the word processor. On the menu, make the insert and picture selections and point to the graphic you wish to include. You can use the window to browse for the graphic you wish to insert. If you select an image from the My Documents folder and were to check the HTML source, you will see that it will contain a full path name with the image. When you save the document, you will be prompted to move the images with a window that prompts you to "save embedded files." It is important that if you do not select the default options, you keep track of where the images are placed. What is important here is how you will save your images. FrontPage will understand that you will need to move the image with the HTML document and will prompt you to place them together, so that later, when they are posted, no parts will be missing.

To create a link you can insert an address directly, then select the insert hyperlink option on the menu. If you wish to turn another line of text into a link, first type the text, then highlight the text and press the select hyperlink on the menu. The insert hyperlink icon is a small globe with a chain "link" on the icon. The window that appears for creating a hyperlink is pictured in figure 11.5.

Place the entire URL, or Web address, in the hypertext box. The selection for target frame determines how the linked page will next appear. For example, if the selection is made for new window, the page will open in a new browser window. You can determine if the link will

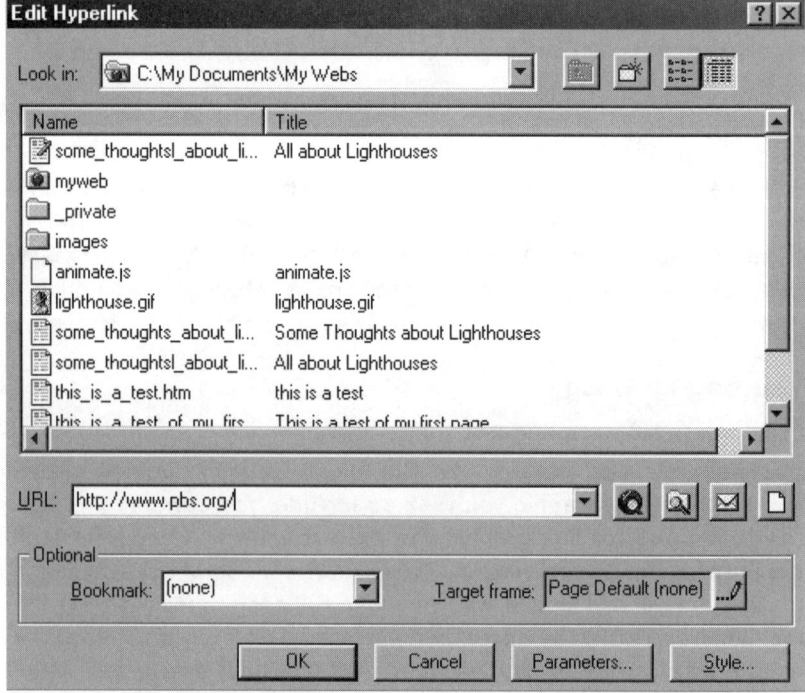

Figure 11.5   Creating a Hyperlink in FrontPage

open to a new browser window or overwrite the current page in the current window.

Often you decide that you want to set up a link to a page that you have not yet created. This window gives you the option of setting up that new page for later modification. To create this new page, select the icon to the far right of the URL box; it appears as a blank document icon. Place the cursor over this icon and you will see the message to create a page and link to a new blank page. This is an extremely useful feature in designing a new site. If the page already exists, it is easy enough to locate and name. When you create names as "placeholders" on the fly, often by the time you get around to editing the new pages, you forget the exact name, fail to get the pages to link properly, and wind up spending a good bit of time debugging the spelling differences!

Creating Tables

Creating tables is a very easy process. Choose table from the menu, and you are then given a cursor to draw the perimeter of the table. The table toolbar will automatically appear on the desktop, and you can increase the rows or columns in the table immediately with the options on this toolbar. In addition, when you enter the cells on the table, the table tools will allow you to adjust the vertical alignments from the toolbar. Use your basic formatting tools for center, left, and right alignment, as well as any formatting, font, or color selections. You can make adjustments to the table itself by highlighting and right-clicking any of the cells and selecting table properties or individual cells with cell properties.

Using Dynamic Effects

FrontPage also gives you options for creating some dynamic effects. You can easily create a "rollover" by following these steps. A rollover is an event that is triggered by the cursor moving or "rolling" over the text or image identified for the effect. Suppose that you wanted the text to change when the mouse moved over the word "Lighthouse." To create the effect, highlight the word lighthouse, then choose format on the menu, and select dynamic HTML effect. Next choose an event, such as a rollover, then choose formatting, and the final step is to make the formatting change selections.

Creating Marquees

To create items like marquees, which are text that scrolls on a page like you see above a movie theatre, select insert on the menu. The next selection is to put in a component. A box for marquee properties then appears on the screen, and you can make the selections for color and size and other formatting options. The text to appear scrolling on the screen is then placed in the text box.

Creating Frames

Frames are used to divide a Web page into separate areas. The frames can be thought of as separate pages within a page and are independently scrollable. Many Web designers in the early days used frames poorly. They were powerful and fun, and many designers went a bit overboard with them. Instead of assisting to make a page easier to navigate, they often had the effect of making the page far more complex than it needed to be. When introducing frames into a page, be careful that they are used for a purpose and are easy for the user to navigate. Remember that if your page is difficult to understand, a visitor will click off to another location in seconds! To create a framed page with FrontPage, you must select a frames page tab while creating a new page. Once there, click the frames option and then click the contents icon. You can then follow the prompts to create the new portions individually within the page. There are many, many more options available in FrontPage. Experiment and have fun creating!

CREATING A WEB PAGE USING INSPIRATION

Inspiration is a package that can be used for many educational projects. Designed as a tool for visual thinking and learning, the program has the capability to create many graphical interpretive devices. One of the features of the latest version of Inspiration is the capability of storing any of the designs that are created as Web pages.

To begin using the program, you must have it installed on your computer. If you wish to preview the software before purchasing, the company provides a trial version that can be downloaded from their website at www.inspiration.com.

Developing Web Pages

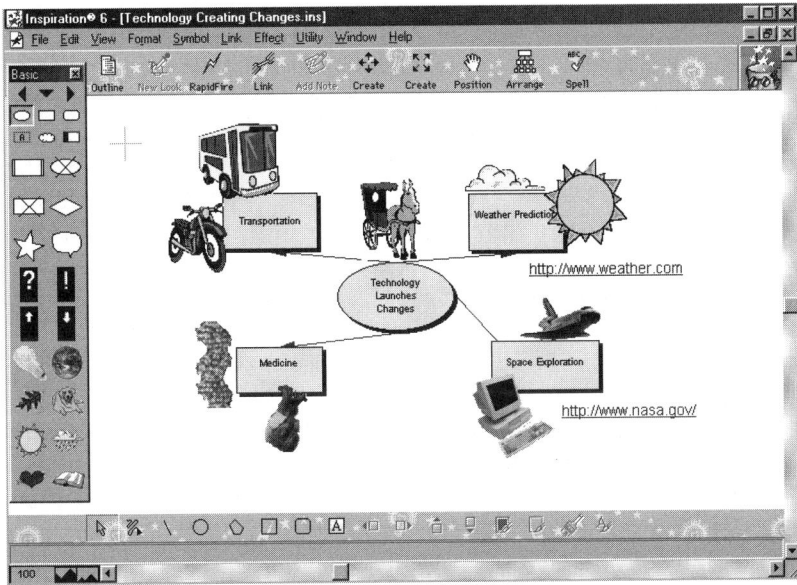

Figure 11.6   Desktop for Inspiration

The desktop for this application is fairly easy to understand. Generally you can use this tool for idea webs and brainstorming about topics. Figure 11.6 shows the desktop for this program.

The main menu at the top offers the manipulation of files, editing tools, symbols, format options, and views. The view selection on the main menu will allow you to toggle on the additional toolbars by highlighting and selecting the choice. Some of the selections also have additional function keys to toggle toolbars to the screen. The toolbar at the left of the screen is a tear-off toolbar and can be moved anywhere on the desktop. This toolbar is called the symbol palette. There are numerous symbols to choose from. To change the symbol libraries (which are grouped by category), click on one of the arrows at the top of the bar. Any of the symbols can be inserted onto the page. The draw toolbar is at the bottom of the window and contains the icons to draw "freehand" on the screen. You can insert lines, shapes, and text boxes with these tools. The toolbar that is most unique to users is the diagram toolbar. The outline tool will shift between the diagram and an outline presentation of a diagram.

The diagram will always begin with one box being placed at the center of the screen. This original tool can be changed, adjusted, and modified by the user. The default placement will be the center of the screen. Most idea webs will traditionally start at the center of the page and grow out. The diagram can be created by clicking the desired tool or shape that will then be placed on the desktop. The link tool will allow the user to create a link between objects. This can be used to create links by hand. There are new symbol tools and they look alike—only one points north, south, east, and west, and the other points northeast, northwest, southeast, and southwest. When you hold the cursor over the new symbol icon, you will notice that one of the four branches will be highlighted. This indicates the direction in which the new symbol will be placed on the page. Additionally, a link in the shape of an arrow will automatically be generated when using these tool buttons.

Once you have placed objects on the page, you can modify their size, location, and text. To move the objects on the screen, you can use any of the "nudge" buttons that will activate at the right of the draw toolbar. The nudge buttons are really helpful in moving your objects around on the screen. To modify the size, when they are the highlighted object move the cursor to the corner of the highlights, and when the cursor changes to an arrow you can hold the mouse button down and drag the image to adjust its size.

Inspiration allows you to insert graphic images from any location. From the main menu, go to insert and down to graphic. Graphic file formats of .gif, .jpg, .bmp, .wmf, and .pic or .pict are allowed.

You may place hypertext links into your documents simply by typing a valid Web address. Adding a link requires auto-detection to be turned on. From the utility menu, choose Internet, and then toggle hyperlink auto-detection. A check mark next to the menu item means it is turned on. The hyperlinks can be triggered in either the diagram or outline views. In addition, hyperlinks can be added to any text. To create a link in figure 11.7 for the medicine symbol, you could highlight the medicine text, then go to utility on the main menu and choose Internet. At this point a box will appear in which to type the URL of the link. You can even specify other text that you want for the link.

Developing Web Pages

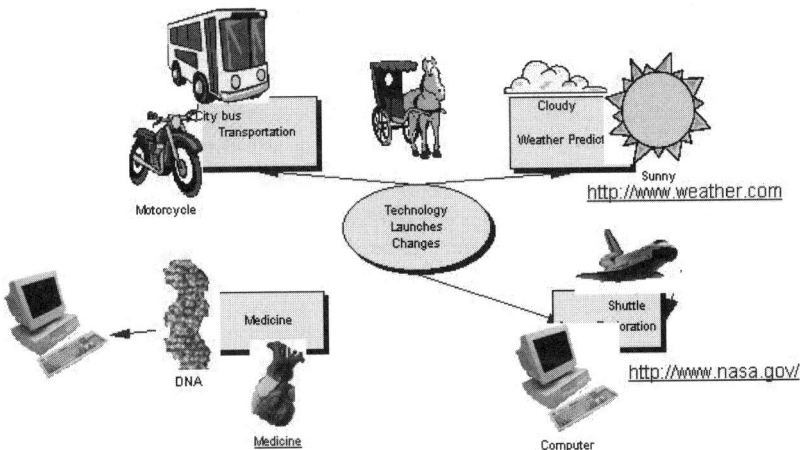

Figure 11.7   The Inspiration 6 Desktop

The last step involves saving this diagram as a Web page document. A "save as" command will only allow you to create an Inspiration diagram for future use. Instead, you will need to export the document, which is also available under file on the main menu. When you arrive at the export options, you may choose between graphic file formats of .jpg, .bmp, .wmf, or .pict. The final option is to choose to export into a single HTML page. This feature also allows you to export outline pages as HTML or word processing pages. Once the HTML option is selected, you will be prompted for the location to place the exported file.

Your final step will be to post the generated page. Posting is the step that loads the page onto a host or computer that has a live connection to the World Wide Web. Be sure to include all of the parts for the generated page; this will include the page as you created it with an .htm extension, and you will need to move any images (in the form of .jpgs) that are associated with this page. They will be created into the same location, and will need to be moved together onto the Web server and still reside in the same folder on that Web server. The images that Inspiration creates in association with the saved page will contain the same file name, followed by a number. For example, the page generated in figure 11.7 was saved as TechnologyChg.htm, and the graphic associated with it was saved as TechnologyChg1.jpg.

This software is a handy way to generate some fairly complex image maps and can have many useful applications. Not only can you use it to generate ideas, but you can also use it to create menus and very creative pages for any Web application.

Whichever tools you have available, you will find that software packages for Web page design and products like Inspiration will be greeted with enthusiasm in your classroom. Hopefully you will have access to one of the packages discussed above for the exercises that follow.

Activity Sheet 11.1
Creating Web Pages

Name: _____ Date: _____

Using one of the Web page applications, design a Web page about your favorite place to go on a vacation. You do not need to have gone to the destination. Create a page that explains what there is to see and do there. Answer the following questions before you create your page:

1. What is the temperature like?
2. What is the best season to go to this place?
3. How can you reach the destination?
4. What are the place's special foods? For what kind of cooking is the place most famous?
5. What sights are available here?
6. What amusements are available here?
7. What famous events happened here?
8. What other special things does this location have to offer vacationers?

Activity Sheet 11.2
Creating Web Pages

Name: _____ Date: _____

1. Pick a destination in outer space.
2. Create a Web page that tells about the features of this location.
3. Make sure that some of the information on this page is presented in a table. An example could be its distance from other locations or the sun.
4. Be sure to include at least three images on this page.
5. Try to find an animated graphic that is appropriate for this page and include it as well. Appendix 2 contains a list of websites that have graphics you are allowed to use in your page.

12
Introduction to Programming

This chapter will take a look at what programming is all about. References are frequently made in computer books to programming languages, but seldom do they explain the logical constructs that are involved in writing programs. We will learn about the process of designing an algorithm and representing it with a flowchart. We will then take a very brief look at some of the programming constructs. We will also discuss programming techniques and look at samples from some of today's more popular programming languages.

PROGRAMMING LANGUAGES

Programs are sets of instructions that are executed by a computer. Software or programs can be divided into the two categories of operating systems and applications. We have learned that operating systems (OS) provide special information to the system. An OS is the language that speaks to the hardware. Applications, on the other hand, can have many different purposes. Some applications can themselves be programming languages, while other applications, though created in a language, do not require an understanding of programming to be manipulated by a user. There are many languages that can be used to create instruction sets that a computer can execute. We have to be careful to not say that a computer can understand instructions, because, as we know, computers can only carry out functions as described and are not capable of reasoning and making choices based upon memory and experience. Remember that the memory and reasoning approach is associated with artificial intelligence.

There are many programming languages, and a person who writes computer programs is often referred to as a programmer. There are even different "flavors" of the same language. Understanding different programming languages is often like understanding different dialects of a foreign language. Different programming languages use the same logic and constructs to create programs. However, the details of how the code is written and interpreted is the main difference of the languages. Languages are divided into three types: machine languages, assembly languages, and high-level languages. Machine languages are those that manipulate the processor of a particular machine directly. They are machine-dependent and are not portable from one machine type to another. Manipulating machine language was very tedious, so assembly languages developed. A translation process needs to happen between assembled programs into machine language. Both assembly language and high-level language programs have an intermediate process that converts the information into machine code.

Compiled or Interpreted

Programming languages are described as being high-level or machine languages. Machine-level languages are written with the instructions that go directly to the processor. Machine language is in no way intuitive, and it is unique to each processor. High-level languages, on the other hand, require another step to turn them into the language of the processor. In this case, the processor needs to use some type of translator to perform its functions. There are two different types of translators: compilers and interpreters. An interpreter translates the program, following through statement by statement. A compiler translates the program into machine language before execution. With a compiled program, the program is left in its translated state. With an interpreted program, the program is retranslated each time it is run. For this reason, compiled programs run much more efficiently than interpreted programs. Compiled languages are more powerful and more efficient languages for writing programs. Usually, however, the compiled languages are more complex to understand, especially for those new to writing programs.

BASIC (Beginner's All-Purpose Symbolic Instruction Code) is a language created in the mid 1960s by Kemeny and Kurtz at Dartmouth College as a way to write programs in a simple form of English. Later, a popular version of Basic was developed by Microsoft Corporation and released as Qbasic for the IBM and compatible computers. Statements in Basic are intended to be easy to understand by people as well as computers. Qbasic was shipped as part of the Microsoft operating system for many years. However, when Microsoft advanced to its Windows operating system, Qbasic was no longer included—probably because there was no demand to use it. This is too bad, because it was a nice, simple language for students to begin to learn to write simple programs.

Many programming languages require the use of a text editor. Text editors are simple programs that treat all the instructions as text. Remember, we used a text editor to create Web pages with HTML. Text editors have useful features like the ability to find and replace text. This feature is useful when you want to make changes to a program and need to be sure that you make the change not in one place, but throughout the whole program. The programming language next executes the information that is stored in the format of a text file. The execution phase is usually described as running the program.

Algorithms

Computer programs are step-by-step instructions to perform a specific task. The process of the instructions as a problem-solving set is called an algorithm. An algorithm is a set of instructions that are well-defined to perform a task. An important feature to an algorithm is that it contains a finite number of steps. Each step or instruction represents an action or calculation to be performed. No steps can be left out or left to chance, because the instruction set must be exact for the microprocessor to be able to perform its tasks.

Algorithms are a convenient way to look at a problem. Creating an algorithm to complete a task will often help you to understand the steps that need to be taken for completion. Programming constructs are the different methods that you can use to work through an algorithm. Constructs can be ways of combining

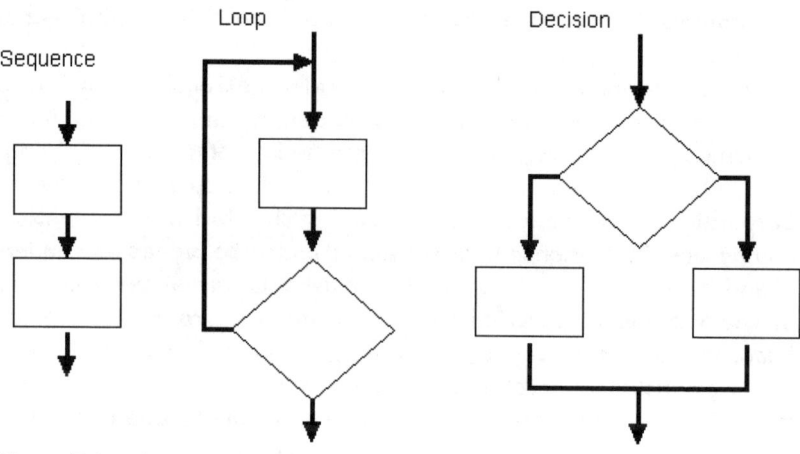

Figure 12.1   Using Constructs in an Algorithm

statements to perform a task. Algorithms are made up of the different constructs joined together to solve a problem. Examples of the constructs can be seen in figure 12.1, and they will be explained in greater detail below.

Flowcharting

In the early days of computing, time spent on a computer was very expensive. There were few computers available, and most would run all through the day and night. It was not uncommon for programming students in college in the seventies and early eighties to have to wait up half the night to have an opportunity to run a computer program. During the day, university computer centers would process the business applications for the school, and students would have to wait to submit their programs or jobs late in the evening. Obviously, when time and money were key factors, you wanted to take every opportunity to ensure that the program would run correctly the first time. In this scenario, having to repeatedly test a program for a minor modification was a very big deal. Probably for this reason, a lot of time and effort were spent on the skill of developing a flowchart. A flowchart is a graphical representation of an algorithm. The flowchart was important to break down step-by-step what needed to occur throughout the course of the program. Flowcharting symbols each had distinct functions that were to be performed.

Today, flowcharting has become pretty much a lost art. Our computing power is now so cheap and easy to access that modifications that would have taken hours now take seconds or even less. Hence, a programmer will just get down to the task at hand and not slow down to write out an entire procedure step-by-step. While there are still many cases in computer science where flowcharting is worthwhile and important, the average programmer no longer spends the time creating these diagrams. So, why bother with flowcharting here? The main reason for learning flowcharting is to understand the incremental development that must happen in creating a program. Flowcharts are a wonderful way to understand and approach logical thinking. Interestingly enough, most students will encounter a flowchart or analogous diagram when taking standardized tests. The ability to follow a flowchart is often used in testing the way a person thinks. Therefore, why not build a flowchart and assist in the development of these thinking skills in your classroom? Besides, drawing flowcharts can even be fun, because today there are so many applications that greatly assist with the development of symbols on a document.

A flowcharting template is a piece of plastic that has been cut out in the shapes of the symbols that were a defined set. The programmer would trace the shapes in succession on a piece of paper and connect every shape together with a series of flow lines, which are arrows that indicate direction. Today, you can create the majority of these symbols with a word processing program. Interestingly, some of the symbols on the templates have become rather outdated, such as the symbols for punched cards and punched tape! However, the main symbols for logic are still with us today. In Microsoft Word, there is a whole flowcharting template available within the AutoShapes selection of the draw toolbar. Using a word processing application for a flowchart is an excellent choice. However, if you have the Inspiration application software available, it is a great product to use for this purpose. The advantage of using Inspiration is that it will automatically create the flow lines and allow you move the other symbols and automatically adjust the flow lines to accompany any modifications. With a word processing or paint program, you will have to modify each flow line and symbol by hand after such a modification.

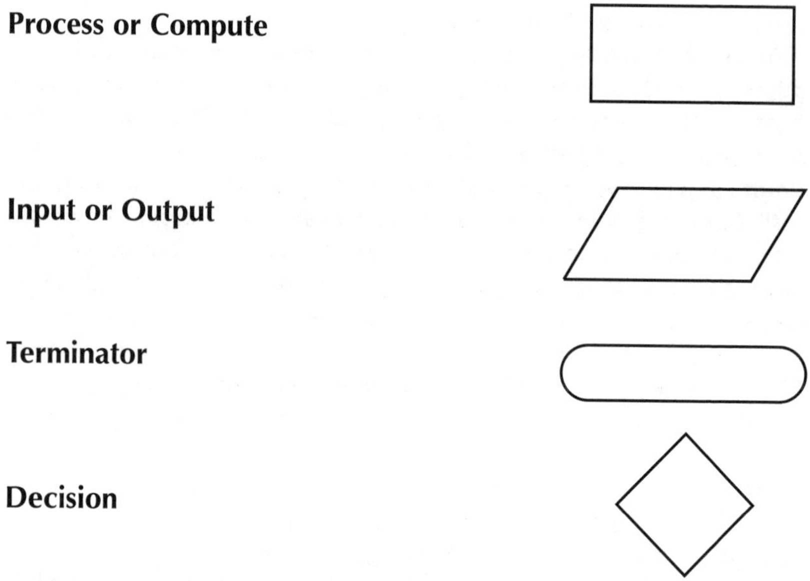

Process or Compute

Input or Output

Terminator

Decision

Figure 12.2 The Basic Symbols of Flowcharting

The basic symbols required for flowcharting appear in figure 12.2. You many refer back to this diagram when we build a sample to perform a task. In the meantime, there are some additional concepts that have to be mastered before a flowchart can be drawn.

A variable is something that can change throughout the course of the program. It is common to refer to a variable by the name it is assigned and to refer to the information it contains as its value. Variables will often change as a result of the functions performed in the algorithm. Naming variables is a very important part in programming. In math, we are accustomed to naming our variables simply: as perhaps x, m, or ab. In programs, however, variable names can be absolutely critical. Variable names should describe something about the value that will change for clarity in understanding the program. Therefore, variable names like price, old_amount, and wage will provide a lot more information to the programmer. All languages have reserved words that are unique to the program. Reserved words have meaning to the compiler or interpreter and cannot be used as variable names. Each language has its own set of reserved words. Be sure to look into

Introduction to Programming

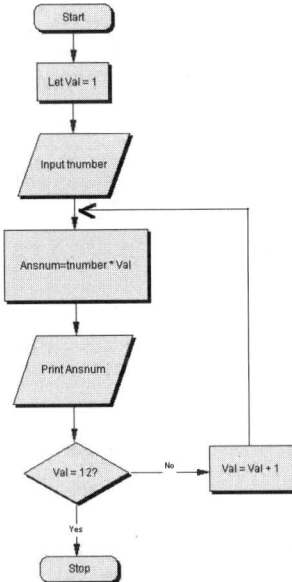

Figure 12.3   Flowchart for Printing a Multiplication Table

the list of reserved words for your language before making assignments. Variables are introduced into programs in assignment statements. There are languages that require variables be initialized before they can be used. Initializing can include setting the type of information that the variable will hold. Sometimes, variables are set to initial values, and sometimes they are set as place holders that will be assigned values later on in the course of the program.

There can be a distinction between local and universal, or global, variables. Local variables are those that only the current portion of the program can understand. Global, or universal, variables hold a wider definition and can sometimes even be used between different programs. Programs often have very strict naming conventions for the declarations of global or local variables. Sometimes you can think of these as place markers that maintain their spot for a short time or over many operations.

Let's design a very simple flowchart to calculate a multiplication table up to twelve. You will need to remember to begin and end your flowchart with a terminator. The flowchart for this problem is fairly straightforward. Follow along with it in figure 12.3.

Begin by describing the problem:

Step 1—First, you need to find out what table the user wants to calculate, which is variable "tnumber." Next, you need to initialize "val." Val will be the number to multiply by to calculate the value for each row of the table.

Step 2—Once we have val and tnumber, we can compute the first value, ansnum, in the table.

Step 3—Next we need to check to see if we have reached the end of our table. For this example, twelve will be the limit to our calculations. If we have reached twelve, we will stop.

Step 4—Otherwise we will need to increment val to the next value for our table.

Step 5—Once val is incremented, we return control back to the point where we perform the multiplication process and print our answer.

The important features to understand here are that the decision tree has one question coming in through the top and then has two branches coming out at the bottom. The two branches need to contain one branch for a no or false condition, and an additional branch for a yes or true condition. It is also important to start and stop the termination of the program with the appropriate commands. The stop feature is often overlooked, but without it, the computer would need to continue processing endlessly.

There is a now-famous example used when introducing computer concepts of how to make a peanut-butter-and-jelly sandwich. This sandwich is used as an example of how important it is to enumerate each step. Additionally, none of the process can be left to memory or chance. A processor needs to process from finite, concrete steps. Therefore, your algorithm must represent each one of these steps throughout the procedure. In the case of the peanut-butter sandwich, students are asked to list the steps in creating the sandwich. They all agree it is an easy task until the instructor starts to "literally" construct the sandwich. Unless the students tell the instructor to take jelly out of a jar on a knife, the instructor could reach in and grab a lump of jelly directly with her fingers. Further, unless students specify to face the two slices of bread with the sticky sides together, a sandwich can wind up with the peanut butter and the jelly facing the outside. For students, the process of placing the bread together is done by a memory that the student maintains of what a sandwich should look like. Remember, once again, the processor does not have this kind of a memory! Therefore, each step needs to be carefully explained and spelled out.

When enumerating steps, be careful not to go too far. When we consider a finite number of steps for a program, we need to keep things thorough, but not too detailed. Consider again the case of the sandwich. You could go so far as to enumerate the planting the peanut, harvesting the peanut, manufacturing the peanut butter, shipping it to market, driving to the grocery store, and purchasing the peanut butter. For the most part, when we write programs we start with concrete variables like what times table we want to generate—not how we came to have the Arabic numerals that represent the numbers one through twelve.

Now think about some other examples of flowcharts. Can you build a flowchart for determining a grade for one of your courses?

Programming Constructs and Statements

Programming statements are the individual instructions to be carried out by the program. The statements usually contain one idea or function and are delineated in some fashion. Delimiters can include a carriage return, so that the statements appear one below each other, the way sentences appear in a paragraph. Other common delimiters can include punctuation marks of some kind. Some languages allow multiple statements to appear within a line, and some do not.

Our multiplication table flowchart included some important constructs. The first things we encountered were the "let" statement and the "input" statement. Let statements are simply variable assignments. Input statements usually halt the program and wait for a user response, usually in the form of entry from the keyboard. These steps are placed in a sequence. The sequence carries out the simplest tasks in the program in order of occurrence. Print statements send the output to the screen or printer. Some languages distinguish between the monitor and a printer and utilize different formats of the print statement.

Arguments are often used in program statements. Arguments are the options that are to be interpreted along with a particular command. Arguments can include items like formatting. Another important characteristic in programming languages is the order of operations. We are familiar with the order of operations in mathematics, and we understand that (2 + 2)*5 is not equivalent to 2+(2*5). The same is true of programming languages. In general, programs will first execute information contained in parentheses, then by the mathematical function in a particular sequence. Languages often have sequences that are particular to the language, which is one important thing to look at when learning a new programming language.

Loops are constructs that perform sequential operations until the completion of the cycle. Loops represent the step-programming construct of repetition. Loops are for tasks that are to be carried out more than one time. Commands that indicate looping and the way they are specified vary within languages. In general, two-part commands like DO and LOOP, FOR and NEXT, DO and WHILE, and DO and UNTIL are the standard words that make up these types of commands. What is also a part of a loop is a condition. Some conditions will need to be examined at each pass of the loop. Without a condition, the loop would never be able to stop. When this happens, we refer to it as an infinite loop. Infinite loops are never intended and are often a function of programmer error. Infinite loops will have the effect of freezing the computer because the end can never be determined. It is important to test the legitimacy of the condition when you create program loops.

Selections also are dependent upon conditions. There are at least two possible outcomes to a decision even though one of the conditions might not require the program to perform any other tasks. The most common execution of the selection process is through an IF statement. IF statements may include more than one condition, and these conditions are identified as ELSE statements. You often see the selection statement identified as IF (condition) THEN (statement). Another option of processing a selection is through a CASE statement. Case statements are useful alternatives when there is more than one condition present for the IF statement. Case statements are a neater way of avoiding nesting your IF statements together. Nested statements are those that are placed one inside another. There is often no limit, save the sanity of the programmer, to the level of nests that a program can contain!

Subroutines are useful methods of breaking a program into separate portions. Subroutines can be thought of as mini-programs that are part of a main program. Subroutines can often be represented by their own flowcharts. All the subroutines are then linked together and called into action by the main program. Program control describes the portion of the program that is executing, and in what order.

Arrays are a special type of variable. So far, the variables we have discussed have only contained one value. There are many occasions where it is necessary for the computer to use more than one piece of information about a variable. We refer to these multiple-valued variables as arrays. The arrays can then be multivalued or multidimensional. Before we think about that, let's consider some examples where it might be useful to place your values in an array. One example might be grades on tests. To calculate some type of class average, it will be necessary to analyze every grade. We can read the data into the program by the use of an array. A single-dimensioned array could contain the individual test grades for a single student. You may wish a multidimensional array, for example, to contain fifteen different test grades for 100 different students. The way in which you specify an array will vary according to the requirements of individual programming languages.

LOOKING AT DIFFERENT LANGUAGES

Today, there are many different languages in use. Traditionally, students were taught Basic as an entry-level programming language. Other popular programming languages of the past included Fortran, Cobol, and Pascal. Basic is based upon algorithms and step-by-step analysis. While Microsoft shipped Qbasic free with its operating system for many years, today their newer product, Visual Basic, is a popular programming language. Visual Basic has expanded the capabilities of the original model and has begun to utilize the now-popular idea of programming objects.

For the sake of simplicity, we will show you what a simple Basic program looks like to create the multiplication table (but this time only for four) that we designed in our flow chart:

```
Val = 1;
    INPUT "Enter an integer to create a table ", tnum
    DO WHILE (Val <= 4)
    Ansnum = tnum * val;
```

```
PRINT tnum; " multiplied by "; val ; " is "; ansnum
Val = Val + 1
LOOP
```

```
Enter an integer to create a table
? 4
4 multiplied by 1 is 4
4 multiplied by 2 is 8
4 multiplied by 3 is 12
4 multiplied by 4 is 16
```

The latest programming model that has emerged is referred to as the object-oriented model. The object-oriented model emphasizes grouping a collection of data and methods together to manipulate the program. The combination of data and methods describe an object and makes up a class. In the object-oriented model, the idea is that by breaking things apart and keeping them in modules, you can have an easier time of understanding how the program fits together. An object is a value that can be created, stored, or manipulated. Groups of objects make up a class. Further, the idea of hierarchy presents order and allows the ranking of information. One of the most popular object-oriented languages is C++. C++ evolved from C language created by Dennis Ritchie at Bell Laboratories in 1972. The C language derived a lot of its ideas from the earlier BCPL and B languages—also developed at Bell Laboratories by Martin Richards in 1967. Bjarne Stroustrup developed C++ in the early 1980s, again at Bell Laboratories. Over the past decades, C++ has become very portable, and programs written on one system will often work on different systems. (The Java language is another language that is being developed to conquer problems of portability.)

C++ programs consist of classes and functions. Classes and functions can be thought of as mini-programs that already exist and that all C++ programmers can reuse, rather than rewrite, with each new program. Classes are a set of objects that share some properties and functions. Rather than have the programmer recode certain procedures over and over again, C++ has standardized them and put them together in libraries that the programs can call and access at any time in their functioning. Generally, any needed libraries are placed at the top of the program and are added to the program when it is compiled or put together to run as a program on its own. C++ programs go through six phases before they can become programs in their own right. Of course, the first step is to create the code in an editor. Next, the code runs through a preprocessor. The next phase compiles the program. This is followed by the program being linked to any of the libraries or classes that the program needs. In the next phase, it is loaded into memory. Finally, in the CPU phase, it is ready to be executed in the processor.

Every C++ must contain a function called main( ). All statements need to be terminated with a semicolon. Comments, which are lines of code that will not be part of the executed program but remain to make the code easier to read by a programmer, are set off by // or enclosed between /* and */. The exact details of how to insert the pieces in the "include" statements are determined by the C++ program that is used. There are several different vendors for C++ program compilers.

A sample C++ program looks like the following:

```
// Our first C++ program
# include <iostream.h>
main()
{
  cout << "This is my first C++ program. \n";
   return 0; // the program ends
}
```

> This is my first C++ program.

The first line of the program is a comment. Comments are lines of notation for the programmer and have no effect on the program. Comments are important to follow along with the program. The second line provides the link to the classes and functions that are needed. The library contains information already that this program is told to perform. In this case, specific instructions to the monitor are called an iostream, which stands for "input-output stream." The brackets mark the program object. The commands of cout and return are common commands for this language. In the case of cout, the arguments for the command appear after the angle brackets. Each line in the program is delimited with a semicolon. We need quite a bit of code to send a single line to the screen.

A simple program to multiply two numbers together would look like:

```cpp
// Multiply two numbers
# include <iostream.h>
main()
{
    int firstnum, secnum, ansnum;
    cout << "Enter an integer \n";
    cin >> firstnum;
    cout <<" What integer to multiply by? \n";
    cin >> secnum;
    ansnum = firstnum * secnum;
    cout <<" The answer is " << ansnum << endl;
    return 0; // the program ends
}
```

```
Enter an integer
9
What integer to multiply by?
6
The answer is 54
```

One of the most difficult concepts when programming in C++ is that the operators are a different symbol than the equality symbols. This means that when we assign a value, such as when we assigned ansnum to be the product of firstnum and secnum, we use a single equal sign. If we want to test for equality between two integers, we would need to use two equal signs = = to perform a test. In addition, C++ has created a sort of shorthand for adding numbers that could be considered counters. In the multiplication flowchart, we increase val by one for each row in the multiplication table. With C++ we could do this as;

```
Val = Val + 1;
Val += 1;
++ Val;
Val++;
```

This is exceedingly useful shorthand, but is sometimes difficult for new programmers to follow.

Our multiplication table would use a loop, and in C++ it would look like the following:

```cpp
// Multiplication table
# include <iostream.h>
main()
{
   int val, tnum, ansnum;
   val = 1;
   cout << "Enter an integer to create a table \n";
   cin >> tnum;
   while (val <= 12)
      {
      ansnum = tnum * val;
      ++val ;
      cout << tnum << " multiplied by " << val <<" is " << ansnum << endl;
   }
   return 0; // the program ends
}
```

```
Enter an integer to create a table
5
5 multiplied by 1 is 5
5 multiplied by 2 is 10
5 multiplied by 3 is 15
5 multiplied by 4 is 20
5 multiplied by 5 is 25
5 multiplied by 6 is 30
5 multiplied by 7 is 35
5 multiplied by 8 is 40
5 multiplied by 9 is 45
5 multiplied by 10 is 50
5 multiplied by 11 is 55
5 multiplied by 12 is 60
```

Like C++, Java is an object-oriented programming language. Java was designed by Sun Microsystems and was introduced in late 1995. Java is an interpreted language. To run a Java program, you use the Java interpreter to execute the compiled codes in segments. Java has been created as a platform independent program so that any Java interpreter can run any Java written code on any hardware capable of running the interpreter. Because Java is so portable, it is becoming an increasingly popular language. The Internet, which connects many types of systems and platforms, is a perfect frontier in which Java can grow and expand. Java code is extremely similar to that of C++, so programmers of C++ can quickly learn to program in Java.

Our simplest program example in C++ looks like the following in Java:

```java
// Our first Java program
public class Firstprogram {
    public static void main(String[] args) {
        System.out.println( "This is my first Java program.");
    }
}
```

```
This is my first Java program.
```

JavaScript is a scripting language that is based upon the Java language. JavaScript is a client-side scripting language, which means it lives on the client's computer. JavaScript has been developed as an enhancement to traditional HTML to provide more interactivity and just generally neat stuff on Web pages. It uses the same logic as Java, in that it allows you to use the classes of objects that have already been defined and exist as part of the language so you do not need to recode when you wish to use them. To include JavaScript into an HTML document, it is as simple as including the following lines. (If you need to, you may go back and review how to create an HTML document in chapter 10.)

```
<SCRIPT LANGUAGE="Javascript">
    place your script here
</SCRIPT>
```

The following example of a short JavaScript program will place a different message on the screen of the viewer, depending upon which day of the week the user accesses the page.

```
<SCRIPT language="JavaScript">
var now = new Date();
```

```
var day = now.getDay();
var daytex;
if (day == 0) daytex = "Hope you are having a relaxing weekend!";
if (day == 1) daytex = "Here we go for a great week!";
if (day == 2) daytex = "I'm so happy it's not Monday!";
if (day == 3) daytex = "More than halfway to the weekend!";
if (day == 4) daytex = "One more day to go this week!";
if (day == 5) daytex ="Let's all say T.G.I.F!";
if (day == 6) daytex = "Saturday has to be my favorite day of the week!";
document.write(daytex);
</script>
```

In this example, the program checks the date and extracts the day of the week. It can do this by using the objects of Date() getDay(). The final object, document.write, is the object that is used to send the output back to the screen. Also notice that like C++, an evaluation of the day is performed with the double equal sign. A single equal sign would result in the variable of day being assigned to each value, and this script, run with all single equal signs, would always result in displaying the Saturday message.

You can do many things with JavaScript for Web pages. Typically, the uses you see most often are for mouse rollovers. Rollovers are messages that pop up or change as a result of the cursor or mouse rolling over them on a Web page. These changes require a dynamic change of content, and JavaScript allows you to do these. Not surprisingly, Web page development packages are growing in their sophistication, so many of these functions can now be added in by a page designer without knowledge of programming. This is a good thing because it indicates we are moving fast-forward in the goal of the interface being as user-friendly as possible. However, it is always nice to have an appreciation for what lies beneath that advancement in ease of use.

Admittedly, this chapter has taken programming languages that could be studied for years and condensed them into a few simplified pages. You may never have the need for programming in your classroom, but certainly an overview of what is involved can only add to the students' appreciation for technology at hand. While the actual programming may not be an important skill within your classroom, it is important that students understand that our computers can only perform functions as have been scripted by programmers.

Chapter 12

Activity Sheet 12.1

Flowcharts and Programming

Name: _____   Date: _____

For this activity, you will need to refer to the information in figure 12.2, the flowcharting symbols.

1. Think about a simple child's game, such as jacks, hopscotch, redlight, or tag.
2. List the rules of the game:

3. Using the flowcharting symbols, design a flowchart for your game.
4. Be sure to place a terminator at the start and the end of the game.

Activity Sheet 12.2
Introduction to Programming

Name: _____   Date: _____

The following code is a javascript sample to create an interactive paragraph on a Web page. The user will be prompted to fill in your blanks with the window.prompt object. Using your text editor, copy this text to create and test your own paragraph!

```
<HTML>
<HEAD>
</HEAD><BODY BGCOLOR="#01004D" TEXT="#11BFB1" >
<H2><center>My Morning at School</center><p>
<SCRIPT LANGUAGE="javascript">
var first = window.prompt("Enter a place:","");
document.write("This morning I was sitting in class thinking about " + first + ". ");
var first = window.prompt("Please enter an adjective:","");
document.write("I started to drift into a " + first + " dream. ");
var first = window.prompt("Please enter an animal:","");
document.write(" I looked out the window and saw a " + first + ".");
var first = window.prompt("Enter an object:","");
document.write(" I saw that it had a " + first + " and it wanted to give it to me. ");
var first = window.prompt("Name a container:","");
document.write("So I walked to the window to get it, and I put it in my " + first + ". ");
var first = window.prompt("Name a phrase:","");
document.write("I then continued my dream. Before I knew it, my teacher said, " + first + " ");
var first = window.prompt("Name an animal noise:","");
document.write("I responded by making a loud " + first + ". ");
var first = window.prompt("Name an adjective:","");
document.write("My teacher said that I was just " + first + ". ");
var first = window.prompt("Name a place:","");
document.write("I realized I better get back to reality. Maybe tomorrow I can dream about " + first + ". ");
</SCRIPT>
</HTML>
```

13

Viruses

> This chapter presents a description and understanding about computer viruses. We then take a look at encryption and how important it is for our future.

COMPUTER VIRUSES

The term "computer virus" was coined by Fred Cohen to describe programs that were capable of attaching themselves to new hosts. In the case of a human virus, a person must come into contact with a virus, and then the virus replicates itself inside the person until it kills its host or is stopped. Computer viruses are special programs that, once finding an entry into a computer, can do damage that is analogous to a human virus.

It is surprising for many people to learn that computer viruses are special destructive programs that are written by people. The individuals who spend their careers tracking and eradicating viruses indicate that computer hackers write the majority of computer viruses. Hackers are a strange breed of programmers that are hard for many of us to understand. Like criminals, they appear to enjoy writing programs that for moral and ethical reasons should not be written. Curiously, the majority of hackers are male and in their teens or twenties. They are described as writing these types of programs because of the excitement of unleashing something that will be known all over the world.

Viruses

Most people find the concept of writing programs with the intent of harming other people's computer equipment—usually people they do not even know—difficult to comprehend. Without dwelling on the psychology of why, we need to understand what viruses are, how to protect against them, and how to avoid catching them!

The majority of viruses are self-replicating. Once ensconced onto a new medium, they reproduce copies of themselves over and over again. The majority of these viruses are categorized as "macro" viruses. Macro viruses are written by combining key combinations to replicate some function repeatedly. Macros are a feature that is included in many different kinds of application packages, and they are easy to master and replicate. This probably accounts for why these are the most common types of viruses. The most common viruses, once introduced into a system, will continue to replicate it endlessly until it fills up all available memory and storage capacity. This type of virus is probably the most common, and it will continue to use up all of a system's resources until it eventually causes the computer to shut down. A computer worm, while not technically labeled as a virus, also continues self-replicating for the purpose of slowing down a system or a network without actually destroying data.

Also destructive is the logic bomb, a software program that sits on a computer and "detonates" upon a preprogrammed trigger. Logic bombs can be set to do their dirty work upon the event of an instruction or the arrival of a preset time. Detonation can occur like an explosive bomb. Someone can "trip" it, or it can explode at a predetermined moment in time.

Infection

So far, the only way to contract a virus is for the infected files to come in contact with your computer. Early viruses were most often spread by infected floppy disks. The offensive files are present on a floppy and lurk there until a computer accesses the floppy. Once accessed, the program is unleashed on the computer's memory and drives. Infection was easier to fight against in the days of stand-alone computing. Now, with Internet access, there are newer ways for computers to be affected. One of the most common types of infection today is through e-mail correspondence. It is typical for a virus to arrive as an attached file to an e-mail message. To date, these files are harmless if they remain unopened. However, most of the damage can now be unleashed by opening the e-mail message, which then allows the attachment to begin its infestation. Some of the latest viruses are so insidious that they will "forward" themselves to the infected persons address book. In this case, a user's address book is attacked and all of the addressees receive a copy of the infected message. What is most distressing about this aspect of infection is that, initially, a user could protect against infected e-mail attachments by not opening attachments from unknown sources. Now, with the forwarding from an address book, viruses can arrive from addresses that are known. The best defense for these situations is to carefully watch the subject line of a received e-mail message. Subjects can now be the indicators of viruses if the user is savvy enough to watch for suspicious topics. There have been incidences of virus transmission through the most popular e-mail software packages and providers, so all users can be vulnerable to these kinds of attacks.

Another way of contracting a virus is through downloaded software. There are many sources on the World Wide Web that offer free games and shareware programs. Some of these files can contain viruses, and when an unsuspecting user downloads them (or copies them from the website onto their own computer) they can in turn infect the computer. This is one reason why it is very important to carefully consider a source before downloading programs. There have been reported cases of people who have had their computers attacked by the lure of playing a free game or even receiving a free music selection. Be sure to download only information from reliable, authentic sources. Feel comfortable about downloading a patch to a software application from the vendor's website. Don't feel confident downloading a "really cool game" from the site of an individual that looks slick! While the individual might not intend you any harm, it is always best to err on the side of caution.

Fortunately, to this point all of the attachment viruses cannot do any damage if they are not triggered by an activity like opening them. Deleting infecting files will eradicate their destructive potential. It is important to remember these days to check the source and subject of your e-mail messages before you open them. Be careful, because many e-mail packages have a menu feature that will automatically open any unopened correspondence.

Wise computer users will first validate subjects and originators before opening messages.

Protection

So with all the nasty files lurking out there to infect your computer, how can you protect against infection? The solution is threefold. The first part of the solution is to be wise in your usage. Only download and open files you feel confident are legitimate. The second part of the solution is to invest in antivirus software. The final part is to be sure to update your antivirus software often. It is estimated that as many as fifteen new viruses are put into circulation each day, so updated virus protection is absolutely essential.

Antivirus software is inexpensive relative to the cost of not having any protection for your systems and data. The cost of losing a term paper you have been working on for two months because of an infected e-mail from someone you have never met outweighs the outlay of paying for good virus software. There are a number of good antivirus software programs from which to choose. Whichever product you choose, the importance of updating the virus definitions is extremely important. Finally, the antiviral software must be run to be able to do its job. Most packages can be set to run each time a system is initialized. Alternatively, they may be set up to run automatically at some predetermined interval. Whichever option you choose, it is important for the antivirus software to run and perform its job to keep your system clean.

Consider this situation. Mr. Jones is really excited about his new computer. He goes out and buys the top-of-the-line model with maximum storage and the fastest processing speeds. His software package includes the SuperDuper Virus Killer. Mr. Jones uses his machine a lot, has become very reliant on his machine, and has months of research for a project he has been working on stored on his new machine. Suddenly, one evening he turns on his machine and not much happens. His heart is in his stomach as he shuts down and restarts the machine to the same sorry outcome. He packs up his machine and takes it back to a store for service. There the technicians inform him that a virus has destroyed all of his data on his machine, and they quote him a price to restore it to the condition he bought it at initially. Mr. Jones is dumbfounded. He screams that this just can't be because he bought SuperDuper Virus Killer. So, what could possibly be the problem?

Although Mr. Jones purchased excellent virus protection with his machine, he did nothing proactive to continue protecting his files and his machine. Since Mr. Jones purchased the machine, there have been thousands of new viruses invented and unleashed onto an unwitting public. Would the SuperDuper Virus Killer from February have any idea how to disinfect viruses from August? The answer is absolutely not. While the version from February is capable of detecting and defeating 14,000 different viruses, six months later there are many new viruses that the February version would not have any instructions about. How to avoid this problem? Download updated antivirus patches (called virus definition updates) often. Find out how your antivirus software makes this information available and then be sure to use it. Download definition updates manually or set up your machine to access updates often.

It is important to emphasize that there is one additional important step. Be sure that the new definitions are loaded, then run the antivirus program. Antivirus programs are designed to identify suspicious-looking file structures and code. The suspicious code can then be deleted or isolated to insure that further infection does not spread. The programmers who work for the antivirus companies are referred to as computer virologists. To date, the number of viruses has been doubling each year. The last virus to make the evening news was unleashed in the Philippines and had reached global proportions within six hours. Now, several months later, the virus is still in circulation.

Encryption

There are also technology weapons that can do damage in other ways than viruses. Trojan horses come disguised as a different application. Trojan horses come embedded in the code of a game or application and allow loopholes for access by their creators later. Samples of destructive technologies include sniffers and herf guns. A sniffer is a program that can eavesdrop or monitor communications. Sniffers are extremely scary to those dealing with electronic commerce because they can intercept credit card and other financial information. A herf gun is a high-energy radio frequency that is designed to disable electronics and cause them to stop functioning or impede functioning.

There are many who believe that terrorism in the next century will become technological terrorism. Terrorists will no longer have to rely on weapons like guns and explosives. Rather, a more terrifying weapon will be the ability to manipulate electronic commerce. Consider the hacker that could suddenly eradicate all of the records of a financial institution. Gone would be any record of how much money a person had in his or her bank account. Your only monetary assets would be the money in your pockets and the money at home tucked away in the mattress! Technological terrorism is very scary to contemplate. One of the ways that we seek to keep data and file transfers safe is through encryption. Encrypting information is the attempt to put the information into a secret code.

The history of encryption is really interesting. The first-known encryption schemes were centuries ago, when the Egyptians created hieroglyphs for many purposes that were a combination of languages. Over the centuries, there have been many attempts at finding the perfect code. With the Caesar encryption scheme, an "a" becomes a "d", a "z" a "c," and a "b" an "e." In this scheme, every letter in the alphabet is moved three positions in the alphabet. The Chinese code changes the direction so that words are spelled out vertically. The English philosopher Francis Bacon invented a code that looks similar to binary, substituting four characters of a and b for each letter in the alphabet. Throughout history, codes were invented that involved the movement of letters or symbols to stand in for something else. During World War II, the Germans built the Enigma Machine to encrypt messages. Their encryption machine was a primitive computer. Later, the work of British and Polish mathematicians developed a way of decrypting the information, while the Germans, not realizing their code had been broken, continued to use the same scheme.

Codes that consist of putting together information could provide long-term employment for linguists. For example, the most frequently occurring letter in the English language is the letter e. To break a code, a linguist would analyze a code and replace the most frequently-occurring letter, no matter what it was, with the letter e. Now, the combinations and permutations of putting together numbers and characters, which once could have taken linguists years, can now be tried and broken by computers in minutes. Henceforth, we need much more sophisticated encryption techniques.

Many consider people to be the weakest link in an encryption scheme. When choosing passwords, we often choose codes that are easy to remember, and we rarely change them. Those trying to break into systems rely on the human elements when trying to break codes. Using the name of a spouse or children will be easy to remember, but also easy for thieves to figure out and try as well.

Today, the best encryption scheme available is one requiring two keys. Keys are used to help in the unscrambling of messages. Invented in the early seventies by Diffie and Hellman, Public Key encryption splits the decryption of a key into two parts, one known to the user that is private, like a bank PIN (personal identification number), and another that is public. The field of encryption is one that has become vital to the world of electronic commerce, making encryption part of our everyday lives and no longer just the stuff of spies and secret agents.

Today in our new age of information technology, encryption schemes are becoming more and more important to society. Consider the times we now live in. What could be more damaging to a society than the destruction of banking records? Many people fear that some of the terrorist attacks of the future will be attacks to our information structures. Consider the destruction of banking records internationally. Contemplate what would happen if, when you woke up tomorrow morning, all of the records at your bank were destroyed. Your only money would be that in your wallet or purse, or under the mattress at your home. Could you not imagine the ensuing panic that would occur if such records were destroyed? Scenarios like this seem far-fetched, but what is clear is that those that are experts in encryption and creating encryption schemes will have job security for some time to come.

The most important point from this chapter is to remember that your virus protection is only as good as its last update. Don't forget to update your virus software often!

Activity Sheet 13.1

Virus Protection

Name: _____ Date: _____

1. What is the name of the virus protection software on your computer?
2. When is the last time it was updated?
3. How many virus definitions does this application have, or how many viruses does this application protect your computer against?
4. How does this application run? Does it have to be initialized or started? Does this application run at some predefined time interval? If so, what is that interval? What happens if the machine is not turned on at the time the software is scheduled to run?
5. What is the name of a famous virus?
6. What did it do to the machines it infected?

14

Copyright and the Classroom

> This chapter takes a look at intellectual property in the classroom. We consider some of the technological copyright issues challenging our society. Finally, we finish with an examination of how to cite electronic data.

INTELLECTUAL PROPERTY

So, what exactly is intellectual property? Pose this question to a classroom of seventh graders, and you will be stunned by their answers. In reality, intellectual property is recognized as the results of our brains that have monetary value. Intellectual property that could not find a buyer would have intellectual merit, but no commercial value. It is the commercial value that requires protection. Today, our laws recognize different categories including copyright, trade secret, trademark, and patent laws. Trade secrets usually result in a company having a competitive edge over their competition. Trade secrets are highly valuable and are the reason why you will never see the details listed under the ingredients of a name-brand cola. Trademarks include things like signs, logos, packages, colors, and symbols that become associated with an entity itself. These are the things that businesses use to identify themselves from their competition. Patent law gives inventors the exclusive rights to their inventions for a period of time. Patents can be extremely valuable to their owners. Copyright law protects all types of original creative expression as produced by authors, artists, composers, designers, architects, and programmers. It is possible that the laws for trade secrets, patents, trademarks, and copyrights can intersect with one another. However, for those of us in today's classrooms, copyright laws are the only ones that seem to affect us daily.

What Is Copyright Law?

Copyright law dates back to the Constitution, when it was recognized that authors should have exclusive rights to their works for a period of time. Our ancestors recognized that these protections would be necessary to promote the progress of our society. Today our copyright law allows protection to an author as soon as a work is set in a fixed or tangible form. The rights to that work remain for the life of the author plus seventy years. The only major change in copyright law in the last century has been that an author no longer has to register a work in order to have it protected. Once the work is set in a tangible form, it is automatically protected. It is important to understand that copyright law protects the unique expression of a work but does not protect underlying facts, ideas, or principles.

First Sale Doctrine

Have you ever wondered why a library can loan you that new novel you have wanted to read without having you pay for the loan? The first sale doctrine gives the owner of a lawfully obtained copy the right to keep, loan, rent, display, give, or even resell it to a third party. This doctrine is the one that gives libraries the ability to loan books and video stores the ability to rent movies. When the doctrine was passed the recording industry lobbied against it, and Congress amended the doctrine as it was applied to records, cassettes, and CDs. This is why you don't see music for rent at your local video store, and there never were record rental stores.

Fair Use Privilege

To those working within an academic environment, it is the fair use privilege that gives the ability to use copyrighted works in the classroom.

While copyright law is intended to protect an author, it also recognizes that the reuse of ideas and facts is the basis for learning and a requirement within our society. In recognition of the importance of copyrighted works to education, this privilege allows academics to legally use copyrighted work.

Fair use allows an author of a new work to quote from an existing work. It also allows the creation of a parody. In addition, it allows for the creation of photocopies for classroom use and home videotaping of television programs.

Fair use is often used as a defense in cases of copyright infringement. While using works for the purpose of research, scholarship, criticism, or journalism is allowed, a copyright owner is free to file a lawsuit at any time. For this reason, it is often best to seek permission to use protected material prior to using it. If a person does not seek permission but believes they are using the work for scholarship, they are innocent infringers. In this case they are instructed to cease using the work, while often there are no monetary consequences. This is the sort of thing that is becoming more common when an individual posts material on their website that is not of their own creation. Often it has been the case that these innocent infringers are asked to stop using the material in question.

There are four parts to fair use that need to be considered. The first consideration, purpose, identifies whether a work is to be used for profit or for nonprofit, educational purposes. The second consideration is the nature of the work. Third is the amount or portion of the work to be used. The last consideration is the effect the use will have on the market value of the work.

HISTORY OF COPYRIGHT LAW

It is important to understand that all of our copyright laws have been the result of interested parties getting together to draft legislation that would satisfy all of the parties involved. Not surprisingly, those parties represented were well accommodated in the resulting legislation, for no party would partake in negotiations and be content to walk away with legislation that did not leave them better off than before than they were before negotiations. What is obvious is that parties who were not invited, or not present throughout these negotiations, were often left with lesser advantages.

Overall, copyright law is considered by many to be complex and often falls short of the needs of those in fledgling industries, who lacked lobbying power at the point that the laws were enacted.

The 1909 Copyright Act

After a decade of conferences and negotiations that included representatives who were the beneficiaries of earlier laws, Congress enacted the 1909 Copyright Act. Interestingly enough, those who were involved in new and emerging technologies, like the motion picture and phonograph industries, were not included. Not surprisingly, the resulting act favored those who were present over those who were not in attendance. As an industry grows and gains commercial success, newer laws are enacted that are more to their liking and favor. This is a pattern that persists to this day in copyright law. New industries that were not previously invited eventually realize that they need protection and lobby Congress to amend the laws. In the case of the motion picture industry, it resulted in the Townsend Amendment in 1912.

By the start of the 1950s, it was clear that emerging technologies were in need of copyright protection. The intervening years were filled with a lack of consensus. Though conferences and committees were convened, it would take years before revision efforts would result in any enactment.

The 1976 Copyright Act

In 1976, copyrighted works were expanded to include literary, audiovisual, graphic works, musical arrangements, sound recordings, and computer software. The author is granted the right to make copies, authorize copying, sell, display, perform, and create derivative works. Further, the author is granted the right to obtain relief in court in the event his or her copyright is violated.

Copyrighted works are granted protection from the moment they become fixed in a tangible form. However, additional benefits can be gained by placing a copyright notice on a work and registering it with the Copyright Office. Those seeking damages in court really need to have taken the additional steps of placing the notice and registration before a suit can be filed.

Representatives for the various industries have long focused on commercial and institutional uses. Interestingly, considerations of private and home uses are often left out of specific regulatory language.

The 1992 Audio Home Recording Act (AHRA)

This act was introduced to address the digital reproduction of sound recordings. As the technology for sound reproduction was advancing in the eighties, it was recognized by the recording industry that audio home recording devices could have an effect on recording sales from the traditional sellers. The change threatening the industry here was that digital reproduction results in perfect copies. There is no loss in quality, as was the case with previous technologies. Suddenly, the industry was faced with the dilemma of consumers having the ability of perfect copy creation. Legislation was introduced requiring the manufacturers of certain devices to register with the Copyright Office and pay royalties. This legislation explains why technologies such as the DAT machines never became big sellers. Not included in the legislation were computer and computer disk technologies.

Shortcomings to this act were immediately identified and an Information Infrastructure Task Force of individuals from government agencies was put together as a result. In 1994, the Conference on Fair Use (CONFU) was convened. The draft papers of these groups addressed classroom use of technology. The resulting Fair Use Guidelines for Education Multimedia focus on allowing students, faculty and staff to incorporate works into a multimedia work, but prohibits making multiple copies or distributing copies. The guidelines allow for the creation of multimedia for class, curriculum, instruction, examination, portfolios and symposia.

The Copyright Extension Act of 1998

The extension act increased the duration of copyrights. For works created after January 1, 1978, copyrights would last for the life of the author plus seventy years. There are exceptions for work created while as part of someone's job. In this case, the copyright can last an additional ninety-five or one hundred twenty years from the date of creation, whichever is shorter. This extension is very easy to understand when you consider a cartoon character that gets created for a large studio. In this case, the studio would own the copyright to the character for the life of the author, who was an employee, until ninety-five years after the employee's death.

For works created prior to 1978, the length differs. If a work was created prior to 1923, it is available for use with no permission required. If created between 1923 and 1963 and not renewed, it is available for use with no permission required. If renewed, it is protected for ninety-five years from the original publication date. For works between 1964 and 1977, copyright extends for ninety-five years from the date of publication. Finally, if a work was created but not published or registered before 1978, copyright lasts until December 31, 2002.

The 1998 Digital Millennium Copyright Act (DMCA)

The Digital Millennium Copyright Act was passed in December 1998. This act sought to interpret fair use guidelines for Internet resources. This federal statute attempts to address copyright issues that have resulted from the expanded use of the Internet and online commerce. Here, the technologies are new and the laws have yet to be well-tested in the courts. This law makes it illegal to reverse-engineer software for the purpose of recreating it. It attempts to give consumers privacy restrictions. Provisions are included that provide protection to internet service providers (ISPs). Here, ISPs are let off the hook if their services are used for the transmission of protected material. Further, it helps them to escape liability if their patrons engage in inappropriate exchanges or postings.

DMCA allows for the creation of a copy of a computer program for the purpose of backup. Special exemptions are also made for the law enforcement communities.

Another provision (effective April 28, 2000) was that all video cassette recorders and camcorders were required to have a type of copy-proof capability before they could be marketed.

To protect work and creations, individuals and companies have the right to seek ownership and rights by way of patents, trademarks, and copyrights. Often machines are patented. Patents require compensation to the owner if you seek to use his or her invention. Trademarks apply to terms that are registered for a particular application or usage that cannot be used by another entity. Consider the names of companies and their products, and you are almost certain to come up with a list of trademarks. Copyrights, on the other hand, apply to works of text and images, motion and sound recordings, dramatic and choreographic works that have been recorded, as well as architectural works. While patents are required to be registered with the government, copyrights are not, but are implied for all intellectual work upon its creation. Owners of copyrighted works have the exclusive rights of reproduction, adaptation, publication, performance, and display. Once a work is created, a notice of copyright does not need to be explicitly stated, as was the case with earlier versions of the law.

It is important to be familiar with the limitations set forth and to only reproduce the portions as set forth in these interpretations. It is also required that proper credit be paid to an author or artist. Credit can be given in the form of a citation, or notice of copyright. There are many formats for creating and using citations. Some disciplines have made a determination of the style sheets and formats that are acceptable for their field. Others may simply choose one style over another. Regardless of the format, the purpose is tantamount: to give proper credit when using intellectual property that is not one's own. Plagiarism occurs when materials are used improperly and proper credit has not been given.

There are special copyright rules that apply to educators and librarians. A detailed booklet can be obtained from the Library of Congress Copyright Office.

Once expired, intellectual property is referred to as being in the public domain. Material that is in the public domain is fair to be reprinted and posted; hence, you can find many classic works on the Internet.

While many of the formats for creating citations have been around for a very long time, we have new resources that are not included in the formatting sources. Consider the changing face of the World Wide Web and new forms of electronic media. Many of these newer technologies have unique aspects that make setting the citation-formatting rules for them a bit more challenging. In the case of the World Wide Web and other Internet resources, people have often referred to these resources as moving targets. Two students could perform the very same Web search and follow paths to very divergent results. Even more unique is the concept that you could visit a Web page at nine in the morning and review a document. You could go back to review it again after lunch and by that time it could have moved, updated, or removed altogether. This is definitely more challenging than referencing a magazine article, which once in print (and later perhaps archived to microfiche) remains a static source in comparison. Dynamic resources are bringing far greater challenges to giving credit where credit is due!

Copyright guidelines for multimedia products were established in 1996. Students wishing to use portions of multimedia sources such as video or audio files must adhere to size limitations. Overall, a user seeking to use copyrighted multimedia material cannot use either more than 10 percent or three minutes, whichever is the smallest, from video clips. Thirty seconds is the maximum for audio format works.

Copyrights also apply to digital materials. Those downloading text or pictures should adhere to the same rules as they do with written or text materials. When using downloaded materials for educational purposes, follow all permissions as stated on the digital source. Some websites will provide permission to download and allow links to their sites. The only caveat here is to be careful when using such resources, because you cannot always be sure that the website has obtained the proper permissions before posting.

Another issue that becomes far more complex is learning how to identify and utilize primary sources. Information that is posted on the World Wide Web is published. Sometimes identifying the source of information on a Web page is a daunting task, especially in the case where you uncover a page that has not given credit to the original source for the information they have used.

CITING INFORMATION

There are numerous respected sources for citations. All make format suggestions and have methods of varying complexity to carry out. The lack of conformity of electronic media makes digital citations even harder to standardize. Citation references seek to standardize referencing. The process of standardizing a nonstandard resource is full of hazards.

Chapter 14

In general, when citing information from a website, most formats coincide in their attempt to include the following information whenever it is available:

- Author's name, which is often the most difficult element to find.
- Title of the website as provided in the title of the page.
- The posting information for the website; sometimes you may find an original posting date, or even a date indicating when the page was last updated.
- Title of the publication.
- Address of the site.
- The date you last accessed the website. Even if you refer to the website at multiple sessions on various dates, be sure to include the most recent date on which you accessed the information you are using.

Citations for listserv and e-mail messages require additional information relative to the posting sources, address, and subject line features.

The most frequently-used formats for preparing Internet citations include the following.

- *The Chicago Manual of Style*
- *A Manual for Writers of Term Papers, Theses and Dissertations*, by Turabian
- *MLA Handbook for Writers of Research Papers*, from the Modern Language Association
- *Complete Guide to Citing Government Information Resources*
- *The Columbia Guide to Online Style*, by Walker and Taylor
- *Publication Manual of the American Psychological Association*

Further complexity is introduced in that there are generally distinct styles when creating references for papers created in humanities or scientific styles. The Columbia Guide provides extensive sample and materials online at www.columbia.edu/cu/cup/cgos/basic.html. The following are fictitious samples, in which June 1996 was the date of the last modification, and March 30, 2001, was the date the information was last accessed.

For the humanities style:

Baker, Dorothy A. "Lighthouses Through Time." 1996. http://www.allightsource.org/~dab/lens.htm (30 March 2001).

The Turabian version for the above example would include brackets around the [URL], followed by the date of March 2001.
For the scientific style:

Baker, Dorothy A. (1996). Lighthouses Through Time. http://www.allightsource.org/~dab/lens.htm (30 March 2001).

Additional protocols are enumerated in much the same way, with slight modifications in the address information.

Online reference sources usually will contain additional information that is similar in nature to conventionally printed media. Refer to the additional hypothetical examples:

Baker, Dorothy A. "Lighthouses Through Time." *A Guide to Lighthouses* Boston: Fresnel Press. 1996. *My Online Service Provider.* (30March 2001).

For electronic communication, such as e-mail:

Baker, Dorothy [dbaker@myprovider.com]. "Lighthouses Through Time." Private message to Guy Dude [whataguy@anotherisp.com]. 29 February 2000.

Electronic publications and online databases require the following form for humanities citations:

Baker, Dorothy A. "Lighthouses Through Time." *ReferResource.* File #82738 (30 March 2001).

For software programs, refer to the following example:

Light Software. *Tons of Great Information.* San Francisco: Really Cool Software, 2001.

If a particular format is requested, then those are the guidelines that will need to be followed. However, if no guideline is required, any of the formats suggested are adequate to do the job. Probably the best suggestion here is to try to remain consistent with the format, realizing that you will often be lucky if you can even identify an author!

While creating a bibliography with electronic sources is challenging, the rewards of using digital information remain great. It would be nice if Web designers could consider the fact that reliable and insightful sources will be used for all kinds of work, and try to provide bibliographic information. It is also fun to wonder what type of digital communication resources will become commonplace in the future. Part of the great beauty of all of this technology is that online resources make me feel as though as long as I am connected, I have the biggest resource library at my disposal; in fact, the globe lies at my fingertips! Go forth, and conquer technology.

Activity Sheet 14.1
Reviewing Copyright and Fair Use

Name: _____ Date: _____

Consider the following scenario:

Dakota and Willa are best friends. They have gone to school together since they were in kindergarten. Willa got a laptop this year for her birthday, but Dakota is still using the desktop model at her home. Willa spends a lot of time on IM in the evening in her room, while Dakota is in her family room when she goes online, and her brothers are always poking in over her shoulders trying to see her conversations to get her in trouble with her parents.

At school yesterday, Willa told Dakota about a really cool new website that she heard about chatting online the night before. Turns out the website allows you to search for music that you do not own. You can find all kinds of music, including some of the latest releases by her favorite artists. Willa said she had a blast with it, and is making an amazingly cool mix. Dakota is excited and can't wait to check it out today after school when they will be babysitting together, since Willa has promised to bring her laptop along.

Later that afternoon, the girls are listening to the music that Willa downloaded off the Net, helping the children they are babysitting for with their homework, and making them snacks. Mrs. Choptank comes in a bit early and sits down at the kitchen table. She observers that Willa and Dakota have things well in hand. She likes the song that is playing on the computer and remarks that she didn't know you could play CDs on a laptop. Willa tells her that she loves to listen to music while she is working on her homework or online. Mrs. Choptank then says the song that is playing is great and could she have a copy of the CD, as it would be perfect for her bookclub that was meeting later that same evening.

1. Do you think it is acceptable to make personal copies of information, especially music, that you find on the Internet? Why or why not?
2. Do you think it is fair to the artists who have recorded the music not to be paid for their work when people copy their information from online sources? Why or why not?
3. Do you think that it is acceptable for you to give away or lend music that you have obtained, but have not paid for in any way? Why or why not?
4. Should websites be allowed to provide sources for people when they know that the users will be tempted to make copies of things they have not paid for? Why or why not?

Appendix 1

File Formats

These are some common file formats, or types:

.aif	audio/x-aiff
.aifc	compressed audio AIFF file
.avi	video file
.bmp	bitmap image file; used for wallpaper in Windows OS
.cgm	Computer Graphics Metafile, vector graphic format
.dbf	dBase database
.dir	Shockwave application files
.doc	Word document
.dxf	data exchange format; for AutoDesk CAD systems
.eps	encapsulated postscript file
.ewk	claris database
.exe	executable and program files (including application programs)
.gem	digital research graphics file format
.gif	graphic image file
.htm	HTML document
.hpgl	Hewlett-Packard Graphics Language; one of the oldest graphic formats
.img	Ventura Publisher graphic image format
.jpg	graphic image file
.mid	MIDI audio file
.mov	QuickTime movie
.mp3	MPEG layer 3, a compressed audio file; also .mpg, .mpe, .mpeg, and .mpa

.msp	Microsoft Paint image file
.pbm	portable bitmap image
.pcd	Kodak photo CD image
.pcx	PC Paintbrush image file
.pdf	portable document format (for Acrobat Reader)
.pic	graphic image file; Lotus Picture File developed this for spreadsheet graphs
.pict	Apple Computer 1984 graphic file image standard
.pl	PERL language source file
.png	graphic image file
.ppt	PowerPoint file
.ps	PostScript file
.qt	QuickTime movie
.ra	RealAudio sound file; also .ram
.rtf	rich text format; also .rtx
.sea	self-extracting archive (StuffIt file)
.sit	StuffIt archive
.snd	digitized sound file
.stk	Hyperstudio stack
.swf	Shockwave Flash file
.tif	TIFF graphic image file; also .tiff
.txt	ASCII text file
.wav	Waveform audio file
.wdb	Access database
.wmf	Windows metafile format; for exchanging graphics images
.wpg	WordPerfect graphic file format
.xll	Microsoft Excel file
.zip	compressed file using PKZip, WinZip, or StuffIt

Appendix 2

Some Great Historical Sites

Some Great Sites for Historical Information by Decades and Centuries

www.goarmy.com/tech/	For a comparison of 1790, 1890, and 1990
www.cfcsc.dnd.ca/links/milhist/index.html	For military history
www.bomc.com/archives/decades/home.html	For a look at different decades
http://lcweb2.loc.gov/ammem/ammemhome.html	Library of Congress has the American Memory Collection
www.tcm.org/html/history/timeline/index.html	For the computer museum 1945–1990 timeline
www.nhmccd.edu/contracts/lrc/kc/decades.html	Kingswood College collection on American cultural history
http://history1900s.about.com/index/	For the history of the twentieth century
http://history1900s.miningco.com/	For the history of the twentieth century
www.fiftiesweb.com	For a look at the 1950s
www.bbhq.com/sixties.htm	For a look at the 1960s

www.invent.org/book/index.html	For a look at individual inventions
www.filmsite.org/filmh.html	For a history of film by decade
www.cbc4kids.com/general/the-lab/history-of-invention/default.html	A large timeline based on recommendations
http://patent.womplex.ibm.com/gallery	A gallery of obscure patents
http://web.mit.edu/invent/	Invention information, links, and resources

Some sites for finding images: Image Resources for Educational Uses

http://sunsite.berkeley.edu/ImageFinder	Berkeley Image Finder
www.webutilities.com/goodies/default.asp	Ulead Systems
www.ase.org.uk/scienceimages	Science Images
www.archives.gov	U.S. National Archives
http://fablevision.com/northstar/make/index.html	North Star ClipArt Resource Library
http://memory.loc.gov	Library of Congress
http://pics.tech4learning.com	Tech4learning collection
www.iconbazaar.com	Icon Bazaar, up to 20

Glossary

Absolute Cell Reference—In spreadsheets, a formula whose specific cell references do not change even if the formula alters upon relocation.

Address—In email, identified by a user name followed by an @ symbol and a location (for example, geminigirl54@greatserver.net); on the World Wide Web, an address or URL indicates the host computer.

Algorithm—A set of specific actions.

ARPA—Advanced Research Projects Agency; a resource-sharing computer network formed in 1970.

ASCII—Acronym for American Standard Code for Information Interchange, the system by which letters, punctuation, spaces, control codes, etc., are encoded into numerical values for interpretation by the computer.

Binary—The fundamental language of the computer itself. Letters and numbers are represented by groups of ones and zeros, which represent the off-and-on flow of electricity through the circuitry.

BIT—BInary digiT, a switch representing zero or one; the smallest unit of information in a binary system.

Boolean—Named after George Boole, English mathematician (1815–1864), who developed tools to express logical concepts.

Boot—Short for "bootstrap"; refers to the initial commands necessary to load the remainder of the operating system. Thus the system is "pulled up by its own bootstraps."

Buffer—A storage device used to compensate for a difference in rate of data flow, or time of occurrence of events, when transmitting data from one device to another.

Bug—An error in a program.

Byte—A small group of bits of data that is handled as a unit. In most cases it is portions of a network.

Case-Sensitive—A program that knows the difference between upper- and lower-case letters. For instance, a case-sensitive program considers "Dog" and "DOG" to be two different things.

CD-ROM—Compact-disk read-only-memory; in CD-ROMs, information is encoded in the form of pits and spacings on a spiral track, and as the disc moves the pits and spacings modulate the reflected laser beam, forming binary ones and zeros.

Cell—Identified by the intersection of a column and a row in a spreadsheet.

Chip—Tiny piece of material intricately etched to produce an integrated circuit.

Compiler—A program that translates a high-level language to a form executable by the computer. Completes translation process before program is executed.

Computer—An electronic device that is capable of recording data, manipulating it as prescribed in a written program, and displaying the results.

Concatenate—To attach one thing to another.

Conditions—Components that specify the parameters; also called criteria.

Constant—An item whose value or assignment cannot be changed during the execution of a program.

CPU—Central processing unit; main part of the computer containing memory and control circuits.

Glossary

Cursor—Special marker or indicator on the display screen designed to direct your attention to where the next entry will appear; also referred to as an insertion point.

Data—Numbers, texts, facts, instructions, etc., which are represented in a formalized manner so that they can be stored, manipulated, and transmitted.

Database—An organized collection of information upon which rapid searches and retrievals can be performed.

Database form—A layout used to enter information, generally one record at a time.

Debug—To identify and correct all the errors in a program.

Default—The original or initial setting of hardware or software.

Directory—A separate folder on a hard disk for storing files. Storing related files in a directory makes them easier to find.

DOS—Disk Operating System.

Download—To receive a file or other information from another computer user or service.

Driver—A portion of the computer's operating system, which handles the input and output to peripheral devices like printers, cameras, and scanners.

ENIAC—Electronic Numerical Integrator and Calculator (completed in 1946); a prototype for today's computers.

EOF—End-of-file; a special marker to signify the end of a quantity of data.

Endless loop—An error condition in a program in which the program enters into a loop to perform a process that can never be satisfied, thereby halting any further functioning.

Expression—A meaningful combination of operators, constants, and variables used in a program to perform a desired operation.

Execute—The carrying out of command instructions by the computer; used interchangeably with run.

File—A collection of related data.

Glossary

Field—A category or type of information identified in a database.

Field name—A name that identifies a database field and the type of information the field contains.

Flowchart—A diagram that uses connecting lines and a set of conventional symbols to show the sequence and flow of operations.

Font face—A set of characters or typeface with a specific design; each has its own name and can be measured in points; also called font.

Font style—The appearance of characters in a font, such as bold, underline, and italic.

Formula—An entry in a spreadsheet cell or database field that performs a calculation in a spreadsheet or database.

Function—A built-in subroutine that performs common data handling operations, in which input is evaluated and a result is returned.

Global—A global setting is one that affects the entire worksheet or environment.

GUI—Graphical user interface.

Header—Information that prints at the top of the page.

Hard copy—A copy printed on paper.

Hardware—All the physical components of a computer system that you can see and touch, such as the chips, drives, monitor, and other devices.

Hexadecimal—Another name for base 16; a compact way to represent binary information.

Icon—The little picture that represents an object (program, file, or command); double-clicked to initiate a function.

Input—Data to be processed that is entered into the computer from a keyboard, disk, or other input device.

Interpreter—A type of translator that converts a program into machine language. An interpreter accomplishes the translation process while the program is running.

Justification—Rearrangement of columns or text to line up with left, right, or both margins

Language—A set of symbols that a programmer uses to encode instruction to the computer. A low-level language requires less interpretation by the computer but is more difficult to program than a higher-level language. The translation is then either compiled or interpreted.

Lock—An action that prevents the contents of spreadsheet cells or database records from being altered.

Logical operators—Logical terms used to evaluate the "truth" of arguments. The item being evaluated will have a value of "1" if true, or "0" if false.

Loop—Repetition of a series of commands until all records are processed.

Machine code—The native language understood by the computer consisting of binary information (0s and 1s).

Megabyte—1000 kilobytes or 1048576 bytes; abbreviated MB.

Microsecond—One-millionth of a second.

Millisecond—One-thousandth of a second.

MODEM—Modulator-demodulator; a device that converts signals generated by the computer into a form that can be transmitted over telephone lines or optical cables.

Module—A set of related commands within a routine.

Multitasking—Running several different programs simultaneously.

Network—A system of computers, terminals, and databases connected by communications lines; allows users to exchange data and make use of shared resources and peripherals.

Operating System—Software that manages the resources of the computer. The operating system provides a uniform interface between application programs and the hardware. It also provides basic functions of formatting and copying disks, editing files, and debugging programs.

Orientation—The position of a document on the page; can be portrait (vertical) or landscape (horizontal).

Parameter—A value supplied to a command, function, tag, or subroutine; also referred to as an argument.

Path—A sentence that tells the computer the exact name and location of a file.

Program—A sequence of instructions ultimately executed by the CPU.

Query—A question asked about the information stored in a database.

RAM—Random access memory; main memory that is easily read and altered, quickly accessed, and lost if the machine is powered down.

Recalculation—Every time in which data or worksheets are modified, requiring other values to change this process; may happen automatically, manually, naturally, column-wise, row-wise or iterative.

Record—A body of related information about a person, place, item, or event; made up of fields.

Relative Cell Reference—A formula in a spreadsheet that is based upon its distance to other cells; will change when copied.

ROM—Read-only memory; a permanent computer memory system containing data and instructions that can be retrieved and used, but never altered.

Routine—A set of commands that performs a particular operation.

Save—To store information in a file on a disk.

Software—Instructions or programs that are used by a computer to perform tasks.

Stand-alone—A computer working independently, utilizing its own internal resources.

Subdirectory—A directory under a directory; used to further organize files.

Subroutine—A routine that is designed to carry out a specific operation or action when called by another routine. A subroutine is subordinate to the master or main program that calls it. The main routine temporarily passes control to the subroutine, which then executes and returns control to the main routine.

Virus—An attempt to sabotage another's computer; created to destroy programs or data.

Worksheet—An electronic representation of a ledger sheet; also called a spreadsheet or a current worksheet.

Index

Aiken, Howard, 6
algorithm, 206
analog signal, 14
ARPA, 120
artificial intelligence, 9
ASCII, 158
automobiles, 5

Berners-Lee, Tim, 121
binary, 16
bookmarks, 145
Boolean logic, 90, 127–28
browser, 122, 124, 143, 157, 163, 168; errors, 150
byte, 16

comments, 211
compiler, 211, 214
computer, 8
computer aided design, 27
computer CPU, 9
computer definition, 8
computer monitors, 23; CGA, 24; EGA, 24; refresh rate, 24; RGB, 24, 167; size, 24; VGA, 24
copyright, 227

databases, 78–99; attributes, 80; Codd, Edgar 83; data definition, 80–81; data integrity, 84; DBMS, 81; entities, 80; fields, 80; filters, 82; hierarchical model, 83; networked model, 83; properties, 86; records, 79–80; relational model, 83; SQL, 82
digital divide, 138
digital signal, 14
digital watermarks, 28
digitized video, 27
dithering, 26
domain name system, 121, 123, 140
dpi, 26

electricity, 5
Electronic Frontier Foundation, 18
Electronic Zoo, 147
e-mail, 220; attachment, 131, 220; download, 220; MIME, 133; POP, 133; SMTP, 133
emoticon, 132
encryption, 222

Index

fair use, 227
FAQs, 126
favorites, 145, 151
file format, 11
first sale doctrine, 227
flowchart, 202

gamma, 24
gopher, 134
graphics: bitmap, 29, 31; interlacing, 30; JPEG 31; LZW compression, 30; PNG, 31; raster, 29; vector, 29
gray scale, 24

hackers, 218
hard drive, 10
hardware, 9
hits, 128
home page, 141, 144
HTML, 157–60, 181–87; anchor tags, 175; attributes, 166; blank space, 184; CSS, 177; gif, 172; jpg, 172; links, 173–74; SGML, 158; source, 184; tables, 170–71; tags, 157–60; web safe color, 166; XML, 158, 178
hub, 18
human interface guidelines, 19
Hyper Studio, 103; browse mode, 104; edit mode, 104; graphic object, 108; paint tools, 105; projects, 104; stacks, 104; storyboard, 108; title card, 105

innocent infringers, 228
input devices, 12
inspiration, 193–96
intellectual property, 226
intranet, 17

IP, 121
ISPs, 121–22, 231

Jasc Paint Shop Pro, 35
Java 137, 210, 213
JavaScript, 214

keyboard, 12

ledger page, 53–54
line break, 163
links, 147
logic bomb, 219

Macromedia, 182
mainframe computer, 6
memory: RAM 15; ROM, 15
microcomputer, microprocessor 8, 15
Microsoft FrontPage, 187–92
Microsoft Paint, 35
Microsoft PowerPoint, 109–16; animations, 114; apply design, 113; graphics, 112; printing, 115; slide sorter, 109, 114; transitions 114
minicomputer, 8
moderator, 133
moire pattern, 33
Moore, Gordon, 8
Moores Law, 8
Mosaic, 124
Mozilla, 122
multimedia, 100; interactive, 101; kiosk, 101; Wagner, Roger, 201

Netscape, 124
network, 17
network topology, 17–18
newbie, 134
newsgroups, 133

Index

output devices, 13

passwords, 224
PC, 8
PC introduction, 8
peripherals, 12
photo-realism, 27
pixel, 25
printers, 13
program: arguments, 207; arrays, 209; BASIC, 201; C++, 210; classes, 210; class objects, 210; constructs, 201–2; execution, 201; group objects, 210; infinite loop, 208; initializing, 205; let, input statements, 207; nesting, 208; object-oriented model, 210; reserved words, 204; subroutines, 208–9; variables, 204, 209
proprietary, 29
protocol, 13
public domain, 232

QWERTY, 12, 41

ray tracing, 27

scaling, 33
scanner, 13, 32
search engines, 126, 148
silicon, 16
software, 9; GUI, 11; operating system, 10; user-friendly, 10
spreadsheets: absolute address, 59; advanced formulas, 60–62; bar chart, 70; cell, 54; chart key, 69; chart legend, 69; data set, 67; formulas, 57; inverse video, 55; pie chart, 69–70; pound sign, 62; printing, 75; relative address, 58; stacked bars, 71; VisiCalc, 53

TCP/IP, 120
telegraph, 4; Morse, Samuel, 4
telephone, 5
text editor, 159, 201
thumbnails, 28
transistors, 6
triplet, 24, 167
TWAIN, 34
typewriter, 39

Unix, 120
URL, 123
Usenet, 133

vacuum tubes, 6
virus, 218

word processing: editing, 43; headers and footers, 47; line spacing, 48; margins and indents, 47; retrieving, 42; rich text format, 43; saving, 42; soft return, 44; spelling and grammar checking, 48; word wrap, 43
worm, 219
World Wide Web (WWW): authority, 137; authorship, 141; banner ad, 142; bias, 142; consortium, 126, 158; controls, 137; dynamic nature, 138; nonprofit organization 142; point and click, 137; validity, 137; webmaster, 141, 157
WYSIWYG, 19

About the Author

Joanne R. Barrett is the middle school computer coordinator and teacher at the Stone Ridge School of the Sacred Heart in Bethesda, Maryland. She has presented laptop computer education presentations at several conferences, including the College Board Regional Meeting; the Microsoft Anytime, Anywhere Learning Summit; NAIS; and AASL. She has a bachelor's degree from Providence College and a master's degree from Georgetown University. She worked as a computer specialist for the Department of Justice before becoming a teacher. She started working with students as a volleyball coach and decided that she wanted to spend more time working with girls to get them more excited about technology.